Dark
Salutations

AFRICAN
AMERICAN
RELIGIOUS THOUGHT AND LIFE

This series provides opportunity for African American scholars from a wide variety of fields in religion to develop their insights into religious discourse on issues that affect African American intellectual, social, cultural, and community life. The series focuses on topics, figures, problems, and cultural expressions in the study of African American religion that are often neglected by publishing programs centered on African American theology. The AARTL program of publications will bridge theological reflection on African American religious experience and the critical, methodological interests of African American religious studies.

SERIES EDITORS
Anthony B. Pinn, Macalester College, St. Paul, Minnesota
Victor Anderson, Vanderbilt University, Nashville, Tennessee

Making the Gospel Plain
edited by Anthony B. Pinn

A Private Woman in Public Spaces
Barbara A. Holmes

Dark Salutations
Riggins R. Earl Jr.

Dark
Salutations

RITUAL, GOD, AND GREETINGS IN
THE AFRICAN AMERICAN COMMUNITY

Riggins R. Earl Jr.

TRINITY PRESS INTERNATIONAL

Trinity Press International, P.O. Box 1321, Harrisburg, PA 17105

Trinity Press International is a division of the Morehouse Group.

Cover art: *Celebration*, Charles Searles, 1975. Smithsonian American Art Museum, Washington, D.C./Art Resource, NY.

Cover design: Wesley Hoke

Library of Congress Cataloging-in-Publication Data

Earl, Riggins Renal.
    Dark salutations : ritual, God, and greetings in the African American community / Riggins R. Earl, Jr.
        p. cm. – (African American religious thought and life)
    Includes bibliographical references and index.
    ISBN 1-56338-358-6 (alk. paper)
        1. African Americans—Religion. 2. Salutations—Religious aspects—Christianity—History. 3. Black English—Religious aspects—Christianity—History. I. Title. II. Series.

BR563.N4 E365 2001
277.3'08'08996073—dc21   2001033305

Printed in the United States of America

01 02 03 04 05 06   10 9 8 7 6 5 4 3 2 1

To Charles H. Long,
a brotherman and friend, who continues to be a Socratic
type of gadfly to black scholars in religion.
Long has challenged us to think beyond the phenomenon
of religions as they are expressed in rituals and symbols.

To Howard Harrod,
a provocative teacher and a friend, who for several generations
has dared to require that his graduate students in ethics
think through the rigorous theories of phenomenology,
rituals, and symbols. He has persistently challenged his
students by precept and example to explore the religious
and moral horizons of marginalized people's worlds.

Contents

Acknowledgments

I am very grateful to all who have assisted me in the completion of this project. Every researcher knows that locating articles and books in obscure places is never an easy task even in an age when technology has changed the nature of academic research and the accessibility of literary resources. Librarians and student research assistants were instrumental in helping me find scarce sources. I am particularly grateful to Sandra Avent, a former student, who assisted in the initial research for this project.

Joseph Troutman, Jacquelyn Daniels, Robert Quarles, and William Holt of the Robert Woodruff Library helped me to access sources from that library and other research libraries. Staff persons in the archives of the Robert Woodruff Library went out of their way to assist me in finding materials. Thanks go to Douglas L. Gragg, Reference Librarian at Pitts Theological Library at Emory University, for his research assistance. A personal thanks goes to those colleagues who have encouraged me in this long endeavor through the years: Victor Anderson, Noel Erskine, Peter Paris, Howard Harrod, Charles Long, and Thomas Ogletree.

Student assistant Renee K. Harrison has been most valuable in helping me to bring this project to completion. Her ability to find sources in libraries around the country, via the Internet, saved me many hours at the computer. This was certainly the case when we needed to know what Islamic scholars had to say about salutatory greetings. Conversing with Islamic scholars via E-mail became a rather adventuresome learning experience for both Renee and me. Although neither of us could translate an Arabic text, Renee solicited Arabic scholars who pointed us to primary sources in English. Renee also single-handedly compiled the endnotes and bibliography.

I am indebted to Ms. Natasha N. Coby for her editorial assistance, in the final preparation of the manuscript for publication.

Special thanks goes to the Interdenominational Theological Center for research funds to help with the completion of the manuscript. I have dedicated this book to Charles H. Long for his provocative contribution to the development of the black religion and theology scholars of my generation. Long, more than anybody that I know, became the provocateur of the first significant group of black scholars who were studying for the Ph.D. degree in religion in the 1970s. I have also dedicated this book to Howard Harrod, who is ending a distinguished teaching career at Vanderbilt University Divinity School and Graduate School of Religion. Harrod brought to the teaching moment a pastoral disposition that gave comfort to the most insecure student.

Introduction

On the first anniversary of the abolition of the slave trade, the New York African Society for Mutual Relief, with which [Henry H.] Garnet had contact, was addressed by William Hamilton, the foremost black intellect of the first quarter of the nineteenth century. Black people then, two decades before Emancipation Day, "carried themselves with a free air which showed that they thought themselves free," and on that occasion caused concern among their white friends, "by their bold action." Before Hamilton spoke, silk banners inscribed "AM I NOT A MAN AND A BROTHER" were unfurled as New York blacks paraded the streets in large numbers, "easily thrusting aside by their own force the small impediments [whites] which block their way." The procession moved from New York's "African Room," according to the records of the New York African Society for Mutual Relief, to the "Universalists Church" to hear the principal speaker.[1]

For it is through our names that we first place ourselves in the world. Our names, being the gift of others, must be made our own. . . . They must become our masks and our shields and the containers of our values and traditions which we learn and/or imagine as being the meaning of our familial past.

And when we are reminded so constantly that we bear, as Negroes, names originally possessed by those who owned our enslaved grandparents, we are apt to be more than ordinarily concerned and mysterious events, the fusions of blood, the furtive couplings, the business transactions, the violation of faith and loyalty, the assaults; yes, and the recognized and

the unrecognizable loves through which our name was hand-
ed down unto us.[2]

Some years ago, I sought to show in *Dark Symbols, Obscure Signs:
God, Self, and Community in the Slave Mind* that the primary
sources of the black religious experience warrant critical scholarly
inquiry.[3] This was the first published volume of a trilogy that I proposed, at that time, on the primary religious language of the black
experience. The first volume sought to identify the foundational
theological and ethical themes of black religious language. These
foundational themes had their genesis in the slave experience. First,
I sought to show how blacks construed from the Christian conversion language of their white oppressors a new liberated consciousness of God, self, and community. They did so in the face of social,
psychological, and often physical death. In a word, slaves struggled,
against alienating forces, to require that the metaphorical religious
language of their slave masters address their own experience of
enslavement. Slaves' religious experiences erupted out of the caul-
dron of their own daily personal and collective sufferings brought
on by the brutality of plantation conditions. The reality of slaves'
human condition demanded that they test the authenticity of their
white masters', although often pious, Christian language of salvation in the context of their own survival struggles. In this way they
were able to separate the kernel of reality from the husk, truth from
falsehood. Slaves were driven by the need to baptize the masters'
metaphorical religious language in the stream of their own consci-
entious awareness of God, self, and community.

Second, I made no pretense in *Dark Symbols* to be doing a theology or ethics of the black religious experience. Instead, I sought to
do a constructive unearthing of, from slaves' first-order religious language, some of the foundational theological and ethical principles of
the black religious experience. In addition, I made the claim that
these principles have critical theological and ethical implications for
the way in which blacks have understood God, self, and community. This claim is predicated upon the belief that such disciplines of
study as theology and ethics constitute reflective second-order, rather
than first-order, religious language.[4]

It is my methodological assumption that scholars of black religious sources must first identify the foundational theological and ethical elements of first-order black religious language. Second, we must use these foundational elements to illuminate the theological and ethical dimensions of the black religious experience. Scholars must tease out of black people's own primary religious language previously ignored authentic meaning structures such as the conversion motif. Failure to do so means ignoring the deeper meaning structures of the black community's primary religious language. Scholars insensitive to this fact stand to silence, rather than release, the authentic prophetic and priestly voices (female and male) of these sources. This will inevitably happen if black scholars merely impose upon these sources the scholarly agendas of whites and thus deem these sources anemic, if not totally valueless, for illuminating academic discourse. Black scholars might dismiss primary black religious sources of their indigenous community as having no positive contributions to make to white scholars' theological and ethical presuppositions about God, self, and community.

This book, *Dark Salutations: Ritual, God, and Greetings in the African American Community*, is the second volume on first-order black religious experience and language. Here I continue my hermeneutical investigation of the luminous darkness of the black religious experience and language. Its primary thesis is that black Americans' ethnocentric verbalized salutatory expressions often dominate their ritualistic moment of social encounter. A classic example of this can be heard in such verbalized salutatory expressions as "brotherman" and "blackman," which are commonly used by black males. Black females, also, are often heard to use such popular ethnocentric verbalized salutatory greetings as "sistergirl" or "soul sister." These are all salutatory metaphors that suggest certain theological and ethical elements that are foundational for the constructive task of theology and ethics.

Black people have often created and re-created these luminously dark salutatory metaphors by creatively compounding words like "brother" and "man," and "black" and "man." These luminously dark salutatory metaphors illuminate the prophetic/priestly dialectical nature of the religious and moral consciousness of blacks. Part of our thesis will show that these salutatory metaphors address blacks' theological and ethical challenges of brotherhood and sisterhood.

Theoretically, the salutatory moment allows for open-ended creativity to take place between the greeter and the greeted. This is why I have chosen the phrase "salutatory metaphor" rather than that of "salutatory epithet," since an epithet can mean an offensive or derogatory expression about a person. A salutatory epithet, as opposed to a salutatory metaphor, precludes the possibility for honesty to take place between the greeter and the greeted. If I might borrow from the reasoning of the philosopher Paul Ricoeur, I believe that the metaphor has being itself. It is the being of the metaphor that helps to transform the being of the speaker and the one being spoken to and vice versa. This might be seen when blacks have created salutatory metaphors by creatively compounding words like "brother" and "man" and "sister" and "girl." These salutatory metaphors seem to reflect the prophetic/priestly consciousness of blacks. Salutatory greetings tend to keep alive the hope and promise of relational beings being for and with each other. I find the words of Raymond Firth, a cultural anthropologist, very instructive for this study. He observes:

> What is of prime relevance is the establishment of a perpetuation of a social relationship, the recognition of the other person as a social entity, a common element in a common social situation. . . . As with a social relationship, reciprocity is important; an expectation in greeting is that it will elicit social recognition in return.[5]

The present study will thematically examine some of the luminously dark salutatory metaphors that are original to the black experience. It will draw upon the primary sources of the black experience from slavery to the present. Readers will note that I have used a number of speeches, sermons, and addresses of black religious leaders that have their origins in the Reconstruction and post-Reconstruction period of America. This is not, however, a historical study of luminously dark salutatory metaphors. It, instead, is a hermeneutical inquiry into the thematic phenomenon of the ethnocentric ritualization of salutatory expressions. Methodologically, my investigative presuppositions about a written text have been greatly influenced by Paul

Ricoeur. During the course of this study, I have found Ricoeur's critical distinction between metaphor and symbol to be very helpful.[6]

The sources that I have used from the black experience, starting primarily following the Civil War and ending with the contemporary period, reflect blacks' preoccupation with the issue of human dignity for themselves. They illustrate the fact that blacks have lived with the burdensome challenge of having to prove their sisterly and brotherly capacities. Succinctly put, blacks have lived with the insatiable desire to be treated as equal siblings in the family of God.

My scholarly training in social ethics, theology, and religious studies has understandably shaped my reading of these primary sources. Such disciplinary exposure has influenced both my presuppositions and conclusions about these sources. Black scholars in the field of religion have often left it to social scientists to have the last word about them. I have undertaken this study mindful of the fact that scholars of religion are interested in the different complex ways that a people's beliefs manifest themselves in the lived world. This means that I am very appreciative of the luminary contributions that social scientists and other humanities scholars make to our understanding of the original social context of the sources. Too few scholars of religion and theology have brought critical faith questions to these sources.

The noticeable religious content and nature of some of these sources drove me to question blacks' understanding of God and brotherhood/sisterhood challenges as revealed in their struggles with such critical questions as the following: Is God a respecter of persons? Have black people understood God to be "faithfully for and with them" politically and spiritually? Have black people understood themselves to be both "trustfully for and with" each other spiritually and politically? In addition, have black people understood themselves to be "trustfully for and with" even whites who oppressed them? Such theological and ethical questions have influenced my hermeneutical presuppositions about these texts.

I call to the reader's attention the fact that much of this study involves materials that were produced in an era when inclusive language was not the norm. Racism and sexism were the rule rather then the exception in both formal and informal speech. For example, if whites used terms such as "brotherhood" and "manhood" when saluting blacks, they did not mean the same as when referencing each other in the salutatory moment. Had this been the case, blacks would have had no need to create their own dark salutatory metaphors. At a later point in the book, I will give attention to the terms "womanhood" and "sisterhood."

Chapter 1 addresses the Christian's and Muslim's salutatory liberation metaphors. The pivotal question is, How have these religions' teachings of proper greetings in the moment of social encounter influenced blacks? Struggles to answer this question will illuminate blacks' brotherhood/sisterhood challenges across the religious divide as well as on each side of it. I will show in this chapter that Jesus' salutatory formula shifts the theological and ethical paradigm for understanding the phenomenon of salutatory liberation. Christian blacks have understood it to be more radical than the notion of salutatory liberation taught by the Islamic tradition.

Chapter 2 of this study will deal with the theological and ethical propositions proposed by what I have termed "ethnocentric dark salutatory metaphors." They illuminate the theological problem of what it means for oppressed people to understand God as being faithfully for and with them and vice versa. This study helps us struggle with the critical question of whether or not God is a respecter of persons. These linguistic creations also illuminate blacks' understanding of being faithfully for and with their white oppressors as well as being trustfully for and with each other.

Chapter 3 addresses the problematic of revelation, race, class, and reason. The main idea is that these concepts must be viewed as inseparable. It shows how the contributions of the black Muslims forged the way for a scholarly theologian such as James Cone to challenge black thinkers' understanding of the relationship between such concepts as revelation, race, class, and reason. Primary sources of the black experience reveal blacks' struggle with the idea of God's being faithfully for and with the oppressed and the latter being trustfully for and with each other.

Chapter 4 explores what I have called "honorable dark salutatory metaphors" that are manifested in the primary slave sources. Slaves used such metaphoric expressions as "little one" and "little man" to refer to themselves in the presence of God and Jesus. In those rare moments of divine salutatory encounter, slaves heard God and Jesus refer to them by such honorable titles as "little man," "little Mary," and "my little one." These expressions characterized the slaves' sense of affectionate bonding with Jesus as well as with God and vice versa. The chapter shows that these honorable luminously dark salutatory metaphors must be heard against the background of masters' dishonorable salutations to slaves.

Chapter 5 examines the way that a minority group of white leaders of the Christian Church responded to the reality of race and the brotherhood/sisterhood challenge following the Civil War. This minority group embodied what some of that era characterized as "brothers in white." These white leaders thought of and referred to black males as their "brothers in black."

Chapter 6 identifies the prophetic/priestly arguments that "brothers in black" used to engage their "brothers in white." Blacks commonly, in their public defense of their humanity, invoked the Bible as the normative source of truth. This was no less true for whites of the minority conscience type. This chapter primarily addresses the priestly/prophetic types of black conscience.

Chapter 7 responds to the ideological claims of the manhood and brotherhood challenge of those I call "black apologists" and "ideologues." It explores the ideological differences and similarities of such premier black leaders of the beginning of the twentieth century as Marcus Garvey, W. E. B. Du Bois, and Booker T. Washington. All of these thinkers struggled with the question of God's being faithfully for and with black people. Equally as critical is the question of blacks being trustfully for and with each other.

Chapter 8 makes the case that Malcolm X and Martin Luther King Jr. symbolize the iconic salutatory brothers of the black experience. Both greeted America in the name of justice, love, and peace. Malcolm and Martin invoked different religious traditions, Christian and Islam respectively, to address the brotherhood challenges of race. This chapter shows that these two powerful leaders symbolize the dialectic consciousness of blacks' religious and moral understanding of God and brotherhood challenges. Malcolm challenged blacks to rethink what it means to be Christian in white America's hostile racist environment. What does it mean to say that God is faithfully for and with black people politically and spiritually?

Chapter 9 examines the creative way that black males have compounded words such as "brother," "man," and "black" to create the words "brotherman" and "blackman." This type of linguistic creation reflects the imaginative way in which blacks in a hostile society have sought in the salutatory moments to remake themselves.

In chapter 10, I make the case that black women individually and collectively have registered their "ain't I a woman" cry just as black men have declared their "I am a man." Black women's luminously dark salutatory metaphors have not always been as explicit in their ethnocentric flair as those created by black men. I have been hard pressed to find in black women's literature the use of the salutatory metaphors as political and religious statements. This chapter will show, however, that black women have created luminously dark poetic salutatory metaphors that reflect the uniqueness of their gender differences and needs. It will show as well that black women have wrestled with the theological questions of God's being faithfully for and with them. They have also struggled with the ethical question of being for and with each other politically and spiritually, as well as being for and with the oppressor politically and spiritually.

In the afterword, I seek to show that this study presents foundational theological and ethical elements that are critical for any reflective study of black religious experience and language.

Chapter 1

Jesus' Salutatory *Peace* and Muslims' Salutatory *Assaluma Alaykum*

This chapter explores both the salutatory expressions of Islam and Christianity and their impact upon black consciousness. Its primary intent is to analyze critically their implications for constructive theological and ethical reflections. I will begin by addressing Jesus' salutatory message of peace; then I will address Islam's salutatory message of *assaluma alaykum*.

Jesus Christ and Elijah Muhammad are two of black Americans most revered savior figures. Their particular influences have generated decades of verbal warfare between the loyalists of each leader. Jesus Christ and Elijah Muhammad are figures that still conjure up in the consciousness of each leader's followers a feeling of enchanted mystery. Followers of each claim that he is the only true liberator of black people. Jesus Christ's adherents boast that he is "the way to God" as well as "the Son of God." Black Muslims trumpet Elijah Muhammad as both God and the only true messenger of God. The primary concern of blacks has been to find someone who could identify with their suffering. Struggles for brotherly manhood and manly brotherhood have been attempts to overcome that suffering. A critical exploration of Jesus' dialectical gift of salutatory peace, brotherly manhood, and manly brotherhood is needed here.

Jesus' Dialectical Salutatory Gift

Black Christians revel in what they describe as "the sweetness of Jesus' name." In the more charismatic churches, preachers and singers are known to say the name of Jesus with such intensity and repetition that it drives the hearers into an emotional frenzy. The sound of Jesus' name works like a magical potion to the ears of the oppressed. It calms,

soothes, and evokes a myriad of emotional responses, some of which
have a hint of eroticism. Price M. Cobbs and William H. Grier, pro-
fessionals in the field of medicine, several decades ago addressed some
of the psychological ramifications of the name "Jesus" in black consciousness in their study *The Jesus Bag.* They were primarily concerned
with the way in which the name itself seemed to electrify and medicate
the painful emotions of lower-class blacks. Cobbs and Grier saw black
church women of the lower class caught in what they called "The Jesus
Bag." In the early sixties, these scholars did not see the name "Jesus"
having the same kind of demonstrative emotional impact on middle-
class black women as it did on those of the lower class. Their finding
certainly is not the case today. Young contemporary blacks of the middle class are seemingly equally as enchanted by the name "Jesus" as
their counterparts of the black underclass, if not more so.

Following slavery, evangelical blacks proclaimed and celebrated
a unique romance with Jesus' name and person. For them, Jesus has
been their salutatory Lord, salutatory friend, and salutatory brother. Every encounter with Jesus was predicated upon the theological and
ethical presuppositions that he shares personally with them the salutatory gift of peace and the moral challenge of responsibility. Because of
these presuppositions, a critical perspective of some of the normative
salutatory paradigms in the biblical text warrants our investigation.
These paradigms have radically shaped blacks' Christian consciousness
of themselves and their disposition toward others. Black Christians have
viewed them as normative because they are Christ centered. For the
black Christian community, Jesus Christ of the resurrection empowers
the oppressed with the salutatory gift of peace and the moral challenge
of responsibility. At the heart of the dialectical nature of the gift is the
presupposition that the recipient of peace is called by Jesus to become a
peaceful warrior. This is the Christlike way that the recipient is mandated to share the gift with a strife-ridden world. Other dialectical
aspects of the gift are that (1) it empowers the servant to become Lord
and vice versa, (2) it empowers the servant to become friend and vice
versa, and (3) it empowers the fearful to become hopeful and vice versa.

These salutatory paradigms have certain theological and ethical
implications for blacks' understanding of God's being faithfully for
and with them both spiritually and politically. In addition, they give

clarity to the question of blacks' endowed trust, or lack of it, primarily being trustfully for and with each other spiritually and politically, and secondarily trustfully for and with whites spiritually and politically. This gives these paradigms normative status.

Normative Christian Salutatory Paradigms

This section identifies Jesus' normative salutatory paradigms and their implications for theological and ethical reflection. It assumes that each paradigm influences faith perceptions of God and ethical perspectives of human relationships. The New Testament's presentation of Jesus as salutatory Lord has influenced both blacks' interpretation of God's being faithfully for and with them politically and spiritually, as well as of blacks primarily being trustfully for and with each other and blacks being for and with whites spiritually and politically. At least three paradigmatic portraits of Jesus as salutatory Lord are presented in the gospel narratives: (1) the Lord/servant salutatory paradigm, (2) the servant/friend salutatory paradigm, and (3) the brother/friend salutatory paradigm.

The Lord/Servant Salutatory Paradigm

Black followers of Jesus are enchanted with his personhood and words. They rejoicingly call him "Teacher" and "Lord." Moreover, most black Christians are unequivocally endeared to him as his servants. The New Testament narratives portray Jesus as "Lord" and "servant" of his disciples; in turn, his disciples are challenged to become servant/lord of others in Christ's name. Authentic Christian lordship is inseparable from authentic Christian servanthood. For black Americans, this has been less of an academic issue and more of an experiential one. They are ever enchanted in the worship ritual by the many biblical titles that are assigned to the savior figure called "Jesus."

The Lord/Servant Dialectic

Black worshipers tend to sense intuitively the Lord/servant dialectic in the worship drama itself. Nowhere is this truth more illustriously taught by Jesus, through precept and example, than in the Gospel of John, where he goes against the grain of tradition and washes his disciples' feet:

> After he had washed their feet, had put on his robe, and had returned to the table, he said to them, "Do you know what I have done to you? You call me Teacher and Lord—and you are right, for that is what I am. So if I, your Lord and Teacher, have washed your feet, you also ought to wash one another's feet. For I have set you an example, that you also should do as I have done to you. Very truly, I tell you, servants are not greater than their master, nor are messengers greater than the one who sent them." (John 13:12–16 NRSV)

The revealing insight in this text shows that Jesus affirms his disciples' salutatory titles of him ("Teacher and Lord"). He challenges them to experience him beyond the surface of these salutatory titles.

In order for this to happen, the disciples must critically understand Jesus in the light of both what they call him and what he does "to them." In truth what he does when he washes the disciples' feet is antithetical to their expected behavior of him as "Teacher and Lord." It is their "Lord" who breaks protocol and becomes their "servant." It is their "Teacher" who helps them to understand what their "Lord" has done "to them." They cannot understand this without seeing their "servant" in their "Lord" and vice versa.

What a challenging lesson in relationality this must have been for the disciples. They must now see the correlation between Jesus' person and their customary assigned salutatory titles of him and vice versa. The word "servant" could never again mean the same for them in the salutatory moment following this event; nor could the titles "Lord" and "Teacher." Jesus' exemplary lesson shows his disciples that real "lordship" reveals true servanthood; the disciples must now see that an authentic Lord is a genuine servant incarnate and vice versa. The dialectical christological lesson is that the Lord is in the servant and the servant is in the Lord. Every Christian salutatory encounter with the other must assume this fact. Theological and ethical transformation are assumed at the heart of this transaction.

Theological and Ethical Transformation

Jesus' radical transformation of salutatory titles gives a new theological twist to what it means for God to be faithfully for and with a stigmatized group of believers spiritually and politically.[1] His actual radicalization of these titles enables a stigmatized group to better understand ethically what it means to be trustfully for and with each other spiritually and politically.

The Johannine "Teacher," "Lord," and "servant" salutatory title combination must now be used to characterize who Jesus really is and what he does for and with his followers. He is "Lord," "Teacher," and "servant" of all liberation relationships. Jesus' followers, also, must use the salutatory title combination to refer to their own newly liberated identity consciousness in relationship to him, themselves, and others.

The Johannine Jesus taught his disciples the need to be and do lordly and servably for each other. He makes them the beneficiaries of a radically new revelatory insight into old salutatory titles as these titles relate to their being and doing. In short, Jesus introduces them to a new Lord/servant egalitarian moral imperative: "You . . . ought to wash one another's feet." This new Lord/servant egalitarian moral imperative must be seen as the norm for being trustfully for and with each other. It is contrary to the old servant/Lord theological and ethical paradigm that demands the servant's unconditional commitment to the Lord of the relationship. Jesus now teaches that disciples cannot be Lords of the relationship without being trusting servants of one another in it.

Clearly Jesus has made horizontal what was once the vertical Lord/servant relationship paradigm. He has turned it on its side. Liberated in Jesus, the followers are now free to serve each other. Washing one another's feet might symbolize the common ground of political and theological compromise. It certainly becomes the place where brothers and sisters, through being Christly servants, can elevate each other to lordly status.

In "Servanthood Revisited: Womanist Exploration of Servanthood Theology," Jacquelyn Grant rightly reminds her readers of the limitations of the servanthood concepts and its negative implications for doing black theology.[2] I would make the case, however, that blacks have almost intuitively understood the dialectical contribution that Jesus made to the notion of lordship and servanthood. Nowhere is this better demonstrated than in Martin Luther King's classic sermon on the interaction between Jesus and the mother of James and John. She asked that Jesus grant one of her sons a position on his right hand and the other a position on his left when he comes into his kingdom. After having explained to her that that was not his to give, Jesus radically redefines for the mother the true price of greatness. He reminds her that they must drink the cup he drinks and be baptized with his baptism. In short, the disciples must become true servants with their Lord/servant. The power of King's sermon is that he dared himself drink the cup of Jesus' suffering and be baptized with the baptism of his death. In doing so, King radically redefined for Americans the true meaning of what it means to be Christian. He reminded us that it entails more than living by middle-class norms and values. In fact, to be Christian demands the critique of them.

This Lord/servant paradigm is viewed as normative for understanding Jesus as the son of God and son of humanity. Jesus' disciples were challenged to assume the duties of servants if they expected to reign victoriously with their Lord and Savior. The commonly heard prayer phrase in the gospel narratives "Lord, have mercy!" can be considered the prayer's normative greeting for approaching Jesus and God.

The Servant/Friend Salutatory Paradigm

The Johannine Jesus no longer calls his disciples "servants" but "friends." Jesus' salutatory greeting has revolutionary implications for the master/servant relationship. His alteration of the customary salutatory paradigm of his day makes Jesus a renegade type of leader. Imagine what would have happened in Jesus' day had a given master suddenly started saluting his hired help as "friend(s)" rather than "servant(s)" in the company of his peers? What happens in any given salutatory moment when the slave salutes his master as "friend" rather than "master" or "Lord"?

Jesus' changing of the salutatory expectation structure, from calling his disciples, not "servants," but "friends," radically affects his followers' mutually valued expectations of each other. He liberates them from the bondage of customary salutatory entitlement. Understandably the Johannine Jesus' new take on salutatory titles defies the customary structures of class differentiation. This fact continues to have a great impact on the religious sensibilities of the oppressed. Imagine what it means to live in a society where you are stigmatized in general as the enemy of the ruling class. Witnesses of this reality understand with a different kind of profundity Jesus' radicalization of the old salutatory greeting: "but I have called you friends, because I have made known to you everything that I have heard from my father" (John 15:15 NRSV). As servant/friend, the Johannine Jesus says to his disciples:

> "This is my command, that you love one another as I have loved you. No one has greater love than this, to lay down one's life for one's friends. You are my friends if you do what I command you. I do not call you servants any longer, because the servant does not know what the master is doing; but I have called you friends, because I have made known to you everything that I have heard from my Father." (John 15:12–15 NRSV)

Jesus makes a radical shift from the traditional salutatory paradigm of his day, which denoted subordinate/superordinate relations, to one of trusting friends. Again he makes horizontal what was once considered a fixed vertical master/servant relationship. While the old social paradigm between "Lord" and "servant" was predicated on distrust bred by the structures of social alienation, the new salutatory paradigm is founded on trust shaped by the reality of intimately revealed knowledge from Jesus to the disciples.

David Rensberger, another of my colleagues, has helpfully observed that members of the Johannine community saw themselves as society's outcasts in the era that the Gospel of John was written. As society's outcasts, the Johannine community needed a Christ who radically defied traditional expectations between "Lord," "Teacher," and "servants." What kind of Lord is this who has the power to give the gift of friendship to his subordinates, thereby elevating them from servanthood to that of friendship? John's Christology makes it clear that this is their eternal heavenly "friend" who became a servant in order that they might become his "friends."

The radicalness of the term "friend" must be seen in the fact that this concept only occurs in the Fourth Gospel twice before its use here. Wes Howard-Brook has noted the use of this term in John: "The first time was when John (the Baptist) spoke of himself as 'friend for the bridegroom,' and in the same context as his fulfilled joy (3:29). Also, Jesus spoke to Lazarus as 'our friend' (11:11)."[3] What then is the difference in the use here when Jesus tells his disciples, "I call you friends"? Howard-Brook observes:

> But now the notion deepens into the primary description of the bond of discipleship. As Jesus tells them in verse 14: "You are my friends if you are doing what I am commanding you." John is already in this relationship. Given the proleptic reference in 3:24 to John not yet having been "Thrown into prison," one can infer that the Johannine community and readers of the fourth gospel ought to be familiar with the tradition of John's death as a martyr. Thus, he can claim to be a friend of the bridegroom because he was willing to lay down his life both in the figurative sense of "decreasing" in favor of Jesus "increasing" and also literally through his truthful witness before the powers. Jesus invites his disciples to share in this intimacy by doing what he commands.[4]

Obedience and trust constitute the new brother/friend structure that now undergirds the relationship between Jesus and his disciples.

The Brother/Friend Salutatory Paradigm

Among the many salutatory metaphors that are assigned to Jesus in the New Testament none has affected blacks' moral sensibilities like the brother/friend combination. Even slaves were enamored by the thought that "Jesus was their only friend" and that "Jesus was their elder brother." Such affectionate images of Jesus, as "only friend" and "elder brother," helped them frame for themselves a dialectical understanding of him.

The Gospel narratives clearly illustrate that Jesus is a "friend" of the outcast. Jesus' marginalized status prepares him to identify with the marginalized. Blacks experience Jesus as the Lord and Savior of the marginalized. This places them in good company. Consequently, blacks of the Christian faith adore Jesus as truly their brotherly friend.

The Elder Brother

In the black community the primal brother has been understood to be the eldest one. Preeminence in the family of God is what gives Jesus primal status. New Testament writings portray Jesus as the only-begotten, the firstborn, beloved Son of God. But according to Paul, he is also the firstborn brother of Christians (Rom 8:29), "the firstborn of all creation" (Col 1:15; cf. 1:18), and "the firstborn of the dead" (Rev 1:5). Black Americans have understandably rejoiced over Jesus' brotherly status primarily because it is absolutely irreversible. Their belief in having been adopted into God's family, through Jesus, gives them similar status. In addition, it gives them the necessary radical religious language for their own corporate and individual social reproduction of themselves. The New Testament language says that God, through Christ, elects to identify with the outcast for their salvation. For this reason, many black Christians have unequivocally concluded that God, even in biblical times, was both faithfully for and with them spiritually and politically. God in Jesus was their chosen brother.

The Chosen Brother

Black Christian leaders have used the exodus paradigm of the Old Testament to buttress their claim of being the favored of God. At times, they undoubtedly have exaggerated the possibilities of this liberation metaphor. Blacks have found it extremely difficult to reconcile the theology of the exodus paradigm with Jesus' unconditional love-forgiveness ethic of the New Testament. The exodus paradigm of the Old Testament is predicated upon a conditional love-forgiveness ethic. Israel does not assume theologically an obligation to love and forgive non-Israelites. The theology of the exodus paradigm gives Israel primal brother status over all the other nations of the earth; it elects Israel as God's premier nation. Theologically, it fosters a suffering-servant complex. The danger of this view is that it might lead its followers to indulge in an insensitivity to the needs of the prodigal brother.

The Prodigal Brother

One New Testament paradigm that has shaped blacks' theological perspective of the elder brother has been that of the prodigal son and elder brother. In the story, the prodigal son prematurely demands his promised inheritance from his father and sets off for a far country. The story shows that, through his stupidity of riotous living, the prodigal learned the true meaning of forgiveness and grace. When he came to himself in the hog pen of a far country, the young son said: "I will arise and go to my father's house" (Luke 15:18 NRSV). His elder brother's misunderstanding of his father's unconditional love-forgiveness ethic made the celebration incomplete. The whole idea of the story in the mouth of Jesus is to teach God's unconditional love-forgiveness ethic. What arrests our attention is the father's love act of forgiveness. The father's act of love and forgiveness mirrors God's unconditional love and forgiveness. In contrast, the elder brother is a prisoner of the conditional love-forgiveness ethic. The unconditional love-forgiveness ethic means that God is both faithfully for and with the prodigal brother unconditionally. Through this paternalistic image, God shows mercy toward both God's housebound elder son and God's returned prodigal son from a faraway country.

The Apocalyptic Brother/Judge

Jesus is portrayed in the New Testament as the apocalyptic brother/judge before whom every soul must stand on the final judgment day. Blacks have drawn heavily upon this portrait of Jesus during periods of unbearable racist insults in America. Preachers preached apocalyptic sermons from such biblical books as Daniel and Revelation to reassure the faithful that God would have the last word in their favor on the final day of judgment. Songsters did the same with their songs. They subscribed to what scholars have called a "compensatory theology." Jesus is portrayed as the divine record keeper of all our deeds in this life. He will come one day to overthrow the oppressor and set the oppressed free. Then God will give crowns of righteousness to the victimized of this world. Sensing political helplessness, apocalyptic blacks have lived with the hope that the kingdoms of this world will one day become those of our Lord and Savior Jesus Christ.

Black leaders of the Church have assumed that they have just as much right, according to the Bible, as any other group to see themselves in God's salvation plan. They have thought of themselves as having equal rights, because of Jesus, to membership in the family of God. Blacks have predicated this belief on the salvific meaning of Jesus' birth, life, death, and resurrection. Their leaders have interpreted these pivotal salvation events of Jesus to have profound political implications as well. Scholars of black America will ever be indebted to James Cone for challenging the academic community to value black America's interpretive reading of the biblical narrative for liberation.

Black preachers have never been reluctant to conclude from Romans 8:28–30 that they have always had a place in God's eternal salvation. These verses articulate for black leaders the belief that God is using every adverse situation in life for believers' ultimate good. They have delighted in the salvation knowledge that Christ shares his privileges with his brothers and sisters. Christ's act of sharing is not deemed as accidental even for them as blacks. Unequivocally, blacks have believed that they are members of God's new creation. This new-creation status has placed blacks in candidacy for being progressively conformed to the image of Christ, who is the image of God (2 Cor 4:4; Col 1:15). Although it momentarily fogs the memory, the phenomenon of institutional slavery has never totally eclipsed blacks' faith of God's being both faithfully for and with them spiritually and politically. Black Christians' memory of Jesus as their brother in humiliation helps them counter the overwhelming theodicy questions concerning good and evil. They reckon with most of this through their empathetic partnering with Jesus as brother in humiliation.

Brother in Humiliation

In his humiliation, the Son of God became the brother of believers (Mark 3:33–35). Yet this designation of Jesus as brother (*adelphos*) occurs only in passages where his humiliation is stressed (cf. Heb 2:17). Even as a brother, he always remains the Lord. So Paul calls himself the *doulos,* "slave" of Christ, and the *adelphoi,* brothers, he entitles *syndouloi,* "fellow slaves" (Col 1:7; 4:7).

Romans 8:29 makes it clear that this new standing as brothers has been made possible by the firstborn of the brothers, Jesus Christ, who died for them all. Because he became our brother, we are brothers among ourselves. The ruling principle in this brotherhood is *agape.* When Paul addresses Christians as *adelphoi,* he prefers to add *agapetoi,* "beloved" (1 Cor 15:58; Phil 4:1). The specific Christian understanding of brotherhood is expressed by linking it with *agape.* The spiritual community is based on the love of God, which creates a new reality from God among men.[5]

In chapter 2, I identify some of the titles that the black community has used among itself for referring to Jesus. One is "little man." Another is "the least of these." These salutatory expressions reflect blacks' way of characterizing Jesus as their brother in humiliation. Whether they use the metaphorical expression "sweet little Jesus boy" or "little man," blacks have been ever finding ways to express their affinity with Jesus.

Blacks have gladly identified with the fact that Jesus chose to assume beggar status with God and humanity in order to save the latter. Jesus brought salvation without using force or war. That Jesus suffered all kinds of injustice made him attractive to blacks. The sermons and writings of black preachers have mirrored this fact for generations. Nowhere is this more evident than in the writings of Francis Grimke. He speaks of Jesus in the finest literary prose of his day:

> Of all the characters in the New Testament, there is something about Jesus Christ that sets him apart from them all. There is a quiet dignity, a majesty, a poise, a perfect command of himself, never excited, never at loss for the right word and the appropriate action whatever the circumstances might be,

bearing about him ever the marks of superiority, of unusual gifts and endowments, and yet mingling with the utmost ease with men of all classes and conditions and with nothing of a condescending, patronizing air—meeting every man as a brother, even publicans and sinners, and sharing with them the best that he had. Marvelous was his patience, tenderness, gentleness, self-effacing love. We stand before him, as we stand before no other character in the New Testament.[6]

The cross on which Jesus died becomes, for the less emotionally expressive generation of black Christians, the principle symbol of our brother in humiliation. Grimke's words are fitting again when he writes:

The center of Christianity is the cross. It is Christ crucified that is the power of God and the wisdom of God to every one that believeth. By his suffering and death an atonement was made for the sins of the world. And that atonement is available for all who will accept it, and who, forsaking their sins, takes Jesus Christ as their prophet or teacher, and their king or Lord. It is out of such a relation to Jesus Christ that the Christian life comes and also the Christian hope.[7]

In the traditional black church, Jesus' crucifixion and death on the cross have been more than a confessional doctrinal statement. They have been the salvation drama that is reenacted in the preacher's sermon during every preaching moment.

Jesus' Salutatory Message and Challenge

Peace, courage, and responsibility are at the heart of Jesus' salutatory message. The New Testament word for "greeting" means to proffer the greeting that is customary on entering a house or meeting someone on the street or parting. We are primarily concerned here with the words that Jesus uses for greeting in the Gospels. An example of this in the Gospel of Luke is when the angel says to Mary: "Greetings, favored one! The Lord is with you" (Luke 1:28 NRSV). Luke's characterization of Mary's response in the next verse is rather intriguing: "But she was much perplexed by his words and pondered what sort of greeting this might be." This idea implies the salutatory rule. The purposes of the salutatory rule is for the greeter to put the greeted at ease and vice versa.

The Rule of Greeting

Jesus was critical of those who exploited the salutatory greeting during his lifetime. Jesus said of the scribes of his day: "They love to have the place of honor at banquets and the best seats in the synagogues, and to be greeted with respect in the marketplaces, and to have people call them rabbi. But you are not to be called rabbi, for you have one teacher, and you are all students" (Matt 23:6–8 NRSV). Jesus does not wish his disciples to be honored by greetings but rather wants them to greet others beyond their kinship circle: "If you greet only your brothers and sisters, what more are you doing than others?" (Matt 5:47). Jesus desires that we should greet on the street those who are not our brothers, and even our enemies, and thus draw them into the circle of our fellowship, not recognizing the enmity.[8] In doing so, we convey the message of peace.

Message of Peace

Jesus' gift of peace to his disciples empowers them with courage and the challenge of responsibility. The message that Jesus' envoys are supposed to give when they enter a strange house is, "Peace." Kiel Hars Windisch says that "This peace is presented quite realistically as a *dynamis*. If the family is worthy of it, i.e., if the messenger is received accordingly (Mt. 10:13), then the power of the greeting comes on it as the Spirit comes on a man, or blood or a curse to his destruction. Otherwise, the *eirene* of the disciples will return to them. The *eirene* (peace) is thus a power with which the disciples can spread blessing but the withdrawal of which has the force of a curse. The power is linked with the word and corresponding gesture. The greeting of the apostles who are endowed with authority dynamis is thus a sacramental action."[9]

In the Gospel of John, Jesus' appearance to his disciples after his resurrection is rather dramatic. His greeting to them is both ordinary and profound. Wes Howard-Brook notes that "the common Hebrew phrase is both the ordinary phrase *shalom alechem* is as everyday as our 'good-bye,' a contraction of 'God be with you.' But just as 'good-bye,' when considered in its root meaning is a powerful prayer for the other, so Jesus' greeting offers the disciples exactly what they need in their locked-up situations."[10] Black Christians have been attracted to this salutatory message of peace because it is not "as the world gives" (John 14:27; 16:33). For his disciples, Jesus' gift of peace gives them courage that dissipates their fears of the world's persecution. The realistic nature of Jesus' peace appeals to the oppressed. Leaders of the civil rights movement came to understand that reality very early. Martin L. King Jr. clearly articulated the biblical perspective of this when he countered critics charges that the civil rights movement was disruptive of the social order. Wes Howard-Brook's observation of Jesus' peace is worthy of note: "Jesus' peace is not the superficial claim that consists of either the mere absence of fighting or the repression and denial of conflict. Instead, it is the centeredness that comes from acknowledging fear but simultaneously trusting in God's victory over the world (John 16:33)."[11]

Finally, Jesus' gift of peace appeals to the oppressed because in John 20:21 the idea conveyed by the repetition of the greeting is responsibility: "As the Father has sent me, so I send you" (NRSV).[12] The truth being taught is that Jesus is sending his disciples to share this peace that he has given them in the salutatory moment of encounter with them following his resurrection.

Jesus' person and name are welcomed in every aspect of the black community, even among black Muslims. Among the latter, however, Jesus is viewed merely as another prophet, a messenger of God. Black Muslims, claiming that salvation will never come from Jesus because he symbolizes the white man's religion, view Christianity as the religion of the white devil because of the evil deeds of its white followers. Black followers of Islam have hailed it as the only religion that will save black people. Black adherents proclaim Islam to each other and the world as the only true religion of salutatory peace.

Preferment versus Equalization

It seems rather ironic that the Christian tradition places an emphasis on equalization with the brother as the other rather than that of preferment. We mean by "preferment" the idea of promoting the brother in social status. The Christian tradition, however, teaches us to love our brother as ourselves. Is it possible to prefer my brother and ignore his rights? Is it possible to advocate a brother's rights and yet not prefer him?

The ideal among Muslims is that the true brothers are co-owners of worldly goods without distinction of status. A real brother must not use the expression "my shoe," thereby attributing it to himself. Where true brotherhood exists, one Muslim can put his hand in another Muslim brother's pocket and take what he wants without permission. Preferring one's brother in the same way that your brother prefers you is really not the highest expression of brotherhood. It amounts really to what might be called "complementary brotherhood." The idea is that preferment is worthier than equalizing. Abu sulayman al-Darani used to say:

> If I owned the whole world to put in the mouth of a brother of mine I would still deem it too little for him.
>
> I feed a morsel to a brother of mine and find the taste of it in my own throat.[13]

Preferring one's brother's material need over one's own need is deemed worthier than giving alms to the poor. The prophet Ali said, "Twenty dirhams I give my brother in God are dearer to me than one hundred I give in alms to the needy."[14] In addition, Ali said, "To make a meal and gather my brothers in God around it is dearer to me than to free a slave."[15]

The brother's needs ought to be like one's own. The brother should not have to ask or reveal his need, for the other must be a sentinel of his needs. One should not see oneself as having earned any right by virtue of what one has done. On the philosophy of brotherly preferment, messenger Al-Hasan said: "Our brothers are dearer to us than our families and our children, because our families remind us of this world while our brothers remind us of the Other."[16]

Al-Hasan observes that eschatological existence is greatly influenced by the treatment of the brother. God responds to the Muslim in the afterlife according to the way the Muslim has treated his brother in this life: "If a man stands by his brother to the end, then on the Day of Resurrection God will send angels from beneath His throne to escort him to the Garden of Paradise."[17] The salutatory response is the initial one in the brotherly encounter. Sa'id ibn al-'As said, "I owe my sitting companion three things; on his approach I greet him; on his arrival I make him welcome; when he sits I make him comfortable."[18]

Muhammad: Salutatory Messenger or Lord?

Central to the Islamic tradition is the idea of peace and brotherhood. The word "Islam" itself means "peace." Traditional Muslims and black Muslims in America all advocate the notion of peace and brotherhood. For some black American Muslim followers, the late Elijah Muhammad was the messenger of God. Others such as Minister Louis Farrakhan, a devout Muslim leader, have hailed him as God incarnate:

> The Lord of Retribution raised a Messenger "produced by the suffering and longing of generation upon generations of black people, whose blood cried out for justice and not only justice—but revenge." God anointed a poor black man who only had finished the fourth grade in school and turned the unlearned one into a teacher. Only God's intervention can make the virgin conceive: the barren black nation produce a savior who resurrected the dead.[19]

The major concern here is to show that for Muslims the notions of brotherhood and peace transcend barriers of race. This will be shown by examining the Muslims' idea of peace in relationship to that of brotherhood.

Assaluma Alaykum: An Islamic Salutatory Metaphor

Scholarly Islamic sources teach that Islam is a religion of peace and security. Mohammad M. Siddiqi asserts that Islam teaches "the security of this life as well as that of the Hereafter. Literally the word *Islam* means complete submission and resignation to Allah Taala and *salaam* means, to beg for security from Allah, the Exalted."[20] Muhammad 'Atiqul Haque observes that "the man who follows this peace is called the Muslim."[21] He further observes another root meaning of the word and concludes that "Islam means complete submission and surrender, and the man who submits and surrenders himself to the will of his Lord is the man who has accepted Allah as his Creator, Sustainer, Lord and Master of the Day of Judgment."[22] The idea is that humankind has chosen to follow peace over chaos, order over disorder, discipline over indiscipline, submission over refusal, surrender over insolence, obedience over disobedience. For traditional Muslims, this is an ethical issue. Muslims who follow peace are expected "to establish peace and what is good, and to prevent chaos and what is evil, and they are the best people" (Qur'an 3:110).

The whole idea of peace in the Muslim religion must be seen in relationship to its objective. Simply put, the objective of Islam is to establish peace on this earth; it is the duty of the Muslim to give full loyalty to this religion of peace. The Muslim aims from birth to death to establish peace over against chaos on this earth. For this reason, traditional Islamic scholars can say that "Islam is the only approved religion of God and truly Islam has been the only recommended religion of God on this earth since the creation of human beings."[23]

Egalitarianism and Timelessness

Traditional Muslims believe that their mode of greeting is unique when compared to the greetings of the followers of all religions and of the nations of the world. Mohammad Siddiqi observes that the salutatory words *assaluma alaykum* "have a deep spiritual and moral significance."[24] Identification of some of its elements is in order.

Assaluma alaykum creates a spirit of social egalitarianism between male greeters of the Muslim faith in the salutatory moment of encounter. Traditional Muslims criticize the way that the order in the ritual of greeting is controlled by the variable of class in most societies. In non-Islamic societies, the poor man, in the moment of ritualistic greeting, is expected to "pay obeisance to a man of riches, or a person having a better position in society, otherwise no wealthy man can ever think of showing such humility to a poor man."[25] Ordinarily, in the greeting ritual between those of the superior and those of the subordinate classes, the latter is deferential to the former. Siddiqi, however, contends that the contrary must be the case for Muslims:

> Among Muslims, there is no discrimination between junior and senior, poor and rich. All say *"Assaluma-alaykum"* (may peace be upon you). To respond to it with the words of *"Wa-alaykum Assalam"* (and may peace be upon you also) is *wajib* (obligatory). They have been advised to add to this expression the words of *"Ramat-Ulla Wabarkatuh"* (and also Mercy and blessings of Allah be upon you) as well, just with the view to excel one another in showing blessings and benedictions. Here there is no problem of rich and poor, employer or employee, officer or subordinate, no difference at all. This method of greeting is a *Sunnah* for all to follow equally. This is the brotherhood and equality which Islam preaches.[26]

The salutation also extends beyond the temporary moment. Muslims claim that when they pray the peace of God upon each other, they have more in mind than those of us who express the prayerful wish of "Good morning" or "Good Night," which convey the sense of well-wishing for a limited time. In contrast, "assaluma alaykum is a prayer for well-being, security and happiness, having no restriction of time. It is a prayer, a good wish, for all the time to come."[27] *Assaluma alaykum* is a prayer of respect and love for the Muslim brother for the sake of Allah.

The Object of *Salaam*

The object of *salaam* is not to show respect for an individual. *Salaam* is a word that Muslim men reserve for use among each other: "It is . . . to admit and display love for a Muslim brother, just for the sake of Allah, the Exalted."[28] The primary object is to wish peace upon the brother being encountered, wishing that Allah may keep him safe and sound in this world and the hereafter. It also wishes Allah's peace, mercy, and blessings upon the other brother.

Some teach that for the Muslim to give and return *salaam* to another is to give him safety. Giving the other safety must be reciprocal. In the salutatory moment, it is as if one Muslim brother is saying to the other, "I am giving you safety and security." The belief is that this prevents any would-be suspicion that might take place among brothers. Ultimately this is predicated upon the Muslims' notion of divine reward.

The Divine Reward

Muslims commonly believe that prayerful salutations, on behalf of the other as brother, generate divine reward. A man stands to earn ten good deeds from every time he says to his brother, "Peace be on you" or "Peace be on you and the mercy of Allah." Imam Al-Ghazal offers one Muslim tradition's understanding of divine reward:

> Imran bin Hussain narrated, that a man came to Allah's Rasool Sallallahu Alaihe Wasallam and Allah's Rasool Sallallahu Alaihe Wasallam returned the greeting, and when the man took his seat, he said: "Ten." (This man has earned ten good deeds due to this greeting.) After a while another person arrived and said "Assalamu Alaykum Wa Rehmatullah (peace be on you and mercy of Allah)." Allah's Rasool Sallallahu Alaihe Wasallam responded the greeting, and when the man took his seat, he said: "Twenty" (this person has earned twenty good deeds). Then a third person turned up and said: "Asslaamu Alaykum Wa Rahmatullah Wa Barakatuh (peace be on you and Mercy of Allah and his Blessings)." He returned his greeting and when the man took his seat, he said, "Thirty" (this man has earned thirty good deeds due to this greeting) (Tirmizi Abu Dawood).
>
> In another Tradition, it is narrated, that the fourth person arrived and further added the words of "Maghfirathuh" (His g(f)orgiviness). Allah's Rasool Sallallahu Alaihe Wasallam said, "He would get the reward of forty good deeds." It is therefore evident, that on addition of each word, reward salaam and the one who responds to it, both can add the words of "Rahmatullah Wabaraktuh."[29]

Muslims believe that *salaam* is the first level of righteousness and the first quality of brotherhood, and it is the key to creating love. By spreading *salaam,* the Muslims' love for one another grows stronger, and they demonstrate their distinctive symbols and spread a feeling of security amongst themselves. It is a security that is fundamental to the understanding of brotherly duty.

Salutatory Brothers and Duties

Muslims value calling another brother by his favorite names, be he absent or present. This is considered crucial to the brotherhood contract. Umar gives three ways of sincere brother love: "Give him the greeting 'peace!' When you first meet him, make him comfortable, and call him by his favorite names."[30] Muslims assume a contractual sense of brotherhood, the awareness that a bond exists between two persons, like the contract of marriage between two spouses. Imam Al-Gazali observes, "The contract of brotherhood confers upon your brother a certain right touching your property, your person, your tongue and your heart—by way of forgiveness, prayer, sincerity, loyalty, relief and considerateness."[31] Muslims pride themselves in creating strong, warm, rich, and durable bonds of love. They refer to themselves as being sons and daughters of Adam and Eve and consequently brothers and sisters, which means they are bound by a law of mutual assistance that has divine sanction.

Mutual Assistance

"God's messenger said: 'Two brothers are likened to a pair of hands, one of which washes the other.'" Why does the messenger choose the simile of two hands? Messenger Imam Al-Ghazil's answer is that "the pair of hands are of mutual assistance towards a single aim."[32] In the same manner, the prophet says that brothers' brotherhood is only complete when they are comrades in a single enterprise. In a sense, the two are like one person. This is the premise that ought to drive one brother to share with another Muslim brother. The Muslim brother, from his surplus, is expected to give to his brother spontaneously. In sharing one's property with one's brother, there are three degrees: "The lowest degree is where you place your brother on the same footing as your slave or your servant, attending to his need from your surplus; at the second degree you place your brother on the same footing as yourself; at the third degree, the highest of all, you prefer your brother to yourself and set his need before your own."[33]

Another brilliant metaphor that Muslims use to illustrate their mutual dependence is that of the mirror. Muslim brothers believe that they serve as social mirrors for each other: "The believer is a mirror to the believer."[34] That is to say, one can see from the other what he cannot see from himself. Imam Al-Ghazil observes the value of this: "Thus a man can profit from his brother by learning his own faults, whereas if left to himself he would lose this advantage, just as he can benefit from an ordinary mirror by becoming aware of the faults in his outward appearance."[35] For this reason, a Muslim brother values preferment of a brother over equalization.

The Salutatory Muslim Brother

For the Muslim, who is the salutatory brother? Muslims unapologetically show special preference toward the Islamic brother even in the salutatory encounter. Muslim brothers are supposed to avoid contention and disputation with each other, which are the enemies of Muslim brotherhood. The prophet Ibn 'Abbas said:

> Do not fall out one with another, do not hate one another, do not envy one another, do not break off love with another. Serve God as brothers. The Muslim is brother to the Muslim. He does not wrong him or forsake him. A man can do no worse than disgrace his Muslim brother. He does not wrong him or offend him or forsake him. A man can do no worse than disgrace his Muslim brother.[36]

Muslim brothers have to guard against Satan, who is the enemy of brotherhood.

The Archenemy of Brotherhood

Traditional Islam recognizes a universe consisting of three realms: heaven, earth, and hell. Governed by the creator-judge, the world is inhabited by human beings and spirits (angels, jinns, and devils), who are called to obedience to the one, true Allah, the Lord of the universe. Satan is at the opposite end of the spectrum from God. Allah is seen as the principle of good; Satan (*shaytan,* "adversary") is seen as the principle of evil. Islamicists believe that Satan has envied humankind from the beginning of creation because Satan's refusal to accept humanity's unique status in the hierarchy of the universe caused Satan's expulsion from heaven. The expulsion led to the fall and to the age-long moral struggle of human beings, torn between the forces of good (Allah) and evil (Satan). The Qur'an's account of the myth is instructive:

> Then the angels bowed all together, except for Iblis who refused to be among those bowing. God said: Isblis, why are you not among those who bow down on their knees? He said: I am not going to kneel before a human being that you have made from clay, from molded mud. God said: Get out of here; you are an outcast. My curse will be upon you until the Day of Judgment! He said: My Lord, let me wait until the Day of Resurrection. God said: You shall be allowed to wait until the appointed time. He said: My Lord, since you have led me astray, I shall make things on the earth attractive to them and lead them astray, except for your sincere servants. God said: This will be a straight path to me. You shall have no authority except over those who are perverse and follow you. Hell shall be their promised place. (15:30–42).[37]

Traditional Muslims believe that humankind's primary vocation is to represent Allah upon the face of the earth, which means that they must represent God to each other. The devil often keeps them from representing God, as when Satan motivates brothers to spread slander against each other. The prophet said: "Satan likes to cast this kind of thing upon your brother, so that you will shun him and break with him. How careful you must be of what is dear to your Enemy!"[38]

The Islamic view of salutatory brotherhood is rather instructive of Muslims' ethical beliefs. They advocate a conditional love-forgiveness ethic, which is contrary to Christians' ideal of an unconditional love-forgiveness ethic.

A Conditional Love-Forgiveness Ethic

The salutatory Christ challenges us with an unconditional love-forgiveness ethic, which is not conditioned by gender, race, class, religion, or nationality. This has been the appeal of Jesus' salutatory message to black Christians in America. That message has been dramatized in the various phases of the struggle for social justice in this country.

Assaluma alaykum presupposes a conditional love-forgiveness ethic. Muslim brothers' first priority is to love and forgive each other, and they are to reserve the *assaluma alaykum* salutation for each other. It is not a saluting that a Muslim brother uses aggressively with a non-Muslim brother.

The Muslims' conditional love-forgiveness ethic is founded on the theological premise that Allah is a respecter of Muslims. Allah is unequivocally both faithfully for and with Muslims spiritually and politically. The Muslim belief is that Allah teaches brothers to defend themselves against their enemies, who are in turn the enemies of God. On the contrary, Christianity teaches that the Christian must love the enemy. The idea is that the Christian must will the enemy good. The Christian idea is that God is both faithfully for and with the brother or sister who sacrifices oneself for the hostile enemy.

Summary

Throughout the centuries of oppression, the theology and ethics of both Christian and Islamic salutatory perspectives have benefited blacks' struggle for liberation. The primary benefit has been that blacks have been forced to think dialectically about God, brotherhood/sisterhood, and forgiveness.

Chapter 2

Ritual, God, and Salutation

"Brotherman," "blackman," and "soul brother" are popularized salutatory verbal expressions of fraternal endearment that black males commonly use in their daily ritual of meeting and greeting. They constitute preelusive possibilities for liberative dialogue in every moment of social encounter. Similarly, black female salutatory metaphors, such as "soul sister," "girlfriend," and "sistergirl," have served the same kind of ritualistic function. All of these salutatory metaphors mirror blacks' creative religious and moral linguistic defiance of such denigrative white racist salutatory epithets as "nigger," "boy," "mammy," and "wench."[1] Countering these infectious racist designations, blacks have created their own luminously dark linguistic salutatory exhortations for and with each other. Their communicative creations have proven to be of prophylactic value against whites' raw racist verbal insults. Reflecting blacks' creative capacity for linguistic improvisation, such metaphoric expressions have contributed immensely to blacks' self-understanding and respect for each other. Blacks have found such salutations to be a constructive alternative to white racists' verbal rituals of dehumanization.

Luminously Dark Salutatory Metaphors

I call blacks' salutatory epithets "luminously dark salutatory metaphors" because they are created out of the darkness of black people's victimized experiences of racism. It is a darkness, however, that illuminates the complexities of the religious and moral aspects of black people's being and belonging in the society. Dark salutatory metaphors reflect black people's creative struggle to free themselves from the society's racist language and illuminate the emotional complexity that black

25

people experience in their social encounters with the realities of race, class, and gender. Some of these metaphors are explicitly ethnocentric both in their origin and purpose.

Blacks have often created and re-created luminously dark salutatory metaphors by creatively compounding words like "brother" and "man" and "black." In so doing, they have produced such powerfully dark salutatory metaphorical expressions as "brotherman" and "blackman." Such creative engineering of words has often enabled blacks to re-create a larger affirmative social image of themselves. In other words, it has allowed blacks to become copartners with God in the sacralization of their humanity and humanization of their sacredness. It is as though blacks, to borrow a phrase from Paul Ricoeur, "empty the language (of their oppressors' consciousness) and re-fill it" with their own consciousness.[2] At best, blacks empty the salutatory language of its white racist insensitivity and refill it with their tenderized religious and moral sensibilities.

These luminously dark salutatory metaphors illuminate the prophetic/priestly dialectical development of blacks' religious and moral consciousness. They have allowed blacks "to make sense with nonsense, to transform a self-contradictory statement into a significant self-contradiction."[3] These metaphors, by their very raison d'etre, prophetically indict whites' false claims of Christian brotherhood/sisterhood. They demand a critical study of the way that white and black Christians have handled, both then and now, the issue of being and belonging in their social encounters. More will be said later about the prophetic side of the salutatory dialectic in a subsequent section of the study.

The priestly side of the salutatory dialectic must be seen in the way that blacks have used their luminously dark salutatory metaphors for ministering unto each other in a hostile racist society. It provides the therapeutic language of blacks' priestly responses to each other; it accents their forgiving-and-being-forgiven disposition toward one another. The priestly side of the salutatory dialectic allows the victimized to embrace each other's dark otherness. It enables blacks to affirm experientially the otherness and sameness of their darkness.

Central to the prophetic/priestly dialectic salutatory metaphor, conscious or unconscious, has been the hope of blacks for a dark religious savior figure—Christian or Muslim.[4] This religious savior figure, whether Jesus for Christians or the once Elijah Muhammad for Muslims, has been seen as the one who salutes them as brother/friend in the darkness of their victimization, the one who brings peace, joy, and love to them in their darkness. In this sense, the savior figure identifies with and becomes the victimized. This savior figure also changes the being of the victimized and gives the transformed a new name. A classic example of this is Malcolm X's account of Elijah Muhammad's changing his name from that of Malcolm Little to Malcolm X.[5] Some have used luminously dark salutatory metaphors mindless of any critical understanding; others have used them unaware of their correlation to such kinship salutatory expressions as "hommie" and "blood." In short, blacks' brotherly/sisterly salutations have all been intended to promote love and trust among themselves. Their salutations must clearly be seen in the scholarly community as constituting more than blacks' verbal rituals of frivolity. In a word, they must be seen as having challenging theological and moral implications.

Theological Propositions

Blacks' salutatory brotherly/sisterly constructs serve as primary linguistic expressions for critically studying the complexities of their religious and moral understandings of God and human relations. A number of blacks' creative salutatory brotherly/sisterly metaphors, such as "brotherman" and "soul sister," constitute a linguistic foundation for analyzing religious and moral dialogue in the black community. This is so because the primary salutation constitutes the initial point in the social encounter for affirming the sacred and the human of each other. The potential for this affirmation manifests itself when greeter and greeted, in the salutatory moment, constructively create and re-create each other socially. In short, every salutatory social encounter for the oppressed has the potential to become an epiphanous moment. This belief drives many black Christian worshipers to esteem good fellowship as being invaluable for authentic worship. Such fellowship becomes the basic criterion for judging God's hospitable presence or the lack of it.

Luminously dark salutatory metaphors that promote healthy brotherly/sisterly relations sound a ritualistic call for dialogue among the oppressed. They call for a critical examination of black people's faith in God's faithfulness, or lack of it, toward them; they call for a critical study of black people's capacities to be trustfully for and with each other. Such metaphors will affirm the community's belief that God is faithfully for and with the oppressed and vice versa. In addition, luminously dark salutatory metaphors beg the question, To what extent can blacks be trustfully for and with their white oppressors without being against themselves? Religiously, this salutatory humanization/sacralization process is driven by the belief that God has created all human beings with the potential for trustful dialogue. Failure to respect mutually each other's humanity/divinity in the salutatory moment of social encounter amounts to the sin of omission (e.g., color or gender) to the other's self-worth. Those committing this sin of blindness have claimed that they could love the soul of the victimized while disregarding his or her embodied self-worth. They have predicated such contradictory belief and behavior upon a false understanding of humanity and divinity. In other words, they have overly spiritualized social reality and have ignored the other as having any human or divine worth in the salutatory moment of social encounter. Those committing the sin of blindness tend to impose, as we have shown above, dehumanizing salutatory metaphors upon the other in the moment of social encounter.

Multiple Prepositional Constructs

Hermeneutical and phenomenological inquiry of blacks' understanding of God being faithfully for and with them and vice versa, as well as blacks being trustfully for and with each other, and blacks being faithfully for and with the oppressor reflect the religious and moral complexity of blacks' consciousness. That fact is seen in the multiple "for and with" prepositional constructs characterizing God and human relationships. Critical inquiry into these prepositional constructs will help illuminate some of blacks' complex religious and moral faith claims. This constitutes the locus of the theological and ethical challenge.

The Theological Challenge

Blacks' struggle for brotherhood/sisterhood has provoked several theological questions: Is God a respecter or nonrespecter of persons? Asked
another way: Does God value the individual's physical attributes at all?
An even more pointed question is: Is God for or against blacks because
they are black? Or is God particularly for and with blacks because they
are oppressed? If God is not a respecter of persons, then the assumption is that God is no more faithfully for and with blacks than for and
with any other ethnic group. This would mean that God favors no one
ethnic group over any others. If this is so, how do we explain the fact
that God permits one group, in God's name, to oppress the other? If
God is no respecter of persons, we must say that God is neutral or
indifferent toward both the conduct of the oppressed and oppressor.
This would mean that the oppressed are without a divine ally in their
suffering, that God is not a God of distributive or retributive justice.

Debate as to what God's exact disposition toward the oppressed
really is has continued to surface in the black community for
decades. Despite this fact, a paucity of scholarly publications on this
subject exists. William R. Jones's publication *Is God a White Racist?*
published almost thirty years ago, generated practically no formal
debate among black scholars on this issue.[6] Recently, Anthony Pinn,
with a rather careful study of primary sources, has revisited the
theodicy question in relationship to the black community.[7]

The primary focus here, however, is to show that black Americans' luminously dark salutatory metaphors reflect a complex faith
understanding of God spiritually, socially, and politically. They
reflect the race's God consciousness. The first theological and ethical
question is, Has God been both faithfully for black people spiritually and faithfully with them politically as their liberator? The second
theological and ethical question is, Has God only been faithfully
with black people spiritually but not faithfully for them politically?
This is what might be called the God being "with-but-not-for"
blacks. Initially, the first question presents a "both/and" dialectical
portrait of God as the unconditional friend of the oppressed. Subsequently, a critical response to the latter question presents a yes/no
portrait of God as an enemy/friend of the oppressed. In a word, the

latter presents God as oppressor/liberator of black people. As unconditional friend, God is unconditionally committed to the freedom of
the oppressed; as the conditional enemy/friend, God is conditionally committed to the liberation of the oppressed. God's conditional
commitment is contingent upon the oppressed's unconditional obedience. Adherents of the latter believe that the oppressed must display a greater righteousness and piety than their oppressors. Blacks of
this view, over the years, have read and interpreted the Bible with the
belief that they are innately a people of high character and deep religious devotion. Periods of severe national white backlash have commonly been interpreted as signs of God's punishment of the race for
its collective and individual disobedience. Many black preachers certainly expressed this belief when Ronald Reagan became president.
Reagan's negative policies against black Americans had many sug-
gesting that God was punishing blacks for their disobedience. Ironically, these leaders failed to make the same assessment of whites.

Social-protest leaders of the black nationalist perspective have
questioned the presupposition that God is faithfully for and with
black people. Some among them have concluded, as did Malcolm X,
that it is absurd to think that the God of the white oppressor is faithfully for and with oppressed black people. "How could the enslavers'
God," they have wondered, "be an absolutely faithful friend of the
enslaved?" Those of this persuasion have frequently concluded that
the God of whites has been an absolute enemy of black people.

The theological and ethical proposition of God's disposition
toward black people spiritually and politically is but one side of the
dialectic. The other side is reflected in the question of whether God
is faithfully for black people spiritually but faithfully against them
politically? The former is a complex theological conundrum; the latter is a simplified one. Neither the position that God is both faithfully for and with black people because they are oppressed nor the
one that God is faithfully for them spiritually but not faithfully with
them politically gets at the whole truth. James Cone criticized the
presupposition that God can be faithfully for black people spiritually but not faithfully with them politically. He emphatically concluded that God, as liberator, must be perceived as being both faithfully
for and with black people spiritually and politically. Did Cone ignore
the different ways in which blacks have metaphorically expressed

from slavery to the present their understandings of God? Critical study of the black religious experience shows that blacks have never, with any degree of consistency, favored one theological belief about God's relational acts toward them over another. Finally, understanding God as being neither "faithfully for nor with" black people suggests that God is unconditionally indifferent toward the oppressed.

The above complex theological perspectives on God's possible relational posture toward black people constitute their primary God-consciousness dilemma. These perspectives show how blacks have critically internalized and applied such biblical beliefs as creation, revelation, and providence to their daily social struggles for brotherly/sisterly and manly/womanly status. This rather complex thesis about blacks' religious belief counters some whites' racist assumptions of blacks being overly simplistic in their religious belief and practice. The general assumption here is that the religious and moral beliefs of black Americans have been shaped by their perennial struggles, in a racist society, for a normative understanding of humanity and brotherhood/sisterhood challenges. The religious genius of black Americans must be seen in their salutatory creative-language response to the challenges of interhuman relationships.

This complex view of God's relational acts toward the oppressed originates from blacks' reading of the New Testament's assertion that God is no respecter of persons (Acts 10:34, NRSV). It counters the Old Testament's explicit theological claim that God favored the Israelite people above all the other nations of the earth. Generally Christians quickly invoke the New Testament's claim about God's liberationist acts on behalf of all humanity to counter the Old Testament's claim that God favored the Hebrew people above others. Ironically, blacks have characterized themselves as the new-exodus people (favored by God) with a New Testament ethic that demands loving the oppressor as God's child. This combination of an Old Testament exodus theology and the love-forgiveness ethic of the New Testament has had a tendency to create in black people a kind of unhealthy religious and ethical schizophrenia.

Blacks in particular have not always been able to resolve this theological and ethical problem with an either/or answer. Historically they have found themselves in the difficult dilemma of trying to wed the New Testament view of "God who is no respecter of persons" with the contrasting Old Testament notion of "God who is a respecter of persons." The dilemma for blacks is how to reconcile the God who favors the Hebrew people, of the Old Testament story, with the God who is a nonrespecter of persons, of Peter's roof-top vision in the New Testament. As many contemporary scholars have pointed out, the exodus story of God's delivering the Hebrew people from Egypt has been black people's theological paradigm. On the one hand, it has been a challenging theological and ethical dilemma for black Christians. On the other hand, it has not been a problem for devout black Muslims, who clearly believe that God is a respecter of persons who particularly favors them above all others.

Blacks' God-consciousness dilemma has affected their social-protest philosophy at every major transitional period in their struggle for social justice. While a good number of the primary black religious sources in American history prophetically speak to this fact, an even larger number totally ignore it. Many of the sermons and essays that black preachers wrote at the turn of the twentieth century and after were often of a rather impressive poetic literary nature. They, however, were generally silent on the issue of social justice. Despite assaults on their race, many black leaders made no specific references to these heinous crimes. These ebony brothers of the clergy chose instead, as did their white counterparts, to quibble over such Christian doctrinal issues as personal sin and individual salvation. Despite this fact, some strain of God consciousness has continued to be the driving force behind blacks' struggle for social justice. This fact is seen both in what might be characterized as the integrationist philosophy of social justice and the antithetical black nationalist philosophy.[8] Advocates on different sides of the social-justice protest philosophy have dreamed and worked, and some have ultimately died, for its utopian realization in America. A critical understanding of the complex theological perspectives of God in black consciousness vitally contributes to blacks' notion of ethical challenge.

The Ethical Challenge

Blacks' perennial struggle for recognition and affirmation of their own humanity has shaped their understanding of God's relational acts toward them. In short, it has structured blacks' understanding of their own social ontology. J. W. E. Bowen, a highly trained black Christian minister at the turn of the twentieth century, cleverly summarized blacks' challenges of manhood and brotherhood. Holding an earned doctor of philosophy degree in religion, Bowen observed that blacks' challenges of manhood and race were no less problematic for the nation. He told an audience: "[T]here are two problems in which we are specially interested to-day, viz, 'The Negro Problem' and 'The Manhood Problem.' 'The Negro Problem' is the 'Nation's problem.'"[9] Recognizing "the Negro" as a major factor, Bowen noted that the nation's future was contingent upon its ability "to incorporate the Negro into its life, so that he shall become a contributing and determining factor in the body-politic; and whether he shall share all the rights, privileges, fruits, blessings and protection of American Citizenship."[10] Bowen did not take lightly the difficulty of resolving this monumental problem, which he deemed as "second in importance to the Manhood Problem."[11] Bowen proceeded to delineate the challenge that the black man must meet:

> This concerns him primarily and the State secondarily. In this he is not only the major term, but the minor also; nay, he, himself is the problem. He must definitely state it and draw its logical conclusion upon the blackboard of the nations before its united intelligence. It is whether the Negro will vindicate for himself a right to stand among the thinking nations of the world, and to claim citizenship by contributing to the thoughtful and material products of civilization in the republic of thought! It is whether he will develop those manly and Christian virtues which are essentials of a worthy character and conclusively prove that the color of his skin is only skin deep and that it does not reach his brain or heart! It is whether he will regain in an educated Christian civilization his pristine position in arts and sciences, in literature and history, in architecture and philosophy; the position that he held in his original home; whether he will come back from the heights from which he had fallen; to a civilization second only to this Christian civilization in that it lacked the touch of a divine afflatus.[12]

The question of the "Negro's manhood" was central to Bowen's view of God and nation. Whether Bowen saw God as being a respecter or nonrespecter of blacks is one specific aspect of this question, which has produced what might be called a complex religio-ethical problematic of black consciousness, one born out of manly and brotherly struggle in a racist society. At least two further religio-ethical questions have subsequently dominated blacks' consciousness on this matter: What does it mean for blacks to be and belong ethically for the dominant white society? Asked from a Christian perspective, this question becomes, What does it mean for blacks both to be lovingly for and to be lovingly with their oppressors? Can they be lovingly for them without being lovingly with them or vice versa? Another question is, What does it mean to be "against" them?

Professing white Christians were not exempt from these questions. They often, claiming to be lovingly for (but not lovingly with) blacks, preached a servile Christ type to blacks. These whites might be characterized as ideal sympathetic observers. The Christ whom they shared with blacks could not turn the status quo upside down on behalf of the oppressed. Such a Christ would have become the enemy of whites themselves. For this reason, whites have often equated blacks' public practice of servile humility with their being Christian and vice versa. In turn, formal expressions of Christianity in Christ have proven less attractive to many black males, in particular.

On the one hand, whites have defined black males as less than human; on the other hand, whites have expected them to obey both the civic laws of the society and the moral laws of the Christian faith. These absurd racist definitions and expectations have often demanded that black males develop and exercise a superbly resilient religious faith and a profound sense of ethical responsibility. This has, indeed, been the case with those black males who have professed Christianity over the centuries. First, whites have always expected that blacks go the second religio-ethical mile in all social encounters. Second, whites' dehumanization of blacks has challenged the latter to reinterpret the Christian language for their own liberation purposes. This has taken place generally when blacks' awareness of their own ethnicity and social location has influenced their hermeneutical reading of the Scriptures.[13] This is evident in the writings of such prominent black American male leaders as Marcus Garvey, Elijah Muhammad, and Malcolm X. Black Muslims have been very clear in their responses to these questions. They have been emphatic in their claim that Allah requires them to be clearly against their oppressors. Being for and with each other as an ethnic group is basic to their religious belief.

The theoretical issue of being and belonging for and with each other provoked the ethnocentric question, What does it mean for blacks to be and belong for and with each other religiously and ethically? On the one hand, black Muslims have stated that blacks must first "be for each other" and "with each other" ethnically. On the other hand, black Christians have, informed by Jesus' teachings of love for the other first, submitted to the Bible's injunction of loving the ethnic other even when she or he is their oppressive enemy. It is the old love-the-sinner-but-hate-the-sin dilemma. This has been the case despite black nationalists' call for black people to love their own ethnic selves first. Black Christian preachers across the decades have strongly encouraged their people to subscribe to Jesus' teachings of love. Their success reached its crescendo under the leadership of Martin Luther King's advocacy of an aggressive "redemptive love" and "redemptive suffering." King taught that such redemptive love would radically change the heart of the oppressor to favor the oppressed.

Black nationalists have been advocates of the doctrine of self-defense. They have based it on the argument that God does not expect oppressed people to suffer at the whims of their oppressors. Malcolm X's famous self-defense statement, "By any means necessary," has become the foundational principle of the practical philosophy of black nationalist movements. His premise was that God expected the oppressed to defend themselves first for their own sake and second for the sake of their oppressors. The question of blacks' loyalty and their love of the oppressor has always produced an either/or ethical dilemma for them throughout the history of their struggle in America. National calls for the sons of America to serve in foreign wars have merely aggravated this ethical dilemma. In response, black leaders have often differed in their answer to the question of ethnic interest versus that of national interest. Twentieth-century voices, from W. E. B. Du Bois to Marcus Garvey, from Roy

Wilkens to Martin L. King Jr, have responded differently to it. They have not been able to escape the either/or dilemma.

An Either/Or Dilemma?

Both theological and ethical in nature, the either/or dilemma has been at the heart of blacks' God consciousness. Its theological side has raised serious questions in the black community about which religion, Christianity or Islam, offers the true deity for the liberation of black people. Christian leaders have responded confidently that God, through Jesus Christ, is the only authentic liberator. Black Muslims have said that Allah, through Muhammad, is the only authentic God and liberator of black people. They have diametrically opposed claimants, unconsciously and consciously, and have affected blacks' philosophy of being and becoming in a racist society. Black nationalist groups, such as Marcus Garvey's Negro Improvement Association and the black Muslims' Nation of Islam, have contributed to the complexity of religious and ethical challenges. This has meant that whites could no longer take for granted blacks' submissiveness to racism. For this reason, during the civil rights movement, whites could not assume that all blacks embraced a nonviolent philosophy. Black Muslims' "by any means necessary" ethic demanded that whites respond to blacks cautiously.

Muslim or Christian?

Continuous debate about which religious tradition is more effective in fighting racism has often created a great either/or religious dilemma for blacks. The dominant voices of this debate have been primarily males in both the black Christian and the black Muslim religions, which sometimes has enhanced the us/them consciousness in the black community between black Christians and black Muslims. The either/or religious and ethical dilemma is born, not of different us/them confrontational perspectives, but of different perspectives of God/Allah. It has often boiled down to a your-God-versus-our-Allah confrontation. This has particularly been the case between black Christian males and black Muslim males of recent decades.

Black males have historically produced different types of religio-ethical responses to the white racists' religious and moral expectations. One religio-moral type has arisen from a view of God as no respecter of persons. Another type emerges from a view of God as a respecter of persons. Despite the obvious difference between the types, adherents of both have conceived that the manhood of the race is at stake. This reality was definitely a driving factor behind the black Million Man March in Washington, D.C., in 1997. The march dramatized the need to respond to the despairing plight of black men in this country. Ironically, at that march, Louis Farrakhan's rhetoric was replete with quotations from Jesus Christ. Many blacks felt that Farrakhan's generous citation of the name Jesus, more than that of Muhammad, was an act of rhetorical manipulation. Black Christians and black Muslims have not been impervious to their own respective differences. Each camp has presumed that blacks must accept either the thesis that God is no respecter of persons or the antithesis that God is a respecter of persons. It has been impossible to concede that God is both a nonrespecter of persons and a respecter of persons. Black liberation theologians, after more than two decades of discourse, have yet to struggle with the complexities of God's relational disposition toward blacks. Constant struggles against the realities of racism, caste, sexism, and class have demanded that blacks construe their own complex vision of God's love toward them.

An either/or theological presupposition of God, be it one of the integrationist or black nationalist perspective, must not muffle the potentially different critical religio-ethical voices of the black community. Appreciation for destiny is fundamental to the constructive task of black theology and ethics. It shows that blacks religiously and morally forged out of the crucibles of their own experiences of victimization a complex both/and response. Different ideological perspectives of avant-garde black leaders have demanded that those of their race rethink God and themselves through both universal and particular constructs. This has been necessary for survival in America during every major era of civil rights struggle, especially during the black power movement of the late 1960s.

Black Power and God

James Cone's introduction to *Black Theology and Black Power* certainly generated among black intellectuals public debate about God's relationship to the oppressed and oppressor. Leaders of theological seminaries could not escape the fiery heat of the debate. Interestingly enough heated discussions about God and race came right on the heels of Martin L. King's assassination. Passion for the issue would permanently change the way that black academics of religion would do God-talk. King's philosophy of nonviolence had advocated a God who was leading black people out of the wilderness of second-class citizenship into a morally transformed American society. King advocated a universal vision of God who transcends race, class, religion, and nationality. While Cone did not deny claims of God's universality, he accented God's particular liberation involvement in the life of black people collectively and individually. If King was concerned about how God was working through blacks to love their white adversaries, Cone has been equally as forceful in his conviction that blacks must love and defend themselves from whites' oppressive power. The latter has devoted his intellectual energy to the theological issue of what God must be doing for black people.

Cone begins with a thesis of God as liberator of black people from the oppression of whites. He perceives that it is God's nature, according to biblical teachings, to be both faithfully for and with the oppressed and unabashedly challenges the black community to rethink the prerequisites of God's revelation to the oppressed. According to Cone, the experience of blackness is the primary medium for God's disclosure to humanity. Given this premise, Christian salvation for whites, who would be liberated from their oppressor status, must be contingent upon their willingness to assume the victimized status of the oppressed. Cone, in short, said that they must become black. It was Cone's provocatively courageous book *Black Theology and Black Power* that initiated the discussion of blacks' religious being and actions in the academy. His pioneering voice about black theology made possible the discussion of such subjects as God, ritual, and brotherhood/sisterhood challenges. It provoked the love debate.

The Love Dilemma

Inherent in the philosophy of the God of the oppressor is the moral imperative that the oppressed must sacrifice themselves for the good of their oppressors. Endemic to the philosophy of the God of the oppressed is the moral imperative that the oppressed must love themselves for their own good. The former advocates the love of the oppressor as a means to liberation; the latter demands the love of one's own ethnic self as the first law that must be fulfilled in the step toward liberation.

The above love dilemma begs the second dominant religio-ethical question, What does it mean for blacks first to be lovingly for and with each other as brothers and sisters? The theological belief that God is a respecter of persons demands that blacks subscribe to the first law of nature by loving themselves first. This belief has for decades characterized those of the black nationalist ideological persuasion. It, however, has been antithetical to subscribers of the theological belief that God is no respecter of persons. The latter belief has mandated that its followers subscribe to the law of sacrificial suffering, symbolized in the death of Christ, by loving others as they love themselves. It has peculiarly characterized black advocates of the integrationist philosophy. The integrationist belief has driven, in addition to the Church, black civil rights organizations such as the National Association for the Advancement of Colored People as well as the National Urban League. Leaders of these secular organizations would certainly find it very difficult to deny the Bible's influence on their organization's explicit and implicit ideas about God, ritual, and brotherhood/sisterhood challenges.

The concern here is to show that a complex either/or theological perspective of blacks' understanding of God's love for the oppressed is fundamental. It will demonstrate how blacks have struggled with the issues of being both lovingly and faithfully for/with God and each other. Moreover, the either/or theological understanding must not eclipse the inherently knotty problems that such metaphorical concepts as black manhood/womanhood and brotherhood/sisterhood have caused.

Black leaders such as Marcus Garvey, Elijah Muhammad, and Malcolm X have taught that blacks must generate out of themselves, collectively and individually, a radically new type of manhood/womanhood and brotherhood/sisterhood for defying the systemic racist system. These black nationalists have also concluded that the race must produce its own mythmakers and interpreters of history in both Africa and America.[14]

Black nationalists in every epoch of the race's struggle have taught that Christianity's turn-the-other-cheek ethic is demoralizing in several ways. First, it demands that the race love and worship a white deity. Second, it demands that blacks sacrificially love their white male oppressors more than themselves. Black nationalists have been emphatic in their claim that both whites and their deity are enemies of black people.

Summary

The theological and ethical implications of salutations have been and remain at the heart of blacks' consciousness in America. The challenge arising from the implications, however, has not been for Christians alone. Black Muslims have also taken on the challenge. Their prophetic contributions have led to a more balanced perspective of what it means for blacks to be manly brothers and womanly sisters in a systemically white racist society. The next chapter's thematic inquiry into the phenomena of revelation, race, class, and reason will be a continuation of this discussion.

Chapter 3

Revelation, Race, Class, and Reason

Revelation, race, class, and reason constitute four inseparable concepts in the consciousness of black American Christians. These codependent concepts are fraught with ideological baggage that has its origin in slavery and invariably provoke the following critical questions: How have blacks factored these respective terms into their understanding of such concepts as manhood/womanhood and brotherhood/sisterhood? More specifically, how do these terms relate to the theological issue of God as a respecter or nonrespecter of persons? Academics of black religion, since the birth of black power and black theology in the early 1970s, have been unable to ignore possible correlations between revelation, race, class, and reason. Following the cue from theologian James Cone, young blacks of that generation unapologetically called for the academic study of religion in the seminary. Historian of religion Charles Long taught us that black scholars must challenge white theologians' experiential and linguistic presuppositions about God and the moral life. In short, Long challenged us to invoke the hermeneutic of suspicion, his presumption being that blacks brought something of substance to the study of blacks' experience and language.

This chapter primarily deals with the issue of revelation, race, and class and reason as reflected in the primary literature produced by black religious leaders in America. Our inquiry requires that we identify some of the metaphorical phrases that blacks have used to name and characterize their own understanding of God's disclosure to them, for these phrases reveal how blacks have engaged the ideological concepts of revelation, race, class and reason. In sermons and testimonies, blacks identified Jesus as the head of the fellowship of God's "little ones." Informed by a compensatory theological understanding of eschatological justice, members of Christ's little ones' fellowship believed that God would reward them on the final judgement day for the

41

unmerited suffering endured in this world. Little ones were buoyed by the eschatological promise that God, on the final day of judgement, would use their testimony to bless or curse the "big ones" of this world: "That which you have done unto the least of my little ones you have done it unto me" (Matt 25:40 NRSV). In brief, God will judge the so-called big ones of this world by what they did or did not do to those of God's little ones' fellowship.[1] The sobering revelation for the so-called big ones of this world will occur when they see that Jesus and those of the little ones' fellowship are inseparably connected.

Theologians have, perhaps, been too quick to use traditional theological and ethical categories from the academy for explaining what blacks are thinking and doing in their religious life and language. They have been reluctant to explore marginal territories of religious experience where blacks have created their own linguistic expressions for naming their own encounters with God. Academics of theology have often been slow to see any constructive value in the unique linguistic expressions of the marginalized, but interpretive insights from the primary sources of the black religious experience are invaluable to the constructive task of theology and ethics.[2]

I have examined primary sources for their insights and have found, for example, that in traditional slave sources the term "dream" is the slaves' primary way of talking about the phenomenon of God's revelation to them. In this case, would it not be better for scholars to use the concept of "the dream" as the relevant analytical construct for probing primary slave sources? It would keep us from assuming that "revelation" is the only construct that we might use to speak of the Christian notion of insight in the sources. I wish to show here that when we talk about revelation and the black experience, we must raise the question, What has it meant for black people to believe that God discloses God's self to those who have been ascribed nobody status in the society? Grappling with such a question raises the issue of universal revelation.

Universal Revelation

Blacks' understanding of God (that is, whether God is a respecter or nonrespecter of persons) provokes critical questions about their understanding of divine revelation. For example, how have blacks characterized the cultural medium of revelation? What aspects of white religious culture and beliefs have blacks adopted as prerequisites for God's revelation? Upon the end of slavery, the objective of northern missionaries was to educate blacks to believe that normative white culture was the only medium for God's revelation. They equated their ruling-class culture as synonymous with God and vice versa. In other words, whites absolutized their culture as the universal medium of God's revelation. Projecting themselves as God's viceroys, northern white missionaries taught blacks that they had little or no culture worthy of God's consideration, which the northerners mainly attributed to what they characterized as blacks' ignorance and superstition. This meant in short that God had no respect for black people; only if blacks adopted and internalized whites' cultural practices would they be acceptable in God's sight. Blacks were expected to emulate to perfection whites' religio-moral beliefs and practices. As subjects of white domination, blacks generally lacked the educational preparation to question critically whites' racist presuppositions about what constituted the cultural prerequisites for God's revelatory self-disclosure.

Conversion for educated black Christians of the postslavery era meant the once slaves exchanging their "slave selves" of ignorance and superstition for new "enlightened selves" that would conform to normative white expectations. New enlightened selves were designed and birthed out of the womb of white missionary education. This birthing experience meant exchanging the God of slaves' crude imagination for the God of the enlightened white ruling class. Blacks were taught that God's revelation was predicated on their abilities to reason from and through whites' rational categories. Until James Cone's public declaration of black liberation theology, the most erudite black public contributors to conversations of religion in general started with the presuppositional questions and answers of whites. Older black religious thinkers, such as George Kelsey and Howard Thurman, were among a few of their race who published their ideas for public consumption and response. They, however, accommodatingly subscribed to those issues of faith and morality that whites deemed worthy of publication. One thing all black scholars of that era had to prove was that they could think in what whites deemed to be conceptual universal categories.

Whites claimed that such conceptual universal categories as "revelation," "faith," and "reason" transcended race and nationality. The black masses did not draw such a conclusion.[3]

Universality and the Black Masses

Common-speech or folk concepts, such as "somebody," "everybody," "anybody," and "nobody," have been pervasive in the black religious imagination since slavery. Despite this fact, little, if any, constructive scholarly attention has been given to their foundational importance to the conversations about black theology and ethics. These common-speech concepts about the different types of "bodyness" tend to dominate the black masses' talk about God and the social self. I would contend that they must be the point of departure for any constructive reflections on the black masses' self-understanding of being and belonging to God. Moreover, the idea of somebodyness is at the heart of the verbal ritual of luminously dark salutatory metaphors.

A nobody/somebody dichotomy is at the heart of black American religious consciousness. It originated in American slavery and continues to the present. Christian slave masters, who valued slaves as nobodies, ironically claimed to present blacks to a God who would transform the worthlessness of their souls while ensuring the servile social status of their bodies.

The nobody/somebody dichotomy has shaped black preachers', and their communities', interpretative reading of the Scriptures. Christian salvation means being transformed from nobody status to somebody status. From Genesis to Revelation, God is portrayed as taking nobodies and making them into somebodies. The devil is portrayed as seeking to reduce God's people, including Jesus, to nobody status. Jesus' triumphant birth, life, death, and resurrection were to transform those of nobody status into somebodyness. Thematic in practically every black worship service is the theological reassurance that God values the victimized as somebody despite race, class, or gender. The black masses have invoked these "body" concepts (nobody, somebody, anybody, and everybody) in referring to the God of everybody in general and each somebody in particular. Blacks have understood God as a caretaker of everybody's needs in general (i.e., "the whole world") and each person's own needs in particular. Although God has not always seemed responsive to each one's own particular needs, the black masses have expressed conviction that this God of everybody/somebody has "the whole world in his hands; he's got everybody here in his hands."[4] Black Christian masses have kept this conviction of inclusivity alive in the face of the intimidating exclusivity cries of black nationalism.

Blacks' poetic affirmation of such understanding of God runs deep in their consciousness although they have often lacked experiential association with other people of "the whole world." For them "the whole world" has meant a generic unit of everybody-in-general in which nationality, race, and gender are not important. Everybodyness is the key variable because it is an anonymous pronoun that refers to one body as a unit in a "whole world of bodies." The anonymous pronoun "everybody" makes the singer a part of the social world.[5] In this epigrammatic faith claim of God's having "everybody here in his hands," black singers recognize that their "anonymity is part of the structure of the social world."[6] That is, the God who holds their anonymity in his hands holds the anonymity of everybody else "in his hands." The anonymity of the singers' sense of everybodyness among themselves creates a universal kinship bond with those of "the whole wide world." Seemingly the black masses have understood that this is what makes them codependent upon God. It is possibly their way of acknowledging that there is some of everybody else in us and some of us in everybody else.

One of the great challenges of claiming universality has been maintaining creative tension between a God who is for and with everybody in general and a God who is for and with each somebody in particular. Songsters of the black spirituals have envisioned a God who is both for and with everybody regardless of their particular size and location in the world: "the big round world in his hands" and "the little bitsy baby in his hands." In addition, God is personally for and with those who acknowledge each other as codependent siblings of the same heavenly parent:

> *He's got you and me brother in his hands.*
> *He's got you and me sister in his hands.*[7]

An intimate relationship with Jesus helped them to reach such a conclusion.

Somebodyness and Jesus

Blacks frequently use the anonymous pronoun "somebody" to refer to every preconscious encounter with God. "Somebody" status in black religio-moral language is often ignored, but it is a dominant concept. Generally folksingers warn their hearers of the possibility of experiencing an encounter with this mysterious somebody whom, perhaps, they can only name after the fact. The sinner has to depend upon associates to identify by comparison the knock of this unnameable somebody: "It knocks like Jesus."[8] Identifying the knocker depends both upon the uniqueness of Jesus' knock as well as upon the community's familiarity with it. No sinner can afford to ignore this one who knocks. First, the probing question "Can't you hear him?" functions as a kind of wake-up call to the sluggish or listless sinner. Second, the question "Can't you trust him?" demands the sinner take self-inventory of his or her personal faith.

Jesus, this primal "somebody," calls the name of "everybody" whether or not she or he responds. The singers ask that complete silence be observed in the presence of the primal caller: "Hush, oh, hush! Somebody's calling my name."[9] Humility is the only appropriate response to this universal somebody. The singers' lamentable refrain, "Oh, my Lord, What shall I do?" conveys a humble confession of absolute dependency upon the caller and suggests a need for obedient surrender. An obedient silent listener can rejoice in the salvific gladness that only the primal caller can give: "I'm so glad I got my religion in time."[10]

The somebodyness aspect of Jesus and God in blacks' God consciousness is fundamental to their understanding of being and belonging. In a racist society that intended to reduce their worth to nobody status, blacks have taken great pride in the knowledge that God and Jesus ascribe to them somebody status. God took God's own son, who was born into nobody status, and exalted him to his original heavenly somebody status. Heavenly gladness is in knowing that God does no less for them.

For blacks, experiencing rebirth in Jesus has meant being ascribed the heavenly gift of somebody status. This rebirth has constituted the ground experience of being favored by God, who is both a respecter of everybody in general and each body in particular.

God for and with Everybody

Intellectuals of the black religious experience such as Benjamin E. Mays, Howard Thurman, Mary McLeod Bethune, Bishop Henry McNeal Turner, and Martin L. King Jr. have strongly advocated the universality of God. Such advocates have sought to maintain the dialectic tension between a notion of God who is for and with everybody in general versus a vision of God who is for and with each somebody in particular. At the heart of black American religious belief has been this dialectical "for and with" idea about God, which best speaks to black Americans' understanding of themselves in proximity to God and vice versa. God as everybody's God, who is incarnate in everybody we meet, is a strongly held conviction in the community of the oppressed.

Everybody's Father

The traditional way that the Christian community has talked about God as everybody's God has been to invoke the biblical principle of the fatherhood of God and the brotherhood of man. Since the women's liberation movement, it is politically correct to speak of the parenthood of God and the brotherhood/sisterhood of humanity. Because of the nature of this study, I will be using the traditional terminology reflective of the historical time of the writings under examination. Formulated here is the theological belief that God, as the Creator, is both for and with everybody. This notion is best conveyed in the lyrics of the familiar spiritual "He's Got the Whole World":

> *He's got the whole world in his hand.*
>
> *He's got the little bitsy baby in his hand.*
>
> *He's got you and me brother in his hand.*
>
> *He's got everybody here in his hand.[11]*

This spiritual celebrates God as both the Creator and Sustainer of everybody here in the world. In the evolving consciousness of black Americans from slavery to the present, this notion of God has remained constant.

Black Christians embraced the idea of God's being for and with everybody because of what God did in Jesus. This view of God and Jesus was proclaimed by such black social and moral leaders as Booker T. Washington, Frederick Douglass, and W. E. B. Du Bois. It was embraced as well by the many clerical leaders of the Christian Church who have generally done so enthusiastically.

Blacks who formally affiliated with the Church generally have had no problems embracing the idea of God's being for and with them. The question is the end for which God has been for and with them. More than one response has emerged. First, there has been what might be termed a compensatory theological response; that is, God uses suffering to prepare the sufferer for heaven. Many have viewed suffering for and with Jesus as an earthly means to a higher end. This interpretation has led many blacks to an asocial philosophy of the Christian faith. Scores of sermons and addresses written and published at the turn of the twentieth century reflect this view. They mirror black preachers' tendency to spiritualize Jesus and the idea of Christian brotherhood/sisterhood. Thousands of black preachers still preach and teach this view.

Another response is that God is both for and with the oppressed by transforming and empowering them to change this world. Whereas subscribers to the former spiritualized view accent the value of being prepared for heaven, adherents of the latter are more concerned about bringing a little heaven to this earth. Forceful representatives of this earthly empowerment view, which dominated black literature both before and after the nineteenth century, include Washington, Douglass, and Du Bois, who wrote and published numerous speeches on it. A number of black preachers, during and since the nineteenth century, have written scores of sermons and addresses on the subject. This study will draw upon those sources. Church and civic leaders of the black community sought to address the social reality of the issue of brotherhood. For them it had to be more than the spiritualization of relationship.

Everybody's Brother and Class

At the heart of black consciousness is the conviction that Jesus is the brother of everybody in general and each somebody in particular. Following the Civil War, the education of blacks by white missionaries had much to do with the way many blacks saw and articulated their views about God's being everybody's father. The acquisition of formal literacy by some after the war created a class chasm between educated and noneducated blacks. It helped to perpetuate the field-slave/house-slave dichotomy in black consciousness. Those who internalized the northern missionaries' educational values system acquired a greater sense of somebodyness than did their unenlightened brothers and sisters.

A former slave's observation of black worship is a case in point. During her training at the Laing School, which was run by missionaries in South Carolina, a student expressed her observations about the worshiping practices of a group of blacks in a rural area of lower South Carolina. Her criticism reflects the either/or consciousness that missionary training fostered in blacks regarding the enlightened versus the ignorant. Characterizing a traditional ritual in black church worship, the student writes to the white editor of the school paper:

> Well they commenced the meeting by singing two or three of those spirituals, such as you like to hear them sing so much. They sing good too. After a short sermon all the members of the church got up and formed a procession in the aisles, and commenced what they called the Christian March, by singing and marching slowly up one aisle, through the pulpit and down the other aisle, out of the door and around the church three times. Then they all formed a ring, and marched round and round, singing and shouting. Then they all shook hands with each other, and separated. I never was to any country meeting before, and it seemed very strange but they all had such a good time, and it really was very solemn, and they enjoyed it so, they didn't seem to want to go home—though some of them had a great distance to go. The way these people here talk is almost like a different language from ours.[12]

The illuminative sentence is the last one. The student finds kinship identity with her white missionary teacher. The irony is that the student was a native of the area.

The mission of missionary schools was to strip ex-slaves of their slave ways and dress them in the new manners and social graces of Yankee civility. William Pickens's autobiography *Bursting Bonds* is insightful for trying to understand this phenomenon. The northern missionaries' educated view of the Christian Church changed his attitude about it following slavery. At nineteen years old Pickens joined the little Congregational church on the campus of Talladega College. Pickens says that he had never been a member of a church before. His rationale for this, which touches on the problem of slave consciousness versus that of missionary enlightenment, is rather insightful:

> In the first of January came the annual week "of prayer," and I joined the little Congregational church which is fostered in connection with the college. Why had I not become a church member before this time? That is a thing worth explaining in the interest of the younger generation of Negroes. I believed in God and the church, and had always been a most faithful worshiper, but I could not dream dreams and see visions. Without dreams and visions no one was allowed to join the average Negro church of the past. The cause that produced many of the Negro songs was the fact that the candidate was required to bring and sing a "new song" to prove that he was really converted by God, for the doctrine was that "the devil can convert you, but he can't give you a new song." Rather suggestive, this idea of the unpoeticalness of the devil. It would amuse more than it would instruct for me to relate some of the ridiculous stories which I have heard accepted in church as the convert's "experiences." At last I had found a church which did not require that I visit hell, like Dante, in a dream, to be chased by the hounds of the devil and made a narrow, hair-raising escape. And I have been a member of this church since my first year in college.[13]

Pickens's testimony reflects the class consciousness that drove a wedge between educated and uneducated blacks. Pickens's attitude about folk religious rituals and beliefs mirrors the position more of a Yale University graduate than that of a former slave.

God and Slave Consciousness

Slaves often likened their personal encounters with God to that of meeting an unknown cosmic stranger, the wholly Other. Their open confession of an ignorance of God's direct involvement in their personal lives, prior to some dramatic revelatory encounter, was not uncommon. Barbaric experiences of slavery challenged slaves to reconstruct personal visions of God that included them as God's elect. These personal reconstructed visions of God affirmed their somebody-ness individually and collectively. In general, slaves used both scriptural fragments, heard from authorized plantation preachers, and the converted community's collective trove of testimonies of personal encounters with the wholly Other to design their own vision of God.

God's Little Ones

Converted slaves characterized themselves as the "little ones" of God. An understanding of this metaphorical expression is necessary for engaging the question of God as a respecter of persons versus that of God as a nonrespecter of persons. Slaves concluded that God, at best, was dialectical in action toward them. On the one hand, God favored them because they were little ones who needed to be and belong in God. On the other hand, God would hold them in disfavor for being disobedient. God's revelation in their visionary experiences clearly signified for them God's favor. Black slaves of the faith community based their favoritism before God on what they declared as their status as "little ones" in the sight of God. They embraced the biblical perspective of a God who favors the little ones of the world. The critical question is whether God created blacks for status as little ones or adopted blacks for such status. Or was it both? If so, what does it mean to serve a God who can empower the oppressed to find liberation even in its stigmatized social status? In spiritual song language, status as little ones seems to be both a salutatory designation from God to slaves and one that they voluntarily accept.

Slaves often said that God was the farthest somebody from their minds prior to the moment of a personal encounter with God. A slave might have confessed having lacked a consciousness of God until the initial moment of having God encounter him/her for the dramatic conversion experience. The slave might be heard to say: "The first time I heard the voice it scared me because I wasn't thinking about God and his works."[14] In their worldview, God as the unknown Other is the one who jump-starts the sinner's focused awareness of the need for God's governance in his or her life. The sinner's narrative of personal conversion makes it clear that God's radicalness toward the sinner constitutes the initiation of the conversion process. Every conversion moment is a constant reminder that God became the "Little One" in Jesus. Awareness of this fact was consistent with a converted slave's humble confession of what it actually means to live conditionally as a Christian: "And if I am a Christian, I am the least of all." It was this humble awareness of God's contribution to their self-worth that motivated slaves to share the message of the gospel of Jesus Christ with everyone: "on the mountain, over the hills and everywhere."[15]

The both/and vision of God's impartial and partial revelatory disclosure for the little ones gave slaves a dialectical understanding of love as well. They construed an ethic that empowered them to love themselves in particular and everybody in general. Slaves were able to deal with their own sense of self in Jesus. "Brother" and "sister" were the salutatory kinship metaphors used to characterize relational love for each other. The ability to love each other was the true litmus test for being a Christian. While slaves did not refer to loving their oppressors in particular, they possibly alluded to them in such a general lyrical inquiry as "Sinner, do you love everybody?" and in the personal confession "Lord, I want to love everybody in-a my heart."[16]

Struggles for the Universal God

Despite the rich language of inclusiveness in the black folk tradition, educated blacks often did not escape the dilemma of culture and revelation. Internalizing the culture of whites as normative certainly complicated the matter of determining what constituted the cultural medium of divine revelation to God's "little ones." This issue becomes very clear in the writings of such early black leaders as Alexander Crummell, Frederick Douglass, and Booker T. Washington and such later leaders as Martin L. King Jr. and Benjamin E. Mays. Understanding Jesus as everybody's brother did not satisfactorily resolve this problem.

Peter Paris, a contemporary scholar in social ethics, rightly observes that the notion of "the parenthood of God and the brother/sisterhood of humanity" has dominated the primary religious sources of the black experience.[17] A God who embraces everybody as somebody is the ideal belief that has been at the heart of blacks' social and religious imagination. The black leadership has not always been able to resolve this dilemma primarily because whites have often worked against, rather than with, them for a resolution to the race problem. Prominent religious leaders of the race worked tirelessly to try and prove to whites that blacks could be universal in their religious perspective. In his book *Disturbed about Man*, Mays characterizes the oppressed of the earth as "the least of these my little ones."

All prominent black church leaders have been careful to note that God does not value the color of one's skin, religion, or nationality. Howard Thurman was so committed to this principle of God's inclusivity that he struggled for universal linguistic expressions of God. The racism of the period demanded that these leaders find ways of countering those racists who sought to universalize themselves as the norm of God's humanity. Moderate black Christian leadership was caught between conservative whites and restless blacks. Unable to placate both sides, black conservative religious leaders accented "good character" over physical racial traits. They have sought to develop in the members of their race superior moral muscle for lifting their morally weak white brothers to a higher level of Christian behavior. These black leaders believed that they could achieve this since Jesus was the primal man who was the "least of the little ones." For them, Jesus became the primal man of the disinherited of the earth in order that they might become exalted. Their theological and ethical point was that whites could not have Jesus of the biblical text and exclude them and vice versa. It was not an either/or theological and ethical proposition. Instead, it was a both/and theological and ethical necessity born of the particularity of their experienced encounter with God.

Particularity and Revelation

How ethnicity factors into God's revelation became a critical concern for black nationalists. Some black leaders not regarded as black nationalists entertained the idea that God had favored blacks with a greater capacity for suffering than other ethnic groups. Late nineteenth-century black leadership was steeped in this idea. In the modern era, scholars such as Joseph Washington have referred to this as the "suffering servant race myth" about black people.[18] Henry H. Proctor, a famous pastor in Atlanta at the turn of the century, cited the "suffering servant race myth" as normative: God had, despite their suffering servant role, empowered black people with the capacity to love sacrificially with a love that white people lacked.[19] Undoubtedly, this theme was rather pervasive in the sermons and addresses of black leaders during the earlier years of the twentieth century. James Cone voiced a radically different perspective on God, blacks, and suffering.

James Cone's Perspective

James Cone was the first theologian in a theological school in America to assert that blackness had positive value for God's revelation to oppressed people. His initial work, *Black Theology and Black Power,* made blacks aware of their own religious language for questioning whites' explicit and implicit racist theological presuppositions. Rather than presupposing that blacks came to know God through the prism of white culture, Cone dared posit the theological premise that "the experience of blackness" is the norm for God's revelation. He dared to claim that the norm is opaque rather than transparent. Cone's more daring challenge for whites was that they must become black in order to know God because Jesus is black. Daringly, Cone questioned any presumed revelation that comes to the black community embodied in the image of the white Christ. His critical assertion would give birth to a radically new way of thinking about God.

For those who studied theology prior to Cone's declaration, European culture, under the guise of the universal, was the only thinkable means of divine revelation. This was taken for granted in every divinity school in the country, even those of African American origin. Cone's thesis constituted a daring attack on the sacred cow of theological education. He defied the traditional claim that God had designed blacks for the role of messianic suffering. Advocates of messianic suffering believed that blacks could change the hearts of white racists through the Christocentric method of redemptive love. Martin L. King Jr. was the chief proponent of this philosophy. Although Cone conceded that God favored the oppressed, he thought that awareness of God's favoritism would motivate blacks to liberate themselves from their oppressors. He adopted Malcolm X's "by any means necessary" ethic. For Cone, God is a respecter of persons who demands that black people fight to be liberated from their oppressor. He called for the black experience to be normative for reading both the Scripture and the lessons of American history. Cone set the stage in theological education for younger blacks to make constructive contributions to hermeneutical discourse.[20] Cone's ideas, as a scholar of religion, were not totally alien from such an earlier leader as Marcus Garvey.

Marcus Garvey's Perspective

Marcus Garvey was the first prominent black leader in the struggle against racism in this country who literally valued the contribution of physical blackness in talk about God. He was unapologetic in his conviction that God was a respecter of persons, of black people. No black leader since Henry McNeal Turner had been as forthright in his affirmation of blackness as a plus in God's created order. Garvey dared to challenge blacks' rational presuppositions about God and the Scriptures.

Characterizing himself as a philosophic statesman of his race, Garvey reasoned that God created blacks with innate capacities equal to those of whites "to see the truth and do the right."[21] He constantly reminded blacks, "You have the same opportunities to rise to the same level of any other man whom God ever made because he was just enough to endow you with the same facilities, the same sense, and more than all the same soul he gave to every other man is yours."[22] For Garvey, the creation becomes the locus of God's revelation. Given that fact, Garvey starts with "the potential" with which God created blacks. He makes the doctrine of creation the point of departure for the oppressed. This is a strong point in his argument because the presupposition is that God gave blacks what they needed to compete with their oppressors. Garvey presupposes that God gave blacks in the act of creation every capacity that they would need for competing with others in the world.

For Garvey, the doctrine of creation became the cornerstone of his philosophy of black self-reliance, which was the gospel that he preached when he emerged upon the scene during the first quarter of the twentieth century. Black self-reliance meant to Garvey that blacks ought no longer subject themselves to the pathological practice of absolute dependence upon their white adversaries. Garvey, instead, called upon members of his race to pursue the path of corporate redemption. He was confident that God had equipped blacks for the accomplishment of corporate redemption. It would require that blacks generate out of themselves what Garvey called "a new type of manhood and brotherhood" that would ultimately have as its common goal the redemption of black people on every continent.[23]

Garvey reasoned that God gave blacks the primal structure of ethnic brotherhood for the actualization of their own global liberation. He noted that intragroup alienation, not skin color, was the curse of the race:

> It was the curse that you brought upon yourselves by your hate of each other, which was not the spirit of love, which was not the spirit of God, and since man is of God by the link of the spirit between himself and God, you voluntarily

separated yourselves from the blessing of God by doing that which was opposite to the will of God.[24]

For Garvey, the means to salvation for the black race was corporate brotherhood, which he institutionalized in an organization known as the Universal Negro Improvement Association (UNIA). Garvey's objective was to use the organization to restore ethnic pride and unity among blacks. (The lack of such pride was one sign that blacks had fallen from God's favor.) Garvey's goals for the UNIA were (1) to improve the conditions of the race and (2) to establish a nation within Africa where Negroes will be given the opportunities to develop by themselves without creating the hatred and animosity that now exist in countries of the white race through Negroes rivaling them for the highest and best positions in government, politics, society, and industry.[25]

Garvey wanted an organization that would bring forth a black race that would be both equally competitive as well as cooperative with each other. It would as well observe the rights and human dignity of other races. Members of the UNIA were expected to "pledge themselves to do all within their power to conserve the rights of their noble race and to respect the rights of all mankind, believing always in the idea of the Brotherhood of man and the Fatherhood of God."[26] This black nationalist ideology is the antecedent to the black Muslim movement.

The Black Muslims' Perspective

Race, revelation, and reason take on a radically different perspective in the thought of the Nation of Islam (NOI). Earlier followers of the Nation of Islam valued race as the predeterminate of both divine revelation and reason and viewed blackness as the primal color of the creation itself. The NOI has taught that God is black and that all other ethnic groups originated from the black man. Leaders of the NOI have sought to liberate blackness from the hands of white racists who have associated the symbolism of color with morality. For the NOI, God is a black man, not an invisible spirit. The African American is, not the inferior so-called Negro, but the original man, god of the universe.

At the heart of black Muslim belief is the idea that the black man is the God of the universe. This belief demands that we approach the question of God as a respecter of persons differently than we do from a Christian perspective. For those in the NOI, Allah is absolutely a respecter of blacks. Allah's respectfulness of the black man is revealed in what God did in creation: "The primeval black civilization was a divine culture from which originated all science, wisdom, and institutions for human progress."[27] Black Muslims have further stated how this all came about: "The black nation of gods lost world supremacy to the white race. The white man differs from the original species in that he is not a creation of God. He is a man-made race, grafted by the dissatisfied black scientist Mr. Yacub approximately 6,000 years ago."[28] What was Yacub's objective for creating the white man? The Muslim myth describes the objective in this way:

Bent on producing a race evil and powerful enough to transform the original harmony into its opposite, Mr. Yacub set out systematically to drain a number of the original of divine essence. In intervals, the brown, red, and yellow races appeared before his goal was reached: to create a race absolutely bereft of divinity. This was a race whose members were evil by nature, incapable of acting or thinking decently, or submitting to the law of Islam: the blond-blue eyed white devils. In his omniscience God gave the Devil 6,000 years to rule the earth. White world supremacy is equated to the evil era of the Devil and explains the experiences of the darker people in late world history: colonialism, slavery, racist oppression, and poverty. The gospel is that the era of the Devil now has expired. God descended in Detroit to reconnect with his lost-found Nation and raised from among them a Messenger. When the mentally "dead" blacks have united in Knowledge of Self and God, white supremacy will fall. God will himself exterminate the white devils from the face of the earth in a global apocalyptic fire. Thereafter—in the hereafter—the world will be transformed into the black paradise it is predestined to become, where freedom, justice, and equality (that is Islam) will be the conditions for eternal times to come.[29]

The Swedish scholar Mattias Gardell, in his very thorough study of the Nation of Islam, carefully notes the problems of reason, race, and revelation:

> If studied carefully, large parts of the elaborated NOI creed appear to be highly illogical. Different statements contradict each other, they are inconsistent and arrive at different, mutually exclusive conclusions. Adam is on the one hand identified as Yacub, the evil scientist who fathered the Devil, on the other hand he is black man and progenitor of the black race. Moses is on the one hand "a God" for the devils, their teacher and leader in Caucasus, and on the other hand he is the black hero, delivering his black nation from the evil pharaoh in Egypt. God is on the one hand the One, without associates, eternal and infinite, and on the other hand we learned of a plurality of Gods none of whom live forever. The apparently contradictory theses are all matters of belief; they are all regarded as true. How can this be possible?[30]

The experience of blackness is a prerequisite of revelation. This means that the only possible way that whites could know blacks would be through the medium of their experience. Also, it means that whites might benefit from that experience by learning to reason through conceptual categories that the black experience gives a certain kind of uniqueness. In the black Muslim tradition the black man was deemed as the norm of all reality. Theirs is an inversion of the conventional way that whites saw the world. Just as whites assumed that the symbolism of whiteness was normative, blacks in the Nation of Islam did the same with the symbol of blackness.

Summary

In significant ways, the variables of race, class, and reason have entered into the black community's understanding of revelation since slavery. Even when the issue of race was not loudly pronounced, the issue of class was. The primary sources of the black experience of both the nineteenth and twentieth centuries make it very clear that for Christians it has been practically impossible experientially to separate race and class. They have both been presuppositions for talking about God's revelatory relationship with black people. The question of whether God has been for and with black people has invariably been dominant in the consciousness of blacks. Also, the more ethnocentric question of whether blacks can be trustingly for and with each other has been less significant. A thematic investigation of how blacks, even during slavery, might have initially processed this issue proves instructive. It will be the focus of the next chapter.

Chapter 4

Dark Kinship Metaphors
Dishonorable and Honorable Salutations

The barbarity of slavery demanded that black Americans improvise unique ways of greeting God and each other. Salutatory honorific titles and kinship metaphors factored into their constructive improvisational language. Kinship greeting metaphors such as "brother" and "sister" conditioned slaves' affective capacities for perceiving and affirming each other's intrinsic worth. They allowed slaves to share in the ritual of empowering each other as brothers and sisters of God. Benevolent salutatory metaphors, as opposed to malevolent ones, provided the structural means for revelatory insight of God and humanity.

The metaphoric expressions "little man" and "little one" became some of the affectionate honorific titles that slaves used interchangeably to characterize their sense of affective kinship with Jesus. For slaves, it was no easy task trying to live creatively between being faithfully for and with God and being trustfully for and with each other while legally belonging to the plantation master. They had to try to live creatively at the divine and the human juncture of social existence. Here they would find themselves in an exclusive disjunctive state of social existence that was contrary to the master's regulative behavior codes of the plantation. We mean by "exclusive disjunctive social existence" one that demands one and only one alternative in an either/or proposition situation. In contrast, an inclusive disjunctive social moment allows for at least one of a number of alternatives to be true and produces a very complex moral and religious either/or proposition situation. The slaves' state of exclusive disjunction allowed one and only one of a number of alternatives to be true. Defiance of this logic placed slaves in direct opposition to the philosophy that the slave master had the absolute truth. Such a claim required that slaves employ the best of their imaginations. This creative use of their imaginations gave slaves at least a marginal sense of self-autonomy.

Since Christianity was the only recognized official religion of the plantation, slave society produced a rather simple moral and religious either/or proposition situation. (Only with the emergence in the black community of an alternative religion did there arise the possibility for a more inclusive moral and religious either/or proposition situation.) Encounters with and conversion to "the wilderness Jesus" were religious experiences that created for the slaves an exclusive either/or proposition situation, forcing the slaves either to forge a faith in God that would enable them to overcome the false consciousness that slavery produced (i.e., forced subjugation of their will to the master's) or to surrender to the structures of oppression. Submission to the structures of oppression required that slaves believe that their master was unequivocally both for and with them, an understandable requirement since the slaves legally belonged to the master as property. The worse scenario was for the slave only to be able to see himself/herself through the master's eyes. Historian Stanley Elkins characterized this as the Sambo-type of personality. His thesis was that the institution of slavery created a pathological kind of paternalism between master and slave.[1,2] The Sambo-type personality reflects the degree to which the master could all but totally destroy the slave's sense of self-identity. The slave who tried to be both for and with her master had to betray her family and herself. Her alternative was to be forced into an exclusive disjunctive either/or propositiona situation.

Young Austin Steward's narrative of his own moral conflict, at the sight of watching a white man flog Steward's sister, is a classic example of this exclusive either/or moral dilemma. It awakened in him a volcanic energy of moral indignation that he could never again fully suppress. Steward's recounting of the incident is instructive:

> The God of heaven only knows the conflict of feeling I then endured; He alone witnessed the tumult of my heart, at this outrage of manhood and kindred affection. God knows that

my will was good enough to have wrung his neck; or to have drained from his heartless system its last drop of blood! And yet I was obliged to turn a deaf ear to her cries for assistance, which to this day ring in my ears. Strong and athletic as I was, no hand of mine could be raised in her defense, but at the peril of both of our lives.[3]

Steward's case above is a classic example of a young slave struggling with the dawn of critical moral consciousness that forces him to live in silent conflict with the master's will. It happens the moment when Steward is forced to experience the painful contradiction of being for and with the master while simultaneously being for and with his sister, who was being physically assaulted by the master. Steward experiences what I would call an irreconcilable "for and with" dilemma that goes against the grain of his religious and moral sensibilities. The heart of the oppressive experience must be seen in Steward's inability to choose, without endangering the life of his sister and himself, to protect his sister. Steward could have possibly avoided the pain of the experience had he seen the episode through the eyes of his master. If so, Steward would have merely concluded that the master was only exercising his rights, when flogging his sister, over his property. Steward, instead, saw the master beating his sister. This slave's kinship affections for his sister took precedence over his master's property-right claim to her. Here is an example of the making of an either/or disjunctive moral consciousness. This type of consciousness must be viewed as being in radical defiance of the title "slave." Slavery required that slaves be with each other for their master's interest only. Masters prohibited association among slaves primarily for the purpose of preserving law and order.

A careful investigation of salutatory bonding in primary slave sources is in order. Initially I draw upon cultural anthropologists to look cursively at the meaning of salutatory metaphorical structures as a cultural phenomenon. Second, I will look at how slave masters' naming, stereotyping, and titling their slaves all contributed to the making of false consciousness in both their slaves and themselves. It created a false bond between slaves and their master. Third, I will show how slaves, religiously and morally, creatively countered their masters' attempts at the falsification of their consciousness. The final section of the chapter explores the constructive possibilities that these salutatory titles and kinship greeting metaphors have for theological and ethical reflections of the black experience.

The Salutatory Phenomenon

Salutatory ethnic metaphors of entitlement can be honorary salutations that groups bestow upon each other. Blacks' rituals of meeting and greeting each other are deemed highly valuable for the life of the group. Among traditional black church worshipers, spirited fellowship is valued as one of the cardinal doctrines of the Christian faith, as reflected in these lyrics from a traditional popular gospel song:

> *He did not have to let me live;*
> *he did not have to let me give.*
> *I am glad to be in the number one more time.*[4]

The song is a celebration of God's gift of grace and fellowship. Fundamental to our discourse here is this question: How might the ritual of sisterly and brotherly greeting work in response to one's need for acceptance and fellowship? Raymond Firth, a cultural anthropologist, makes a helpful observation when he writes:

> A social relationship is then created only by some exchange of signs, as by a word or a nod. Forms of greeting and parting are symbolic devices—or signs if they are specifically descriptive—of incorporation or continuance of persons in a social scheme. A greeting or parting sign is often represented as conveying information and/or expressing emotion—an announcement of presence or intended departure, a statement of pleasure at someone's arrival, or of sadness at his going away. Granting that this may often be so, the informational or emotional content of the sign may be highly variable, even minimal. What is of prime relevance is the establishment of a perpetuation of a social relationship, the recognition of the other person as a social entity, a common

element in a common social situation. . . . As with a social relationship, reciprocity is important; an expectation in greeting is that it will elicit social recognition in return.[5]

Salutatory verbal expression regarding brotherly and sisterly relationships, rather than signs or body gestures, is the critical focus of this study. This is not to minimize the emphasis that blacks place on such bodily gestures as ritualistic handshakes and embraces. When black males and females encounter each other, they often enjoy most the mutual recognition of the spirit of fellowship. Among black church leaders this phenomenon takes on an almost sacred aura. Black males' mutual recognition of the spirit of fellowship among themselves has been valued since slavery to counter systemic dehumanization in a racist society. This phenomenon was very evident during the civil rights struggle in the South in the first half of the 1960s.

Dishonorable Salutatory Metaphors of Masters to Slaves

How did slave masters meet and greet their slaves? Sources do not always place masters in the positive light of being humane in this ritual. Some assumed absolute power to be able to say and do what they pleased with their slaves. An Arkansas slave, Sallie Crane, painted a grave picture of just how dehumanizing this process was: "We hardly know our names. We was cussed for so many bitches and sons of bitches and bloody bitches, and blood of bitches. We never heard our names scarcely at all."[6]

Masters saluting their slaves with a stereotype, rather than a name, was a common practice inherent with its own complexities. John W. Blassingame, a Yale sociologist, has observed that the popular literary stereotypes were "Sambo, Jack, and Nat."[7] Blassingame points out that

Sambo, combining, in his person Uncle Remus, Jim Crow, and Uncle Tom, was the most pervasive and long lasting of the three literary stereotypes. Indolent, faithful, humorous, loyal, dishonest, superstitious, improvident, and musical,

Sambo was inevitably a clown and congenitally docile. Characteristically a house servant, Sambo had so much love and affection for his master that he was almost filio-pietistic; his loyalty was all-consuming and self-immolating. The epitome of devotion, Sambo often fought and died heroically while trying to save his master's life. Yet Sambo had no thought of freedom; that was an empty boon compared to serving his master.[8]

In summary, Sambo was a victim of false consciousness, believing that he was living both with and for his master. He refused to struggle with what we have categorized here as the inclusive or exclusive either/or propositional situation religiously or ethically. This was not the case with Nat or Jack, whose "customary obedience often hid his true feelings, self-concept, unquenchable thirst for freedom, hatred of whites, discontent, and manhood, until he violently demonstrated these traits."[9]

Some planters subscribed to what contemporaries call the doctrine of behavorism. These planters advocated that slaves would behave according to their masters' treatment of them. A Maryland slaveholder, who was an exception of his era, observed in 1837:

The man who storms and curses his Negroes, and tells them they are a parcel of infernal rascals, not to be trusted, will surely make them just what he calls them; and so far from loving such a master, they will hate him. Now, if you be not suspicious, and induce them to think, by slight trusts, that they are not unworthy of some confidence, you will make them honest, useful, and affectionate creatures.[10]

Some benevolent advisers admonished that planters study the range of personality among their slaves. These admonishers suggested that planters look at "their slaves' temper and disposition" and, when necessary, "coax and flatter slaves with good words."[11]

One of the more interesting facts is that often among themselves slaves gave each other such honorific titles as "Mr. So and So," but before their masters slaves did not speak of their titles at all. The incontestable fact was that their masters often thought of black men as "boy," "uncle," or "nigger" and of black women as "mammy" or "wench."

The term "boy" was used by the slaveholder for all grown male slaves. It connoted the slave master's value judgment of all slaves who were too young to be called "uncle." Calling the slave "boy" was intended to characterize black males as devoid of the spiritual or mental capacities for being manly equals to whites. "Uncle" was a fictive kinship term that many masters used to address the elder male slave on the plantation who was too old to work. Joel Chandler Harris's literary figure "Uncle Remus" and Harriet Beecher Stowe's "Uncle Tom" are classic examples. The fictive kinship term "uncle" might have been a psychological way for the master to control the "for and with" dynamics between him and his slave. Ironically, masters gained a sense of superiority out of claiming kinship with the old broken-down male slaves of his plantation. The same was the case with the term "a'ntie." It was a fictive kinship term the master often used when greeting an elderly female slave. All of these fictive kinship terms were used for the purpose of psychological control. Names like "Uncle Joe," "Uncle Buck," and "Uncle Tom" became popular stereotypes in the slave literature, but none of these appellations became more popular than "Uncle Tom." This stereotype of elderly black manhood was best presented in Harriet Beecher Stowe's *Uncle Tom's Cabin*. The fact is that on the plantation the male slave could make the quantum leap from boyhood to old age without ever being recognized as having experienced the interim years of manhood.

Blacks were expected to use honorific titles when referring to their masters and mistresses. Among these were "Master," "Mistress," "Miss Ann," and "Mars Bill." After their emancipation, old ex-slaves obviously found this practice difficult to break. Younger ex-slaves might resolve the dilemma by using "Old Master," "Boss," or "Cap'n."

No salutatory title has been more confusing than that of "nigger." Scholars have observed that blacks have used it among each other as an expression of both endearment and condemnation. During slavery, blacks used the term to attack slavish personalities as well as to express their affection toward each other. However, most blacks detested its use by whites.

The expression "nigger" was equated during slavery with being devoid of a soul. An elderly black women defended her use of the term to a Quaker missionary from Massachusetts in the following way: "We are niggers. We always will be niggers, and we always shall be; nigger here and nigger there, nigger do this and nigger do that. We got no souls, we are animals. We are black and so is the evil one." The missionary interrupted her at this point to explain that nothing in the Bible indicated that the devil might be black. "Well, white folks say so," the free woman replied, "and we are bound to believe 'em, cause we see nothing but animals and niggers. Yes, we'se niggers! niggers!"[12]

To the mind of pro-slavery such ideologues as Charles Carroll, the expressions "nigger" and "beast" were synonymous. Carroll sought to make the case because in his words "niggers were beasts" and blacks were totally cut off from God. There was no need for the slave master to try and communicate in his behalf because blacks had no soul. Who was the God of the "nigger"? understandably became an inevitable question.

Dehumanizing salutatory metaphorical designations such as "nigger" placed the slave in a nonhuman category. They reinforced the idea of the slave's being absolutely subjugated to the master. This meant that the slave's being for and with the master was an absolutely unilateral decision of the latter. The slave was devoid of the capacity either to affirm or disconfirm the master's decision for his or her life.

Honorable Dark Salutatory Metaphors

Slaves characterized their redemptive encounters with God and Jesus as being positive experiences of restoration. They were restored from the status of shame and disrespect, caused by slavery, to that of honor and respect as bequeathed by the gift of Jesus Christ. A conversion experience for slaves constituted a transformative encounter with the salutatory voice of God, Jesus, the Holy Spirit, and often other subordinate heavenly agents. For slaves, authentic conversion and realized brotherhood/sisterhood in Christ were inseparable realities. Since membership in the body of Christ was predicated upon this principle of brotherhood and sisterhood, the converts' acts of meeting and greeting each other were expected to be no less than brotherly and sisterly. Slaves spoke anthropomorphically, as many voices do in the biblical text, of what brotherly/sisterly relations meant in Christ. They concluded that "God could talk based upon humans capacity to do so."[13]

Legally denied the use of the Bible, slaves designated the individual's conscience as the locus for God's revelatory voice: "God speaks to us through our conscience and reasoning so loud that we seem to hear a voice."[14] In other words, they canonized the idea of the Christ-anointed conscience of the believing community of the oppressed. It was against this canon that every individual was expected to distinguish his or her hermeneutical suspicions about the true voice of God from false ones. There was always the danger of confusing the voice of God with the voice of the slave master. The following is a case in point. Characterizing his initial encounter with God, the slave Morte recalled, "I jumped because I thought it was my master coming to scold and whip me for plowing up some more corn."[15] Morte learns later that this anonymous voice, which he first thought was his master's, turns out to be God's.

Morte's encounter with the voice of God is one of a rare kind in a hostile context. God's salutatory voice personally greets the slave by name ("Morte! Morte!") and bestows upon him the honorific designation "my little one." God's directive to "my little one" is, "Fear not . . . I come to bring you a message of truth."[16] The honorific designation "my little one" is a recognizable theme in slaves' conversion stories. Slaves heard it, perhaps, as a divine compliment that was suggestive of God's respect for and honor of them, which countered the notion of plantation customs.

God's Little One

Jesus as Little One

The honorific designation "my little one" also suggested God's favored posture toward the victimized. It assured that God cared for him or her before the foundation of the world. Slaves probably found "my little one" to be more digestible than the traditional concept "servant" since the latter was a synonym for "slave." This honorific designation, through which the greeter affectionately recognized the slave's precarious state of existence in the institution of slavery, was a radical contrast to such dehumanizing salutatory designations as "nigger" and "darkey." The slave community perceived being called "my little one" as signaling God's possessive and protective care for the individual. It denoted God's way of helping the slave overcome a state of paralyzing fear: "Be not afraid." In this salutatory moment God's summons and promissory note illuminate the darkness: "Follow me for lo, I am a swift messenger and I will ever be thy guide. Keep thy feet in the straight and narrow path and follow me and all of the demons in hell shall not be able to cause thee to stumble or to fall."[17] Here God's "little one" is summoned to obey and trust God as a swift messenger, a constant guide, and a defense against Satan's tripping tactics. This is the promise of the savior figure, whom slaves affectionately called "little man" and "little one."

Jesus as Little Man

As correlative metaphorical phrases, "little one" and "little man" are best understood in the slave narratives when juxtaposed to each other. The latter is critical to the way that slaves understood the phenomenon of revelation. The characterization of the "little man" in slaves' conversion narratives is fascinating. The "little man" generally appears to assist the slave at his or her most difficult moment during the conversion rite of passage, as indicated in the following episode: "Then I began to cry and as I wept and there by my side stood a *little man,* very small with waxen hair. His eyes were like fire, his feet were like burnished brass. On his shoulder he carried a spear and on the end of it was a star that outshone the sun."[18] The "little man" appears both to counsel the fearful soul and give reassurance. The slave's portrayal of the unnamed "little man," who is obviously Jesus, is fascinating. Jesus is an apocalyptic tribal warrior, as the combination of an African tribal chief and the apocalyptic Christ of the book of Revelation in the Bible.

The salutatory expression "little man" seems rather ironic given that they needed a liberator in a society that valued size and power.

One rationale for slaves' description of Christ as the "little man" might have very well been their need for a Christ figure who could personally incarnate himself in the lowliness of their own ethnic social status. They needed one who was antithetical to Satan, whom they also called the "little man."

In another account the slave tells less of what the "little man" looks like and more about his liberating power in absolutely hopeless situations. The slave said that he himself died the sinner's death and "saw his body lying on the edge of a deep gap." While he was in this precarious situation, the "little man" appears to him and initiates a dialogical encounter: "A little man came up and said, 'Arise and go.' I said, 'Lord I can't get up or move else I will fall.' He reached out His hand and anointed my head and said, 'Arise and follow me for I am the Way, the Truth and the Light. I will make a way where there is no way.'"[19]

The stranded victim's use of the honorific title "Lord" clearly reflects his or her awareness of the true identity of the "little man." In the narrative the little man rescues his "little one" from the precipice of life, which is revealed proof that he is "the Way, the Truth and the Light." The metaphorical phrase "the Way, the Truth and the Light" clearly identifies the "little man." Equally crucial is the little man's high priestly function: "He reached out His hand and anointed my head."[20] Jesus, the little man, is portrayed as the high priest of liberation for all of those who are caught on the cliff of life.

Study of the "little one" and "little man" metaphors might very well illuminate the slaves' understanding of the kinship bond between Jesus and themselves. They must have cherished the idea of Jesus' being revealed to them as the "little man" or the "little one." This way of characterizing God's disclosure must have given an oppressed people a needed sense of security in the presence of the divine. It appears to be their unique way of describing the theophanic moment.[21] Bonding was possible with Jesus as the "little man" or the "little one." Indeed, both metaphors point to the possibility of nonthreatening intimacy with God. Such a perception of God or Jesus is critical for those oppressed, for those who had been forced into "little one" status by the system of slavery itself. Encountering

Jesus as the "little one" or the "little man" gave slaves radically new insight into the status of social being. In Jesus as the "little man," converts met one whose incarnational status equipped him with a unique understanding of their minority situation as little ones. Further, their assignment of "little one" status to Jesus might reflect their way of dealing with what would otherwise be the incomprehensibility of the divine. In fact, Jesus was the Cosmic One who appears to the oppressed in a nonthreatening form.

The metaphorical identification of Jesus as the "little man" demonstrates an affectionate kinship between Jesus and those he calls "my little ones." Jesus as the "little man" symbolized the operative norm in the lives of his "little ones," which must have been the most radical aspect of their revelatory experience of Jesus. Slaves could proudly take on the "little one" status of Jesus, who was the Son of God. Having a "little one's" disposition toward God placed believers in a unique relationship and allowed them to share in fellowship with Christ. Being born into Christ qualified every believer for "little one" status, and surrender to the call of God was a major prerequisite for being accepted into God's "little one's" fellowship.

Slave narratives reveal that oppressive plantation conditions possibly did much to sensitize slaves to God's revelatory presence in their lives. This conditioned sensitivity could very well explain the slaves' openness to the one whom they affectionately called the "little man" of their conversion encounters.

The Primordial Evil Man

One convert's description of Satan as a man of bizarre appearance is rather suggestive: "His head as white as cotton and a club foot red as fire."[22] The subjects's salvation is the other "little man" in his vision: "I looked up and saw a man, unlike anyone I have ever seen before. He showed me a little path and said 'follow me.'"[23] Again one might confess that "God came to me as a 'little man.'"[24] This anthropocentric way of characterizing both Satan and God is rather instructive about black consciousness. Satan is also a complex personality type who can manipulate the strongest mind.

A Complex Personality

The spiritual songs portray Satan as a real person, although invisible and untouchable, with a multiple personality. Slaves seemingly become hard-pressed to find enough metaphors to adequately describe Satan's deceitful nature. John Lovell characterized slaves' consciousness of Satan in the following way: "First, he is a liar, a conjurer, a trickster, and a snake in the grass. As liar, he will tell the slave, 'de God I seek I never find.' He will tell him to stop praying because it does no good."[25] Satan's primary objective as a liar is to breed distrust or doubt about the nature of God's dependability. Many believers in contemporary churches still find this language of Satan most appropriate for expressing their convictions about good and evil.

The slave community also used the salutatory metaphor of "conjuring" to characterize Satan.[26] In the slave community, no one was to be feared more than the conjurer. Slaves were to handle conjurers, because of their vulnerability to conjuration, with great care. They warned especially the novices of the faith of their vulnerability to Satan's conjuring powers: If you don't watch out he'll conjure you, cut you in two, or cut you through.[27] For slaves, Satan's power of trickery could be traced all the way back to the Garden of Eden. It was only through Jesus Christ that brothers and sisters could counter Satan.

Community, Jesus, and Satan

Brothers and sisters in Christ were summoned to unite in prayer against old Satan because he was deemed to be the personification of cosmic evil. Jesus' name has been deemed critical among traditional believers for fighting Satan. Harold A. Carter has rightly observed: "The one source of power to wage war on the devil was the name of Jesus. Imaginary or real, many a battle has to be fought or won, using Jesus' name in prayer."[28] The author of the following contemporary prayer realizes that it takes a communal effort on the part of prayer warriors to wage war against the devil:

> We gather here tonight to declare war on Satan and to put
> an end to the power of sin.

Satan, God rebuke you, and we declare you to be a liar through the blood of Jesus Christ.

We know, oh, Lord, that Satan is busy going to and fro in the streets of the city, devouring whom he may, but we thank God for the victory we have over Satan right now.

We thank you, Lord, that you got up one morning from the grave and declared your power over sin, death and hell, and declared, "Whoever will, let him come." We thank you for it.[29]

Another contemporary prayer, gathered by Carter, from the black church tradition illustrates the sense of unity that grows out of the prayerful struggle for united warfare against Satan. It was prayed at the close of the Annual Hampton Minister's Conference:

Almighty God, we thank thee for the hours we have spent on this campus. Every now and then when the way seems dark, you give us a little sample of what is better further along. We have been encouraged this week by the fact that what we have received is a sample of that which is waiting for those who hold out and prove faithful until the end. We are like the ox who is pulling the load up the hill, and about to give out; when the driver gets out of the ox cart and carries a little food up the hill—and the oxen know the food is up there, by faith they pull harder. We are gonna pull harder now. We are gonna cut more deeply. We are gonna believe more firmly. We are gonna hold more assuredly, because one thing you told Peter, "that the gates of hell will not prevail against the church."

Help us to go back now. When Samson wanted to burn down the wheat fields of the Philistines, he got a hundred or so foxes and tied their tales. He struck one match and lighted all those fiery tales and turned them loose among the wheat fields of the Philistines. When the foxes got through, the enemies of God didn't have nothing to feed on. We have been tied together here this week.

The servant of God has lighted our hearts with the candle of Thy Word. He's turning us loose now! We are going out into the world, and we are going to burn down hell and the kingdom of Satan in this age![30]

The Salutatory Secret Community

Slaves' verbal greetings to each other in the brush arbor meetings, or secret meeting places in the woods, gave them a radical sense of being and belonging in the face of alienation and death. During such precious stolen moments, their meeting and greeting each other verbally set the stage for the formulation of what can be called the structure of salutatory inquiry/confession. In the first place, no gathering among the oppressed was deemed complete without those gathered first confessing to God and each other. Then, those gathered would inquire about each other's total state of being. Love for God and each other was the driving force behind both their inquiries and confessions. Communion rituals such as this kept slaves in the meetings from developing a nihilistic disposition. They structurally permitted the opportunity for slaves to display honesty to the Lord and each other. Honest self-disclosures that took place between the gathered brothers and sisters in the brush arbor were the very opposite of what could take place between slaves and their masters. Deception was the expected rule of conduct between slave and master on the plantation. Brush arbor meetings afforded a place for worshipers to develop structures of trust between each other.

Former slave Peter Randolph's account of his brush arbor memories best illustrates this. One of Randolph's stories illustrates the workings of the inquiry/confession structure of the meeting and greeting ritual. Upon the initial encounter, the gathered "first ask each other how they feel, the state of their minds." This salutatory inquiry mirrors the profound way in which slaves mutually valued each other's total being. Slaves used their free moments in secret gathering places to inquire mutually about the welfare of each other's minds and bodies. This clearly demonstrates what it meant for them to be and belong for and with each other in God. It was also a time for slaves to renew their physical and spiritual bonding with each other. Randolph's description of slaves' bodily ritual of greeting and parting is equally as insightful: "They pass from one to another, shaking hands and bidding each other farewell. . . . as they separated they sang a hymn of praise."[31]

The Spiritual Songs

The inquiry/confession structure of meeting and greeting is illustrated clearly in many of the spiritual songs. "Brother" is a salutatory kinship metaphor that dominates the language of the black spiritual songs. Used both in greeting and parting rituals, "brother" is also the salutatory greeting that one uses when making a plea to the sinner about his need to confess his sinful state and receive salvation: "Brother, didn't conscience come and tell you, to go down in the valley and pray?" The one making the plea openly confesses his or her position regarding Jesus and salvation: "No, I ain't ashamed to honor my Lord. No, I ain't ashamed to go down in the valley and pray."[32]

Brotherly cooperation was needed in helping a poor soul make it from homelessness to home in the spiritual song "Brother Guide Me Home." One has only gratitude and appreciation for the brother who will guide him or her home. The pilgrim has only to anticipate the ecstatic joy awaiting him or her: "What a happy time, children?" An inquirer might ask: "Brother, have you come to show me the way? Show me how to watch and pray." The inquirer wants to know the way to enter the chariot traveling along, which is, no doubt, the chariot of the underground railroad.[33]

Slaves viewed confession of their common brotherhood as critical to being a Christian; such is the case in the song "You're My Brother So Give Me Your Hand." In fact, the slave community valued brotherly relations above local church membership and denominational differences:

> *It makes no difference what church you may belong to,*
> *While traveling through this barren land.*
>
> *We may not belong to the same denomination,*
> *While traveling through this barren land.*

Membership in the body of Christ is what made men brothers in the slave community: "If you are working for Christ my Redeemer, you are my brother so give me your hand." Brotherly cooperation is the condition for Christ-centered brotherhood: "But if you take my hand and lead me home to my Lord, You're my brother so give me your hand."[34]

The Parting Ritual

One of the great parting ritual songs was "Goodbye, Brother." In the moment of separation during slavery, those left behind told the one being sold off to another plantation or the one catching the underground railroad, "Goodbye, Brother/Sister." These goodbyes were generally conditioned by the awareness of the unpredictability of fate itself. Subsequently parting rituals were always tempered with the thought "If I never see you no more." God's blessings are invoked for the one taking involuntary or voluntary leave. The goodbye formula was colored by a theological understanding of the body and soul relationship:

> *We part in body,*
> *But we meet in spirit,*
> *We'll meet in heaven*
> *In the blessed kingdom.*

One slave song gives the parting formula for a single brother; another uses "brother" in the plural.[35]

Summary

Despite the negative salutatory metaphors that masters produced to dehumanize them, slaves ingeniously countered with their own constructive salutations in the moment of social encounter. In other words, slaves Christianized the salutatory moment. In doing so, they created the milieu that allowed them to be trustingly for and with each other both spiritually and politically. This is seen particularly in the way that many slaves cooperated with each other in the underground railroad. Salutatory metaphorical expressions from the slave culture, especially christological phrases such as Jesus as the "little man," enabled them to put a different theological spin on Christology. These expressions prepared slaves spiritually and politically for dealing constructively with their potential "brothers in white," who were their oppressors, even the benevolent ones.

CHAPTER 5

Brothers in White
The Minority Conscience of Salutatory Paternalists

Whites viewed the proclamation of emancipation as the year of freedom for blacks. Until then blacks had been viewed as chattel. The historic emancipation event prompted many white professing Christians to rethink such crucial social notions as "brotherhood" and "manhood" in relationship to emancipated blacks. For whites to rethink these concepts meant that they now had to struggle with the human potential of those they previously had deemed as chattel. Whites now were being forced to recognize blacks as social beings who dared speak for and with each other as men and women created in God's image. Significant black voices would speak for and with the white community about the importance of freeing blacks. Rhetorically they sought to reshape the consciousness of the nation toward black Americans' worth as people. Inevitably whites found it increasingly difficult to ignore black voices crying for recognition in the body politic. A minority of white Christians showed some compassion for blacks' cries for freedom.

A Minority's Perspective

Whites who professed any degree of Christian affinity for blacks were often unwilling to recognize them as their social equals. Some did, however, think that blacks might have the intellectual potential, after many generations of exposure to character-building education, to develop gradually into persons worthy of equal citizenship recognition and rewards. These whites invested economically and otherwise in the Yankee missionary enterprise of educating recently freed slaves for civic duties. Their challenging educational pursuits, on behalf of slaves, were driven by the philanthropic philosophy of being followers of Jesus Christ, who obligated them to lift their subservient black brothers from ignorance and depravation caused by slavery.

Debates among whites were alive over whether freed blacks had the potential rational capacities for being gradually developed over the generations into a manly and brotherly race. Benevolent whites expected that such an evolutionary development could only take place through character-building education and character-building religion. The anticipated result was a race that could prove that it merited respect of its white adversaries. Rhetoric about blacks' manly and brotherly capacities thematically dominated the public discourse of both the late nineteenth and early twentieth centuries. It set the political stage for white racists to take full control of the public debate about blacks' destiny in America. Formally this came to be known as the era of Jim Crowism. So-called benevolent whites were forced to debate both their theological belief about blacks' nature and destiny and their ethical behavior toward them. Jim Crowism bred an absolute hostile climate toward blacks that was almost irreversible.

Professing white Christians, during and following slavery, faced both a theological and an ethical dilemma. Framing the theological dilemma, they could not admit that blacks were their social equals without having to admit before God that slavery was wrong and amounted to a sin against God. Framing the ethical dilemma, white Christians could not admit that blacks were their social equals without having to admit they had failed in their duties toward God and those they had enslaved in God's name. Ruled by their own false pride, whites sought to justify their enslavement of blacks on the grounds that the latter were inferior by creation. Christian whites relied upon spurious reasoning to ground their beliefs about God, blacks, and themselves.

Whites of every political viewpoint believed that God unequivocally favored those of European origin over every other ethnic group upon the face of the earth. They and their descendants celebrated this belief in what scholars have come to call the doctrine of "manifest destiny." Proponents of this doctrine, which was grounded in a skewed reading of the Bible, argued that God had created the white man to rule other races of the world. They were meant to save and keep the souls of the lesser ethnic brothers of the earth. Subscribers to this belief were absolutely convinced that God was a respecter of persons. Had whites believed otherwise, they would have undermined their own philosophy of manifest destiny.

Moderate whites, especially in the North, were more inclined to embrace what I am here calling the probability theory of blacks' potential for citizenship-equality. They too advocated a brand of white benevolent paternalism that said that God was *for* blacks but not *with* them. God was only for blacks through whites whom God had ordained to be their spiritual and moral guardians. Whites embraced this for-but-not-with dichotomy because of their inevitable theological belief in the white man's burden and manifest destiny. They believed that God had made blacks only for a subservient role in the development of human civilization. Such white advocates, in addition to black advocates, of this subservient theory reasoned that blacks, when living in Africa prior to their enslavement in America, were totally ignorant of the enlightened God. These advocates concluded that God had ordained the Africans' enslavement as a means of exposing them to the gospel of Jesus Christ. The Old South left little, if any, room for neutrality about what God's position was toward blacks. Moderate whites believed that God had created blacks with inferior intellectual and spiritual capacities, a spurious belief that prevented whites from seeing that blacks had manly and brotherly capacities comparable to their own.

The racist ideology of the Old South demanded that whites embrace the belief that God could only be either *for* black people, through whites, or *against* them, through whites. Benevolent whites embraced the theological belief that God is for blacks spiritually but not politically; malevolent whites held the hard-core theological belief that God is against blacks spiritually and politically. In short, both of these two radically different perspectives of God's being for and with blacks said that God lacked faith in blacks' intellectual, spiritual, and emotional capacities. Having originated in institutional slavery, which was predicated on the myth of the white man's burden and manifest destiny, both the "God for" and "God against" philosophies have been used to justify different degrees of racist paternalism.

Whites answered the ethical question of blacks' capacity for trustworthiness with a resounding "no!" For racist whites, this negation of the idea that the Creator had endowed blacks for trustworthiness originated in the myth of the creation itself. Benevolent whites sought to justify their racist paternal relationship to blacks on the grounds that God had elected the former to remake the latter, through character-building education, in the cultural image of whites themselves. That God had made the "brothers in white" salutatory saviors to their "brothers in black" was the normative belief of the day. Benevolent whites believed that it was God's expectation that the "brothers in black" mimic their beliefs and practices totally. Missionary members of this type modeled themselves proudly before their "brothers in black" as the norm of true Christian humanity and brotherhood.

Brothers in White

Whites' use of such a salutatory metaphorical phrase as "brothers in black" spoke volumes about how they comparatively referred to themselves in relationship to blacks. It undoubtedly suggested the racial superiority of one group over the other even in the natural order of things. Salutatory metaphorical phrases such as "brothers in white" or "brothers in black" suggested that the subject had been permanently clothed in his natural racial existence by God. Whites assumed that God valued their whiteness over blacks' blackness. Given such a presupposition about God and color, whites could always justify their mistreatment of blacks as inferior beings, for such was in keeping with their understanding of the divine law of nature.

Without doubt, theological assumptions had an effect on behavior. What, indeed, was the relationship between whites' theological understanding of God and their ethical duties toward God's black inferiors? How did whites' idea of God's being totally for and with them affect their notion of Christian duties toward those whom God was only "for" through them? The answers to these questions would determine whites' treatment of blacks. Benevolent whites, according to primary sources, tended to show some sensitivity to the problem of the devaluation of blacks but malevolent whites lacked express appreciation for it. Benevolent whites sought to show some sign of a semigood Samaritan ethic for the blacks that their slave system victimized. Following institutional slavery, these whites at least saw themselves as "helpers of moral lepers."

Helpers of Moral Lepers

The critical ethical question facing whites who saw themselves as helpers of moral lepers was the extent to which benevolent white missionaries and former abolitionists, following the freeing of slaves, would practice being for and with blacks. If they believed that slavery stained blacks' souls and characters, how did this influence the way that whites of goodwill related to blacks? Atticus Haygood, who was a white moderate conservative minister of Atlanta, sought to set the brotherhood/manhood issue in theological perspective following the slaves' emancipation. He did so by publicly saluting the black man, in speech and written word, as "our brother in black." This was the salutatory title of Haygood's book *Our Brother in Black: His Freedom and His Future* (1881).[1] Haygood reasoned that southerners failed to understand that emancipation was a part of the providence of God, just as slavery was. He concluded that blacks, although stained by the ignorance of slavery, had brotherhood/manhood potential in Jesus Christ. For Haygood, the probability/potentiality theory of blacks being made worthy of citizenship was possible through character-building education in Jesus Christ.

Contemporary scholars of the history of social ideas and race in America, such as James MacPherson, have contributed greatly to understanding white missionaries' philosophy of character-building education. His scholarly works have illuminated the Protestant work ethic that drove many Yankee missionaries to give up the comforts of their own places in the North to work among the recently freed slaves of the South. Being missionaries among blacks in isolated rural areas of the South, which cut them off from their white colleagues, often created in white missionaries a painful sense of ethnic identity and alienation. One missionary from Massachusetts sensing such alienation wrote a letter to the American Missionary Association requesting a reprieve from his venue at Talladega College in Alabama.

He stated his felt need to "breath the briny air of the ocean . . . look upon the mountains and inhale the life-giving breezes—see and converse with cultivated men and women—be recognized by Christians of my own race—feel that I am no longer a leper."[2] White missionaries of this type often saw themselves as good Samaritans who dared work with God's outcasts for the purpose of exposing them to the cleansing power of God. They worked with the conviction that giving blacks character-building education was more important than teaching them ideas about social equality and citizenship rights.

Character-Building Education

MacPherson observes that "most missionaries generally avoided the inflammatory words social equality, or social rights."[3] He proceeds to say that

> though they associated with blacks that southerners could only regard as social equality, they probably did not in any strict sense consider most of the freedmen socially equal to themselves. No matter how sincere their equalitarianism, missionary teachers could never completely bridge the racial gap. To the black community they were inevitably outsiders. And the teachers' frequent references to black people as they or them are evidence that they could not escape the consciousness of being outsiders.[4]

The missionaries' dilemma of outsider consciousness invariably affected the way that they understood their sense of being for and with "ignorant blacks." What in the gospel could cleanse blacks of their wretched condition of moral leprosy? What could clean these poor creatures from their stain of ignorance and sin? It was the reality of ignorance and sin that had dirtied their souls and bodies. Optimistic moderate whites believed that it would take character-building education, which for them had salvific power, to clean up the slave and place him in evolutionary candidacy for manly and brotherly rights possibly equal to those of whites.

Here I have used the phrase "evolutionary candidacy" intentional-
ly. I have done this primarily because most white missionaries were not
convinced that blacks had the capacity to become men and women
equal to white men and women. Some missionaries believed that
racism's mark of oppression on blacks constituted "internal diseases
which could be remedied by external forces."[5] A long-standing secre-
tary of the American Missionary Association observed that "the root of
the race problem was not in the Negro's color or party, but with the
man himself—with his ignorance, his degradation."[6] He further
observed, "The remedy then is not to change his color or his party, but
his character."[7] Changing the black person's character would make him
or her acceptable to the white fellowship of Jesus Christ.

Christ as Brother Man

A few white leaders of the Protestant church, North and South, held
to the ideal that Jesus Christ was the paradigmatic "brother man" of
humanity. Leaders such as D. G. W. Ellis claimed that "every man
upon the face of the earth is related to every other man by ties of
blood." Convinced of the relational ties-of-blood theory of the creation of humanity, Ellis opposed the hypothesis that "there were several distinct sets of progenitors of the human family." He wrote in
the premier church quarterly of his day that "Christ, as His human
nature, is a *brother man.* He was 'born of a woman,' and hence his
relationship is based upon this fact, and not upon the fact of having
'a like moral nature,' etc."[8]

Ellis used Paul's assumption about Christ's divine and human
nature to address the racial problem of Ellis's day. A prominent
southern cleric, he concluded that all people are related because they
have their origin in Christ. That is to say, all people regardless of race,
have a Christocentric relationality to each other. Ellis observed this
when he conclusively wrote: "If, then, Christ is a *brother man*
because he is related to the race by ties of blood, the same thing that
makes him a brother to me makes me a brother to every other man.
We are related by ties of blood; we are children of the same original
ancestors."[9] Ellis countered the racists of his day who sought to make
brotherhood and the unity of the white race normative. He did so by

noting that unity between the races is predicated upon "a like moral nature and a like sense of moral responsibility, a common theistic conception, a common intuition of immortality, and most of all of the scriptural declaration that Jesus Christ by the grace of God tasted death for every man and not at all on the 'physical unity of the race.'"[10] In short, Ellis was more interested in a Christology of "sameness" rather than one of "likeness" when it came to Christ and the human race.

Inevitably missionaries' subtle, and sometimes explicit, racist practices reflected the cultural ethos of the day. Being for and with blacks was always a challenge that often tested missionaries' Christian faith and practice. It was not easy for missionaries to be for blacks socially and politically in a Jim Crow society. Fear of racist violence demanded that missionaries, even of the liberal persuasion, compromise to southern customs, whatever moderate notions they might have had of Christian brotherhood. It was necessary that they do this in order to protect both themselves and the blacks whom they worked among.

Missionaries who worked within the South's Jim Crow ethics of uplifting blacks saw themselves as having everything to give blacks and nothing to receive from them. This philosophy of unilateralism often prevented whites from seeing blacks' undisclosed intrinsic value. Such whites subsequently became prisoners of their own blind racist paternalism. Viewing themselves as second to Christ in the order of the family of God, white missionaries believed that they were keepers of blacks religiously and morally and expected blacks to present themselves as "empty dark pitchers" before "filled white fountains of civilized knowledge." Whites predicated this assumption upon a faulty notion of a Christ whom they believed had elected them to civilize and save all other subordinate races of the world. This belief gave whites a sense of having special rights and duties in all the world. A small group of whites did accept the ideal of common spiritual brotherhood and sisterhood with blacks in Christ. For example, Haygood, a white clergy leader, made the case that "our brothers in black have been redeemed by God through Jesus Christ. Christ's redemption gave them the right for potentially becoming manly brothers with the contemporary white man."[11]

God, Race, and Character Building

God, race, and character became inseparable social concepts in the theological language of nineteenth-century white leadership when referring to blacks. Whites constantly debated whether blacks had been endowed by God with the innate capacity for adopting and practicing the moral principles of European civilization. Hard-core racists concluded that blacks were even less capable of being taught the morality of whites. They likened any such effort to casting pearls before swine. A small remnant of white missionaries believed that they ought not forfeit their "duties as a higher race to subordinate blacks." This remnant struggled under the burden of conscience to try to understand what constituted the higher race's duties to those they categorized as the lower race.[12]

The Big Three

George Rawlinson, Beverly Bond, and Haygood constitute three major leaders who gave significant interpretation to the whole issue of Christianity and race during the post-slavery period. Rawlinson, the distinguished historian of Oxford University, took seriously what he described as the distinction between "the higher race and the lower." "Higher Race and the Lower" is the title that Rawlinson gave to a published article in the latter part of the nineteenth century. Arguing conclusively for the unity of the human race, Rawlinson took the position that the resolution to the race problem was through intermarriage between the races. He believed that intermarriage between whites and blacks would soon erase the distinction of race. Understandably, Rawlinson's idea of amalgamating the races did not sit very well with the majority of whites of his day.

Beverly Waugh Bond, a southerner, emphatically denounced Rawlinson's proposition for amalgamation of the races as the solution to the race problem of the day. He reasoned that the duty of the white Christian was "to labor in behalf of all of his fellow-men, and for none more than the ignorant and the depraved."[13] Bond's rationale was that amalgamation would go against the self-interest of what his generation called "the higher race." He concluded that whites

could save themselves by fulfilling their God-given duties to those of
the lower race. In the words of Rawlinson: "the claim of benevolence
toward the lower race, may be met by a similar allegation of duty we
owe our own flesh and blood, to transmit to them and their poster-
ity the full yea, added, mental and moral blessings we ourselves have
inherited."[14]

A rather hard-core racist, Bond advocated a notion of duty that
protected the interest of the white race. He concluded that whites'
paramount duties were to themselves rather than to blacks: "The
claims of our own race are at least equal to those of another; that the
higher races have paramount duties to themselves, and that like individuals their first business in the work of elevating others, is to see
that they are not degraded themselves."[15] Bond appealed to the mandate of the law of benevolence itself. His reasoning was that attempts
"to regenerate and save will do harm, and not good, if he (the white
man) is not himself regenerated and saved."[16] Bond's style of reasoning informed his theological and ethical understanding of duties to
those of his day described as "the lower races." He wrote with racist
conviction that "the good of the lower races themselves demand that
the higher shall maintain and advance all their civilization and culture, physical and mental, and moral."[17]

White missionaries were emphatically convinced that God
favored their race above others. They reasoned, as well, that blacks'
experience of slavery itself was a sign that God, too, had favored
blacks. Whites saw slavery as God's way of bringing Africans to "the
great light of civilization."[18] Even moderate whites could denounce
the barbarity of slavery while simultaneously affirming it as an institution necessary to introduce blacks to "the higher religion and
morality of the civilized world."[19] Slavery was perceived as God's
providential school for shaping the moral character of those of
African descent for the New World.

Haygood reasoned that "providence was Blacks coming to
America as slaves and their being emancipated."[20] From reading the
Bible, he concluded that both the enslavement and the emancipation
of blacks were ordained by God. He daringly reminded southerners
that "God has set them free as well as the Negroes, and now the
'truth' should make them free altogether and forever."[21] Courageous-

ly, Haygood struggled to read God's revelatory acts in the South's troubled history and admonished whites to respond brotherly to their "brothers in black." Haygood was less tolerant of the popular idea that whites enjoyed divine preeminence over all other races of the world. Black religious leaders of the nineteenth century found consolation in Haygood's intolerance.

Black leaders' susceptibility to the unilateral philosophy that whites had "nothing but good" to offer blacks violated any expectation of mutuality, as expressed in terms of being "for and with." The critical question was whether the relationship between the races would be unilateral or bilateral. A bilateral philosophy of one race being for and with the other required a religious and moral structure that elicited mutual expectations of brotherly agency. Such a philosophy of mutual brotherly expectations fostered racial and social equality and suggested a type of fraternal equality between the races that whites were unready to embrace because of their unwillingness to partnership with blacks socially. Even white missionaries who claimed to be spiritually for and with blacks were not ready for bilateral relationships. Their unilateral view was predicated on their narrow perspective of paternalism, which assumed that it was enough to be for and with blacks spiritually. The bottom line of this presumption was that whites knew what was best for blacks. By assuming the role of the Christian elder brother of blacks, white missionaries assigned themselves older brother status over blacks.

Race, Morality, and Religion

The either/or disjunction that arose from whites being for and with blacks spiritually but against blacks politically bred an exclusively racist kind of paternalistic religion and morality, which implied that God is the creator of the permanent social and natural inequalities of the races. Proponents of this paternalism, arguing that possessors of power automatically had the right to define religiously and morally what constituted true brotherhood, prescribed a unilateral philosophy of brotherhood. They excluded all assumptions that Christian brotherhood was predicated on a Christology that called for mutual sharing in the body of Christ. Indeed, such social sharing in Christ was prohibited in a white racist society. The prevailing view was that Christ was both for and with whites spiritually and politically. Had they done otherwise, whites would have given blacks a radical Christ who would have undermined their own self-interest as the dominant race, which would have prevented whites from romantically concluding that they and blacks worshiped the same Christ of faith.

Worthiness of Character

In the minds of most whites, blacks totally lacked intrinsic worthiness, which disqualified them of all political rights. Even many abolitionists advanced the idea that "the most urgent endeavor was not to pass more civil rights laws, but to lead these Negroes into higher intelligence; to reform and elevate their standards of morality; to teach them industry, temperance, thrift; to preach to them the pure religion of Christ," the whole idea being that "the Negro had to be made worthy of freedom and able to maintain it."[22] The burden of the missionary educator was thus to prove the Negro worthy for freedom, which for many meant curing the Negro of what some missionaries identified as "lying, petty thieving and sexual promiscuity."[23]

Debate over the methodology of character transformation was not uncommon at the time. Some argued that blacks could be transformed from their state of degradation and shame by salvific methods such as learning the skills of literacy; others said that it would take an internal salvation method such as the blood of Jesus. The debate was often over whether the external salvation came before the internal or vice versa. One missionary observed that "the Negro's elevation and progress like all others, are first internal, then external . . . first in character, then in environment; first intellectual, moral, spiritual, then, industrial, financial, social."[24]

Tension also existed between the social Darwinists and missionaries of the gospel of Jesus Christ as to how best transform recently freed blacks. Those influenced by social Darwinism believed that "time plus education and moral regeneration were necessary to cure the political and social ills of the South." S. R. Thornton advocated a theological perspective of character during the latter part of the nineteenth century.

Thornton's Perspective

Nineteenth-century leaders saw the problem of the formation of character in partnership with Christ as the supreme question of the ages. For whites, the theological issue of character became a primary theme of public discourse. Church leaders and theologians raised such questions as

> What is character? From whence does it emanate? Is it something given to man in his creation, or is it formed by his own volition or will-power? Is he responsible for its existence, or only for its kind or quality? Has an infant character, or is it only the possession of a being capable of moral action? Is character, like the mental powers, a natural endowment, or is it the result of human effort? What relation does it sustain to regeneration, and how is it affected by it? These with many other questions, enter into the merits of this subject.[25]

In addition, Thornton asserted that "God is the embodiment of good and perfect character. In him character is original, uncreated, essential, indispensable to his being. . . . Character is a primeval endowment given to man in his creation. It was the very best type— spotless, pure, and God-like."[26] But if God created humanity with good and perfect character, how did humankind come about a flawed one? Thornton answered that this happened when God told Adam and Eve not to eat from the tree of the forbidden fruit; this moral prohibition was a test of his character. Adam's disobedient act brought about the ruin of humankind's moral character. The fall of Adam, and hence of humanity, means that he is "no longer in possession of that noble and pure character."[27] Humankind's challenge following the fall has been to restore the primeval relation and to restore that fallen character to its original beauty; to thus rise is humankind's supreme work and highest glory. Thornton observed, "The supreme importance of this work is seen in that without this spotless character all the other wonderful faculties and endowment of the soul must of necessity fail to carry out the divine purpose and accomplish their designed end. It is said that the chief end of man is to glorify God forever."[28] Thornton believed in the restoration through Jesus Christ of all that was lost in the fall.[29] Humankind was to be Christ's partner in working out this end of the restoration process. Humanity's failure to cooperate with God in this project was to set us up for shame and everlasting ruin and to deprive us of true character.

Character and God

Christian leaders of the late nineteenth and early twentieth centuries argued that character was "the mightiest spiritual force, and hence the most potent thing in the universe. It is not what a man is reputed to be, or professes to be, but what he is."[30] In short, character is the ontological self. Bishop Eugene R. Hendrix of the Methodist Church of the South proceeded with his definition of a man's character to say that it was "the embodiment of what he thinks, of what he feels, of what he wills. Intellect, sensibility, and will all combined find their truest expression in man's character."[31]

Character building is the cultivation of the seed of regeneration and the development of it to perfection: "Regeneration restores the divine image to the soul, and man develops or establishes the new character. Unaided by grace, man cannot purify his character, else the atonement would not have been a necessity."[32] Thornton further observed:

> A character perfected in Jesus Christ is the one thing that we shall take with us into eternity. It is the only thing that shall stand the test in the judgment. This exalted character is the crown that we shall wear. It's the soul's exceeding reward. It is the inheritance that is incorruptible and undefiled and that fadeth not away. It is the glory that shall be revealed in us. It is the highest wisdom.[33]

Human Will

Discussions of character invariably include consideration of human will. The two appear inseparable. W. S. Reese, at the turn of the twentieth century, defined will this way: "The will is the synthesis of knowledge and feeling, the concrete fact of soul-life and energy. It is the fit exponent of manhood, for it is the essence of the self."[34] Reese argued that the will could be developed because even in fancy it existed in potential. In other words, humankind, through self-assertion, could make actual what is only possible. Reese said, "God has given the potential and the opportunity to make it actual. Man must make himself. . . . By following the law of growth that God has written in our very nature."[35] It is a universal principle of life that power grows only by exercise. Reese proceeds to observe the distinction between the will and impulse. The individual self has to be freed from impulse in order for the will to develop. Reese states this in relationship to rational choice:

> Will grows out of impulse, but it grows away from impulses. So far as a man acts under impulse, his will is still unformed, he has not control of himself, and his conduct has unsteadiness and unreliability betokening the lack of character. Deliberation must take impulse. An act must be chosen or rejected, performed or suppressed, as it furthers or hinders the purpose chosen. In this way habits of thought and habits of choice are formed; that is, our mental and our moral self are organized for the attainment of the chosen end or purpose of life, and choice becomes seemingly immediate and intuitive. This organization of the self into habits of choice we call character. What a man's character is, that he is. It is his will realized, the self made actual.[36]

A Remnant's Perspective

The painful reality is that the white Christian majority has never forthrightly embraced blacks as equal brothers and sisters. They have never embraced a Christ who would mandate them to include those of other races as their social equals. For the most part, white Christians have reduced the notion of equality to the spiritual level only. At best only a minority of whites went on record speaking out against the lynching of blacks. A Baptist minister in South Carolina singled out for condemnation lynchers who sought to justify their action in the name of defending virtue. He charged that they made a mockery of virtue, for some lynchers were guilty of having relations with black women, which helped to provoke "the crime leading to the lynchings."[37] A white Mississippian undoubtedly went to the source of the problem when he observed that "the only way to keep the pro-lynching elements in the church is to say nothing which would tend to make them uncomfortable as church members."[38]

The contemporary scholar of church history Ralph E. Luker has placed in critical perspective what he calls the "social gospel movement in black and white." Luker's study covers the philosophy of racial reform in the years 1865–1912. He shows how a small group of white minority Christians helped to form the nexus for producing such social-protest organizations as the NAACP in 1910 and the National Urban League in 1911. Luker's book traces the role of American social Christianity in racial reform during the period between emancipation and the civil rights movement. He contends that after emancipation the heirs of antislavery sentiment created a series of organizations aimed at racial reform, but all had floundered by the mid-1890s, when lynching was at its peak. As racial conflict and urban problems worsened, black and white reformers, many of them spokespersons for American social Christianity, explored a variety of uniracial and biracial solutions. The denominations organized the Federal Council of Churches in 1909. Central to Luker's thesis is the idea that theological personalism played a major role in curbing racism in American thought. Although some social gospel prophets supported radical forms of cultural imperialism and racial separatism, Luker shows that personalism equipped a few southern white racial moderates and a larger group of northern white evangelical neoabolitionists to challenge racism's central claims.[39] They sowed the seed for what in the second half of the twentieth century would become the full-blown civil rights movement.

A Paradigmatic Breakthrough

The emergence of the civil rights movement in the 1960s was a coming-out moment for white minority Christians sensitive to the race problem. It constituted a paradigmatic breakthrough in race relations for many whites who had been locked in the psychological prisons of their own fears. Also, it provided them with a forum for making a social witness that they lacked previously. One of the more intriguing narrative studies of white minority Christians' contributions has been captured in Taylor Branch's book *Parting the Waters*.[40] Scholars who have studied the history of civil rights organizations such as the Student Nonviolent Coordinating Committee and the Southern Christian Leadership Conference have demonstrated that each of these organizations received significant moral and economic support from minority groups of white Christians.

The birth of the civil rights drama of the 1960s provided the social theater, so to speak, for the consciousness of a Christ figure who dared move back and forth across the color line of race. There emerged a Christ figure who embraced the notion of "black and white together" even in the South, where the color line was expected to control Jesus' behavior.[41] The more whites chose the status of ones they had called "nigger," the more some were embarrassed by their own lack of brotherly and sisterly behavior.

Summary

White Christians who fostered the spiritual welfare of blacks were in the minority. They, however, made a significant contribution, though viewed as conservatives by today's standards, to the discussion of blacks' brotherhood/sisterhood potential. Those of the white minority conscience chose, for fear of political backlash from their community, to be for blacks only spiritually. For this reason, they promoted character-building education and character-building religion as the panacea to the race problem. Their contributions, as priestly in nature as they were, undeniably made it possible for the preparation and emergence of black indigenous leadership. Their "brothers in black" would dialectically embody in themselves, in the best sense of the word, a type of prophetic/priestly conscience of humanity and brotherhood/sisterhood.

Chapter 6

Brothers in Black
The Priestly / Prophetic Type Conscience

Being and belonging for blacks following their emancipation became critical to their new adventure into freedom. Several critical questions were at the heart of the "brothers in black" struggle: What was blacks' understanding, as Christians, of their priestly/prophetic duties to white America and each other? How did Christian brothers in black deal with the dichotomous belief of God's being for and with them spiritually and God's being for and with them politically? Blacks unquestionably credited the God of their weary years with having emancipated them from slavery and set them on the high road of race elevation and purification. Primary black literary sources (sermons and addresses) are not always clear about what the connection is, if any, that blacks made between the god of their preslavery existence in Africa and the "God of their weary years" (i.e., from slavery to the twentieth century). Many black Christian leaders, before and after slavery, adopted the philosophy that suffering was the means that every oppressed group must take in its climb up the ladder of civilization.[1] Slavery was attested to be but one of the serialized experiences that uncivilized people had to endure.

God and Serialized Experiences

Was God authoring and using blacks' serialized experiences of slavery, emancipation, and segregation as character-building episodes for making them a great people? This would constitute blacks' premier theological question for the nineteenth and twentieth centuries. How would blacks know that God was in the serialization of their experiences of victimization? Was God, in fact, the initiator and serializer of these events? These questions were all generated by theological debate of whether God was for and with blacks spiritually and politically. Most black and white Christian leaders concluded that God was using black people's serialized experiences of slavery, liberation, and segregation to make them a great people. It was God's way of bonding with them.

J. W. E. Bowen, the premier black scholar/preacher of the turn of the twentieth century, stated his philosophy in classical terms when he told blacks of his generation, "You must remember that the plane upon which our brother in white stands to-day, has been reached by generations of slavery, toil and sacrifice, afflictions, discipline and adversity; war, pestilence and death."[2] Bowen's logic was that God was using the white man to train them for the journey into the civilized world.[3] Northern white missionaries sought to instill within blacks a Calvinistic theology of perseverance and sacrificial suffering that would make them worthy both for the kingdom of God and the kingdom of America. This would inevitably bridge the gap between God's being for them and God's being with them spiritually and politically. It was the aim of these servants of God to transform the "moral lepers" of slavery into "civilized Christians."[4] Sensing the urgency of this need for his race, Bowen told his audience: "We do not need moral lepers, or men whose religious life will not bear inspection. We need and must have Christian and educated leaders."[5] It seems to have been common knowledge that such new leaders would be "in the position to begin the work of elevation."[6]

The Comparative Method

Black leaders of Christianity invariably compared their race's serialized experiences of suffering in the New World to the story of the Israelites, the almost mythical people of the Old Testament. This meant that blacks had to reassess, at each critical epoch, what it meant to believe in God and Jesus Christ. For instance, what did it mean to have been politically freed by the God of liberation after the Civil War only to have that political freedom taken away with the inauguration of the segregated society? What happened to the God who had been faithfully for and with them both spiritually and polit-

ically as symbolized in the events of the Civil War and the proclamation of emancipation?

Many whites, before and after the Civil War, taught that God
was faithfully for and with black people spiritually. Yet these same
whites taught that God was not faithfully for and with black people
politically. Blacks often found themselves struggling on the horns of
this theological dilemma. If God was not faithfully for and with
them politically, what did this say about blacks' status of personhood? How could they be brotherly and manly in a society that
sought to negate their very existence? Where was the God of blacks'
liberation in this new inhumane social experiment of racial separation? Was God in collusion with the architect of this drama of social
evil? Was this the same God who brought blacks out of the bondage
of slavery? Or had God become the premier teacher for blacks to be
tolerant in this dark and painful historical moment?

God as Schoolmaster

Black religious leaders, both before and following the Civil War, saw
God as their schoolmaster. That is to say, they saw God as using one
of the most negative modern-day social experiments in human suffering to teach them the great lessons of Christian religion and
morality. Black Americans saw themselves as God's new Israelites in
modern Egypt. Pastors such as the Reverend L. M. Beckett, a prominent minister in Washington, D. C., made theological connections
between enslavement in the ancient world and in the modern one.
Clerics of his ilk, black and white, were often attracted to the biblical writers' teachings of obedience and disobedience, blessings and
curses. Blacks' enslavement was often interpreted as punishment for
the collective sins of the dark race's African past, as a necessary school
of adversity that God required even blacks to undergo.[7] That large
numbers of black leaders saw slavery as a necessary preparatory
school for readying the race for the white man's civilization created a
constant dilemma in black consciousness.

The black intellectual preacher Bowen quickly admitted his
inability biblically to justify the practice of slavery. Theologically,
however, he invoked the biblical paradigm of Joseph's love-forgiveness

response to his brothers as the method that blacks ought to use. Bowen, speaking for himself, said: "I am willing to close the whole chapter forever with the noble chapter of Joseph to his brethren: 'But as for you, ye thought evil against me, but God meant it for good.'"[8] Bowen posited that the suffering of black people was necessary to make them socially equal with their white brother: "We have to suffer yet more before we are thoroughly purged and made the equal of our white brother."[9] He believed that this redemptive suffering made blacks God's special students in the university of adversity.

God's Special Education Students

Redemptive suffering was the thematic theological concern at the heart of black preachers' sermons of the late nineteenth century and practically all of the twentieth century. Some have even argued that the benefits that blacks derived from Christianity have more than compensated for the suffering that slavery caused them.[10] God was credited with using white abolitionists and philanthropists and the slave master in the educational experiment. White abolitionists, missionaries, and philanthropists were expected to lift former slaves into the dawn of a new day of brotherly manhood and manly brotherhood. These whites might have been guilty, too often, of equating the kingdom of America with the biblical notion of the kingdom of God. They interpreted Christian outreach (i.e., missions) to slaves as the preparatory stage for making America the kingdom of heaven.[11]

Blacks, understanding themselves as God's special education students in the great school of human suffering, easily made a connection between themselves and the Israelites of the Bible. They often used numerous metaphorical phrases from the Bible to characterize their own liberation from both slavery and the snares of a segregated society. Although it is one of the most commonly referred to, the exodus is just one such biblical metaphor that blacks have invoked. Another such biblical metaphor with which blacks have found great spiritual and political affinity has been "jubilee." It became one of blacks' premier theological expressions for characterizing what the event of emancipation meant to them. Blacks celebrated emancipation as "a jubilee of freedom, a hosanna to their deliverers."[12] Additional biblical metaphorical expressions became part of blacks' language of celebration: for example, "Babylon had fallen"; "Golly! De kingdom hab kim dis time for sure—dat ar what am promised in de generations to dem dat goes up tru great tribulations."[13] These terms arose from the belief that slaves had a special relationship with God and Jesus.

Jesus as Emancipator

The folk imagination of ex-slaves viewed Jesus as the key liberation player, the emancipator of the newly emancipated, affirmer of the nonconfirmed, reconciler of the alienated. Affirmation of this can be heard in the following lyrics:

> *Now no more weary trav'lin',*
> *Cause my Jesus set me free,*
> *An' there's no more auction block for me*
> *Since He gives me liberty.*[14]

Slaves hearing for the first time the news of having been freed often responded with praise. One woman recalls:

I jump up an' scream, "Glory, glory, hallelujah to Jesus! I's free! Glory to God, you come down an' free us; no big man could do it." An I got sort o' scared, afeared somebody heard me, an' I takes another good look, an' fall on the groun', and roll over an' kissed the groun' for the Lord's sake, so I's so full o' praise to Master Jesus. He do all dis great work. De soul buyers can neber take my two chillen lef me; no, neber can take 'em from me no mo'.[15]

Freedom from slavery for the ex-slave was a sign that God had started the progressive process of raising blacks from the pit of inhumanity to the high road leading toward manly brotherhood. Blacks were very much aware that the laws that made whites great actually degraded blacks. Newly freed blacks interpreted their freedom to mean that they had been lifted up by the providence of God to manhood. Many blacks interpreted this as "the right to come forward, and, like Men, speak and act for ourselves."[16] This was another way of saying that black men now had the right to be prophetic on behalf of themselves.

The Prophetic Type

Christian social-protest preachers, such as Reverdy Ransom at the dawn of the twentieth century, believed that God had made black people the instrument of the divine will in American history. He confessed his personal faith in the God of the oppressed (in his discourse "Afro-Americans Seek to Share in Freedom, Culture, and Goodwill") in the following credo:

> I believe the hand of God is in human history, that He makes people the instruments of His, that races and nations may become the high currents of His power to bring men back to that song of good-will which heralded the advent of Jesus Christ, and to the achievement of that love for which Jesus Christ both lived and died.[17]

Ransom advocated the popular theory that God had placed blacks and whites together in America to be both with and for each other to work out a great historical example of human liberty unlike the world had known: "God has given us a splendid heritage upon these shores; he has made us the pioneers of human liberty for all mankind. He has placed the Negro and white man here for centuries to grow together side by side."[18] Ransom thought of it as a theological experiment of coexistence that would benefit both races with intangible moral virtues and material rewards: "The white man's heart will grow softer, as it goes out in helpfulness, to assist his black brother upon the heights whereon he stands, and the black man will take courage and confidence, as he finds himself progressing by slow and difficult steps upward toward the realization of all the higher and better things of human attainment."[19] Ransom consequently envisioned the two races becoming, collectively and individually, the world's moral schoolmasters of the exemplary doctrine of Christocentric brotherhood. He wrote:

These two peoples one at last will become the school masters of the world, teaching by example the doctrines of the
brotherhood of man. If the new Jerusalem tarries in its
descent to earth, coming down state, the church, or society?
We know that it is not, from God out of Heaven, then we,
not like some foolish tower builders upon the plains of Shi-
nar, but taught from heaven in a better way, shall build upon
the teachings of Jesus, with the doctrine of human brotherhood as taught by Him, until fraternity realized, shall raise
us to the skies.[20]

Another social-protest preacher of the era, Bishop Robert E.
Jones of the Central Jurisdiction of the Methodist Church made the
following observation about black people's seemingly intuitive
knowledge of the inseparable connection between their oppressors
and themselves: "The Negro knows well the philosophy which teaches that both oppressed and oppressor are joined together. He knows
that not of his own choosing that all are inseparately linked; that we
rise and fall together."[21]

Black Christian social-protest leaders of the nineteenth century
saw God as the master forger of human persons and history and
viewed God's means of forging persons and human events as a progressive evolutionary process. This God of the forging process was
believed to be in partnership with all who allied themselves with the
black oppressed. Blacks conceded that God used even the fires of
slavery to forge a new black man out of an old black man. Invariably
black Christian protest leaders interpreted this as God's way of making their race worthy of being, doing, and belonging in America.
They admonished blacks to work in partnership with God so as to
prove themselves worthy civically, religiously, morally, and politically. Black leaders, following the Civil War, were products of Yankee
missionary education. They also carried on the work of Yankee missionaries in character-building education in subsequent decades.
Like their missionary mentors, black Christian leaders claimed to
have heard God's voice directing them to serve their race.

The prophetic leader believed that "the voice of God so speaks
and the hands of God so directs."[22] Dedicated to the idea of what he

called "the purification, and elevation of my race," Bowen thought it mandatory that black people "clearly and fully believe that there is a 'divinity that shapes our lives, rough hew them how we may'; and that he presides and directs in the destinies of nations, races and individuals; and that, in our particular history, the hand of Providence is as manifest as it was in the ancient Hebrews."[23] Black leaders deemed the philosophy of the partnership with God as inseparable from the philosophy of self-help.

Self-help Philosophy

Self-help philosophy was integral to black leaders of both the prophetic and priestly religious leadership types, who recognized it as a vital ingredient for making the race a key partner with the hand of Providence. Bowen gave the condition that his audience must meet before God: "Moreover, if we would purge ourselves from the evil that is among us, and return or destroy the golden wedge and the Babylonian garment, that same hand will ever be our guide and protector."[24]

It had been necessary for those of both types to be loving critics of their own race as they challenged it to self-purification from the ignorance and superstition of slavery.[25] Select leaders in every epoch of American history have admonished blacks to concentrate less on their negative memories of the victimization of slavery and more on the positive lessons derivable from that experience. The following is one such admonishment: "My friends, don't harp on slavery always: remember its lessons; study its truths; root out its truths; root out its prejudices; and pass on to the exacting present, with its aims and surroundings—nay, to the more glorious future, with its magnificent possibilities free to every man in the race of life."[26] Black leaders' instructions for blacks to use the memories of the slave experience in a positive way was prerequisite in self-help philosophy: "let us translate ourselves from the infernal regions of slavery, prejudice, and immorality, to the elevated plane of life, with its happy, busy, and pregnant callings and issues."[27]

Generally black leaders believed that God had been at work in the lives of their people since the beginning of slavery. Prophetic Christian leaders, such as Bishop Henry McNeal Turner, conceded that God had been a willful co-conspirator with whites in bringing blacks into slavery for the salvation of the latter's soul from their state of nature. This was God's method of bringing what black leaders of the nineteenth century called "a race of ignorant and superstitious people" into the light of Christian civilization. Black prophetic Christian leaders generally concluded that the God of their slave experience used slavery as an evil means for the spiritual salvation and civilization of blacks. In short, the reasoning was that God used an evil means to an ultimately good end, for slavery was necessary to "purge blacks of their sinful backward ways that they fell prey to in dark and uncivilized Africa."[28] Blacks of this persuasion, who were the rule rather than the exception, obviously started with their oppressors' biblical presuppositions about God's actions in human history. In so doing, black leaders could not escape the knotty theological problem of God and slavery. They refused to entertain such questions as these: What was the theological correlation between the God who allowed blacks' enslavement, as the preparatory stage for the white man's civilization, and the God of their African ancestors? How could God be a co-conspirator with the enslavers and a friend of the enslaved simultaneously? If God is both enemy and friend, how will God ever reconcile master and slave into a family of Christian brotherhood/sisterhood? Such questions go without a clear theological resolve even among contemporary leaders of the black church. Black scholars often leave such questions unattended. The black faith community often finds priestly answers more placating than prophetic ones.

The Priestly Type

The Christian priestly black preacher, particularly in the racist South, often sermonized the value of the pious life in Christ over any prophetic denouncements against the political order. This was in keeping with the southern white church's emphasis on otherworldly biblical perspectives. Accenting the personal salvation of the soul, in the face of the most disruptive social vices (e.g., sexual promiscuity, gambling, drinking, stealing, and lying) took priority over any prophetic call for communal salvation.

Whites created, following the Reconstruction era, such a hostile social and political climate against blacks particularly in the South that black preachers mainly addressed their sermons to spiritual matters. Black preachers stood to place their lives at risk had they declared racism one of the seven deadly sins. Fearful for the lives of other blacks, as well as their own, these preachers chose to remain silent on the matters of the gospel and social injustices. Instead, they accented a personal spiritual relationship with Christ as the antidote for coping with the harsh realities of racism. Spiritual transformation in Christ was viewed by the personalists of salvation as the biblical means of purging the society of racism. In other words, being in Christ was advocated as the absolute panacea to all social ills. Black preachers taught that Christ fortified the soul of the believer with a suffering-servant capacity. Their priestly preaching definitely advocated a view of Christology that was impotent in the face of systemic racism.

Most black preachers' primary objective was the transformation of individual character rather than that of the social order. Every convert to Christ was expected to subscribe to the social doctrine of racial self-help rather than that of any prophetic chastisement of the power brokers of the society. Priestly type black preachers produced a plethora of sermons that admonished the virtues of the spiritual life in Christ and accented what constituted the personal pious moral life in the body of Christ. Their instructions were deemed as salvation recipes for the elevated success of the race. In the South, it was not politically correct for blacks to suggest that being transformed in Christ mandated them prophetically to become agents of social change.

Educated preachers, black and white, of the priestly type have tended to believe that an individual's aristocratic character is the best antidote to systemic racism. Bowen echoed that sentiment when he wrote that "nothing in this world compared with strong, pure, intelligent character."[29] In addition, he concluded that "God esteems good character; that he 'searcheth the heart,' and gives the 'crown of life' to them that keep his word."[30] Many of these leaders advocated what Bowen called the need for "an aristocracy of character" that signifies the genuine morality of "the least of these."[31]

The Morality of "the Least"

Self-identification as the "least of these," a biblical expression that values the marginal status of the oppressed, has been a long practice of blacks. Most blacks, individually and collectively, have found these words to be comforting in the most severe racist situations. Priestly type leadership has undoubtedly invoked the metaphorical phrase to boost the self-esteem of lowly and downtrodden blacks, while black leaders of the prophetic type have used the phrase both to soothe the spirits of the victimized and to counter whites' arrogant presuppositions of superiority. Bishop R. E. Jones's writings at the turn of the century reflect a priestly/prophetic use of the phrase the "least of my little ones." Jones argued that we are saved through Jesus Christ by helping others. He reminded white Americans that God had saved them in order that they might save others, even black Americans. Asserting his saved-by-being-saved principle, Jones wrote: "As we are saved we in turn become, by the fact of our salvation, a force to help save the world. Our duty in this is not debatable."[32] Convinced that it was clearly a theological imperative, Jones wrote, "If we will not help save others then we will be lost."[33]

Jones illustrated "the Christ of the least of my brethren" principle in his story of "two saints who sought to enter the portals of heaven." The first saint came to the portals of the heavenly world with unstained garments unsoiled by service and unmarred by contact with the throng that crowded the upward way. Questioned by the keeper of the heavenly gate as to why he was able to reach there so well groomed and without a sign of toil, the first saint answered, "I shunned contact with the rebel by walking on the extreme limits of polluted humanity." He explained that he could not afford to associate with those along the way who needed help. The keeper of the heavenly portals, before telling him to depart, answered with Christ's least-of-my-brethren principle: "Inasmuch as you did it to the least of these My brethren, you did it to Me" (Matt 25:40 NKJV). The second saint appears at the heavenly gate showing evidence of toil and struggle. When the keeper asked for an explanation of the wrinkles, the saint replied: "Enroute I found many struggling ones, being stronger by grace than they, I gave them a helping hand. In some instances I knelt in prayer, again with an outcast I put my arms around him and told him of Christ's great love, and in another instance I brought one soul a part of the way with me. He is enroute now full of strength, of hope and good works."[34] Jones concluded that the latter was the real saint: this is the one who hears "the keeper reply well done thou good and faithful servant, enter there unto the joys of the Lord."[35]

Bishop Jones believed that the saved-by-saving-others principle prevented the selfish from claiming that salvation is personal in the sense of being strictly selfish. He wrote that "salvation is personal—but not personal in the sense of selfish safety from punishment and the ease and comfort of eternal life."[36] Qualifying his definition of salvation as personal, Jones said: "Salvation is personal in its equipment for service. 'He that loseth his life for my sake shall find it.' This is the stating of the truth in paradox. We have by giving; we increase by diminishing; we grow rich by becoming poor; we live by dying."[37]

The least-of-my-brethren principle has been at the heart of black Americans' understanding of what it means to be for Christ and belong with Christ. It has also been the guiding principle for blacks deciding whom Christ is for and with. What did leaders mean when they invoked Christ's the least-of-my-brethren principle? Did they think of themselves as being the lowest on God's totem pole of humanity? How did the metaphorical phrase condition their understanding of Jesus Christ's incarnational existence? Jones pressed upon those of his generation the priestly meaning of the least-of-my-little-ones principle. He reasoned that the least of my little ones have been "committed to us for special care."[38] It is for this theological and ethical reason that Christians should take the gospel to the marginal ones of society. Jones labeled the enemies of this theological and ethical imperative as selfish: "It is high selfishness to refuse to share with the lonely and discouraged mass of humanity about our joys. So by turning from others we discard the highest possible means of adding to our own stock of good cheer."[39] Jones believed God had made the white man the stronger brother for the purpose of placing the Negro, who was the weaker brother, in his hand. He warned his Anglo-Saxon brothers of the seriousness of this responsibility: "If the Anglo-Saxon refuses to grant a fair chance to the Negro he belittles himself and makes himself thoroughly unworthy of the world leadership which God Almighty has placed within his hands. Will he be recreant to the trust?"[40] It would be to betray what was authentically human, to reject Christ as the norm of human brotherhood and sisterhood.

Christ as the Norm

Jones believed the resurrected Christ was the anthropological norm for evaluating what was authentically human and brotherly. Jones advocated what he termed "Christly culture," which had its origin in Christ's cross and the resurrection, as the norm for measuring all people: "He is an abnormal man, whatever may be his intellectual powers, who has not the culture that cometh from association with Jesus the Christ and the inspiration that cometh from Christ's ideals."[41]

Black religious leaders who invoked the Christ-of-the-little-ones principle did so for the purpose of self-reinforcement. The principle served as an antidote against the victimization of this world. Following slavery, black preachers accented the power of spiritual transformation in Christ for the purpose of making good character. Being a manly brother and brotherly man in Christ meant advocating what might be called the yeast-in-the-dough philosophy. Leaders such as Bishop Reverdy C. Ransom asserted, "The cross of Christ is the symbol under which it goes forth in the way of life taught by Jesus for the reconstruction of society by moral and spiritual conquest."[42] The prophetic ministerial leader believed that Christianity had the power to transform the social order through character transformation. Subsequently, a call for an aristocratic character was not out of the ordinary. The eminent preacher and educator Benjamin E. Mays valued the biblical teaching of the little-one salutatory metaphor. It inspired his philosophy of educating underprivileged black males at Morehouse College. Mays expresses his philosophy of the little-ones in a sermon.[43]

An Aristocratic Character

The priestly minister placed the primary theological and ethical accent on what the word of God could do for the individual's soul and character. Hardly anything was said of using God's power radically to change public policy. Christ was expected to change the wretched self into a new righteously conforming self. Priestly leaders derived from the Scriptures the idea that God is no respecter of persons. They believed, however, that God is a respecter of good character and that "strong, pure, and intelligent character" is the prerequisite to being favored by God.[44] Bowen was so convinced of the value of good character that he called for "an aristocracy of character."[45] Aristocratic character, in the mind of the Christian idealists, took precedence over color, class, and race. The Christian idealists supposed that whites would value blacks' character above all else. This was, of course, not the case.

Bowen emphasized the connotation of "character" (from the Greek word *charasso*) that meant "to sharpen," "to impress," and "to stamp or cut out." It was not uncommon for ministers to chastize blacks who placed concern for political office or anything else above character; in Bowen's words, "The god of times has filled our eyes with his dust—the dust of politics: —and we have not been able to discriminate between the essentials and the accidents of race—strength and power."[46] Bowen believed that "personal excellence in character is the mightiest safeguard to any nation."[47]

Self-actualization through the development of good character constituted the core of the gospel of uplifting the race during the last half of the nineteenth and most of the twentieth centuries. Preachers urged self-actualizers to defy the opposition of a racist society and become the chief architect of circumstances: "The individual must dig out of himself the resources of power, and then must give himself to the work of lifting up the race. He must not be discouraged by oppositions, but he must become the master of circumstances, it would be nearer the mark to say that he is the architect of circumstances. It is character which builds an existence out of the circumstances."[48]

Most black church leaders of both centuries have encouraged loyalty to the race despite a lack of clarity about its constitution. Indeed, many have considered such loyalty to be indispensable to the formation of good character. But what is true loyalty to the race? For some, it has been to imitate what Langston Hughes has called "the ways of white folks."[49] Others have defined it as freeing themselves from everything that tends to remind them of white people. Some church leaders at the turn of the twentieth century, such as Bowen, admonished blacks to let neither color nor class alienate them from each other: "Be true to your colors and do not try to draw away from your poor people, as soon as God gives you wealth and earning."[50] In other words, blacks being trustfully for and with each other was contingent upon their possessing and being possessed by Christly character.

Christly Character, or Christ?

Priestly type church leaders and college educators believed that good character would make good Christians. The inherent danger of this belief was that white and black Christian leaders, both consciously and unconsciously, made it synonymous with the gospel of Jesus Christ. An assumption that the gospel of Jesus Christ would make the "bad nigger good" dominated the work of missionaries among ex-slaves from the proclamation of emancipation to the present. During the civil rights movement, however, blacks used the notion of Christ and good character in a rather radical way.

Northern missionaries had taught a view of Christ and character that predicated brotherhood on class values such as education, skin complexion, and liturgical worship styles. This meant that blacks of the folk tradition were not made to feel welcome among those blacks who were the beneficiaries of the missionaries' education and culture. The Christ and culture issue took hold in the black church of the college trained and is reflected in the life of such a radical church leader as Richard Allen, in the unconventional intellect of W. E. B. Du Bois, and in the back-to-Africa rhetoric of Marcus Garvey.

Refusal to sing the gospel and spiritual songs of the slave heritage was one concrete act that separated recipients of white missionaries' education from uneducated blacks. Booker T. Washington's success in educating the blacks of the rural South might have been because he encouraged the singing in the Tuskegee Chapel of the field ditties of the slaves. The Tuskegeen encouraged the students to sing the songs in the dialect that slaves sang them. Yet he had no tolerance for what he publicly called "the ignorant black folk preacher."[51] In Washington's chapel talks, he espoused the Christ of character and culture and encouraged the students to become professional servants of ruling-class whites, for he believed that this would convince whites that blacks were worthy of being treated with brotherly and manly respect.

Some black leaders reacted negatively to white missionaries' characterization of blacks. Thomas Fortune wondered whether "the black man had any manhood left after the missionaries and religious enthusiasts finished caricaturing his debased moral and mental condition."[52] Others charged that missionaries were guilty of "too much pitying" and "too little love" toward recently freed slaves. In reality missionaries came to the freed slave as the "eminently high to the almost hopelessly low" and did more to make him feel his degradation than "to make him feel that he is a man and a brother."[53] Some teachers demonstrated their condescending attitudes toward recently freed slaves through their references to them as "these people," as echoed in this statement by a nineteenth-century missionary teacher: "The way to win the hearts of 'These people' is not to talk down to them as if they were children; it is not to treat them as they know you would not treat white pupils."[54] James McPherson correctly observes that "many, perhaps most missionaries never did fully reconcile the conflicting impulses of brotherhood and fatherhood."[55]

Summary

The dialectic of priestly/prophetic type conscience has been at the heart of black Christian consciousness. Leaders embracing the prophetic and priestly types have envisioned bringing forth a community of brotherhood and manhood reflective of biblical principles.

Black Christians have understood clearly why there has appeared to be an antithesis between the idea of God's being for and with them spiritually and God's being for and with them politically. Arising out of political expedience rather than theological misunderstanding, the antithesis has been driven by a survival ethic. In the face of political oppression, blacks have sought to be for and with each other spiritually. In every era of the struggle for justice, black leaders have advocated a spiritual transformation or purging of their race through character-building education and character-building religion. They have, as well, called for the moral purging of the American society. The reality is that a creative tension between the need for the moral transformation of the race's character as well as of the society itself has always existed. The former appeals to personal soul salvation; the latter relies on the notion of the salvation of the corporate soul. This whole struggle thematically is taken to another level by black apologists and ideologues who engaged in the rhetoric of manhood and brotherhood.

Chapter 7

Apologists and Ideologues of Black Manhood and Brotherhood

The issue of being and belonging created ideological baggage for blacks in both the nineteenth and twentieth centuries. Ideological differences over the methodological question of the place of blacks in America's social space reached its zenith around the turn of the twentieth century. Booker T. Washington and W. E. B. DuBois represent the first dominant black public voices of the ideological polarization movement in black America's consciousness and have become icons of divisiveness in black America's collective consciousness. Their different strategies over the resolution to the race problem bred unnecessary enmity between blacks.

Two different strategies for solving the race problem were popularized in the American mind. Marcus Garvey and W. E. B. DuBois differed primarily over whether the best place for blacks to advance themselves was in America or Africa. Garvey raised critical questions about God's favoritism or nonfavoritism toward black Americans. In addition, he drew upon Scripture to forge for blacks a hermeneutic of suspicion regarding the creation and redemption of the black race. Garvey questioned the hermeneutical presuppositions that blacks derived from the Bible about themselves.

Martin L. King Jr. and Malcolm X represent the second strategy of the public ideological polarization of black America's consciousness. This strategy was rooted in the question of whether the God of Christianity was an enemy of black people. Malcolm declared that Allah was the true God who favored black people. He condemned King and his followers for relying upon the God who favored blacks' oppressors to liberate them. The first two phases of the polarization focuses primarily on the problem of blacks' capacity to be and belong in America.

Each of the above leaders had to struggle with the question of black manhood. At the turn of the twentieth century, the question of black manhood was just as critical, if not more so, than that of brotherhood. Questions of manhood and race were brought to the forefront of public discourse in America by President Theodore D. Roosevelt in his writings about nature and culture.[1] The existential realities of suffering, due to race, invariably forced black leaders to address the issue of their capacity for manhood. They could not escape this question, which had been at the heart of the slavery debate. The Civil War had been fought over it, and it had driven white racists to respond to Reconstruction in the South. The manhood question has troubled blacks at every turn of their journey and required that black leaders defend their race's manly and brotherly potential.

I will make the case in this chapter that two strategies of the ideological polarization of black consciousness have produced at least four types of responses to the question of black manhood: (1) the generic type, (2) the utility type, (3) the dialectic self-conscious type, and (4) the self-confident type. Critical understanding of all these types will help us better understand the different ways in which blacks have struggled with the notions of God, creation, and redemption. Each one is typified by a black leader whose influence extended over both the nineteenth and twentieth centuries.[2]

The Generic Man: Frederick Douglass

Did God create black men equal to white men? This question has proved problematic for blacks from their earliest existence in America to the present. Public figures, from Frederick Douglass to Jesse Jackson, have had to struggle with it and have spoken for decades against the practice of discriminating against blacks because of the color of their skin. Men such as Douglass, Booker T. Washington, and others have triumphantly asserted generic qualities of manhood. They themselves became, for many, public demonstration that God is no respecter of persons. Ironically others interpreted their feats of triumph as a classic example that God is indeed a respecter of persons.

Those espousing a generic manhood philosophy embraced the biblical notion of the one-blood-one-race creation theory. Leaders such as Douglass, for example, stood diametrically opposed to Martin Delany on this issue. The latter emphasized being a black man first. Douglass, however, emphasized being a man first and a black man second. For Delany, ethnicity was fundamental to social existence; for Douglass, it was coincidental. Delany publicly referred to himself as a "representative black man" and desired to make black people competitive equals with their white adversaries. Douglass, to the contrary, saw himself as a representative man who happened to be a Negro. This is not to say that Douglass resented his ethnic heritage. Douglass was more concerned that the American society salute his manhood qualities first rather than the color of his skin.[3] Douglass valued the generic type man over the ethnic type. The former was valued preeminently for having such intrinsic character attributes as truthfulness, beauty of the soul, love, loyalty, wisdom, and courage, which took precedence over those of race, nationality, and religion.

Douglass's position provoked consternation among his black contemporaries. Some criticized him for lacking what they called "race pride," particularly following his marriage to a white woman after his first wife's death. His position invariably affected his popularity rating with some black leaders. Douglass countered his critics by invoking his tenure of "fifty years of uncompromising devotion to the cause of the colored man in the country."[4] This did little to neutralize the vitriolic words of some of his black critics. Rather than be drawn into a "more-ethnic-than-thou" contest of race pride, Douglass challenged critics to study his tenure of service to the struggle for black freedom. He valued good character over racial pride.

The theme of good character has dominated the consciousness of black leaders in every phase of ideological polarization. Even Booker T. Washington and W. E. B. DuBois were definitely not exceptions to this fact. It is certainly pronounced in the speeches of Malcolm X and Martin L. King Jr. Nowhere is this more evident than in the "I Have a Dream" speech that King made at the 1963 march on Washington. In that celebrated speech, King dreamed of a day when his "four little children would not be judged by the color of their skin but by the content of their character."[5] Malcolm X, a kingpin of the Boston underworld before being converted to the

Black Muslim movement, was known for his verbal attacks upon blacks' moral laxity.

"Possessing manly character" became a popular expression in the mouths of many black religious and social leaders during the late nineteenth and early twentieth centuries. A primary objective of churches and schools was, through character-building religion and education, to bring forth a black self of good character and, in turn, a black people of good character. This concept of a self of good character was predicated upon the biblical one-blood-one-race creation theory. Black social-protest leaders have commonly affirmed this creation principle of equality as foundational for social and political existence.[6] For Douglass, this one-blood-one-race creation theory had to be seen in light of certain distinctions. He rationalized that there were two distinctive kinds of equality: "One potential and the other actual, one theoretical and the other practical."[7] The doctrine of equality was embodied in the Declaration of Independence. Black people were challenged with making the theoretical practical.

Complex problems derived from the generic manhood type beg several theological and ethical questions: Did blacks of this type understand normative manhood as a gift of God? Or did blacks perceive normative manhood as a potential to be accomplished through evolutionary exposure to the white man's educational process? Asked another way: Was manhood believed to be a natural right given by God? Or was it an ascribed right from whites? We have here the issue of social ontology. Most black leaders assumed that definitive manhood was contingent upon their exposure to whites' character-building education. Another question is whether blacks viewed definitive manhood for themselves both as having been created within them by God and to be achieved evolutionarily in them by whites' educational process. Did they see definitive manhood within the context of an actual/potential dialectic? If so, this actual/potential dialectic merely created a greater complex theological and ethical challenge, for it portrays God as the principal collaborator with whites in the project to enslave Africans and names God's objective as exposing them to the normative criteria of manhood. The driving idea was that God made Africans with an exceptional flexible nature so that they would be susceptible to Christianity from their slave masters.[8]

Leaders such as DuBois and Douglass were equally seduced by this idea, primarily because they were unable to see the theological and ethical dilemma it caused.

The inherent theological danger of the generic manhood type is that it stood to deny that God's creation of blacks was good. It suggested that God flawed them in the creation process and sought to correct this flaw by permitting their enslavement at the hands of those who were the chosen of God. This type said in short that blacks must remain dependent upon whites to make them in their own image. The more susceptible that blacks were to this generic premise of manhood, the greater was their susceptibility to partnering with whites as comakers of themselves. Whether conservative or liberal, most black leaders, for almost one hundred years following the Civil War, saw this as the rule rather than the exception. They embraced as normative whites' biased historical comparative method of evaluating the development of races and nations. Most black leaders, employing this method, concluded that blacks of the African continent were inferior to whites. Some, such as Marcus Garvey, DuBois, and Delany, argued that civilization started in black Egypt. Most, however, merely accepted the premise that Africa offered very little to what they called "high civilization."

Advocates of the generic manhood philosophy held that blacks could, through the white man's evolutionary educational process, be made to conform to the same definitive manhood expectations as whites. Given this understanding, it is not an accident that blacks of the generic manhood philosophy concluded that God really used slavery as a preparatory school to prepare them for the long evolutionary journey toward a New World manhood. Further, it is not a surprise that even a leader like DuBois succumbed to the white man's biased historical comparative method of evaluating racial and national development in the world.

God, Jesus, and Agency

Advocates of generic manhood philosophy have a unique way of seeing God and Jesus. They presume that God is not to be seen through the ethnic eyes of those of African descent, but they fail to realize that

European culture and civilization condition their perceptions of God and Jesus. Another assumption is that the generic Jesus is every ethnic group's brother in general and no ethnic group's brother in particular. Their other false assumption is that the generic God is everybody's God in general (universal) and nobody's in particular. This would mean that neither God nor Jesus is a respecter of persons.

The generic man type fosters the notion that to be your brother is to be color-blind. That is, the true brother sees, not the color of another's skin, but the content of his or her character. Ethnic characteristics are of neutral value in relationships with others. Why is this so? If God is no respecter of persons, then "I," as an agent of God's, must be no respecter also. Therefore, being for and with the generic Christ and God is to be against any particularity in the name of universality. So what does it mean for God to be for and with someone? God is for and with the potential the person has in redemption from his or her ethnic self rather than for and with the created self. The generic type views the ethnic self as an aberration of the Creator. The utility manhood type had a different perspective.

The Utility Man: Booker T. Washington

Frederick Douglass and Booker T. Washington placed more emphasis on a person's usefulness than his/her ethnicity. Douglass preferred the generic man as the representative of universal humanity rather than the ethnic one. Booker T. Washington, Douglass's successor, valued the utility man over the ethnic man. He concluded that utility skills would equip the ethnic individual to evolve into the universal mainstream of humanity. Advocates of the utility theory posited that usefulness gave a people status in the market place of humanity rather than their race. Subscribers to the philosophy of industriousness, leaders such as Washington, believed that industrial usefulness would qualify an individual or race for authentic membership in the fraternity of civility. It would win a respectful place for them in the modern world.

Being its chief apostle, Washington made the idea of industrial usefulness the cornerstone of the gospel of racial uplift. Washington's paternal influence over black America enabled him to sway the minds of black preachers and teachers of his day. Industrial usefulness was not advocated merely by conservative leaders such as Washington. DuBois was an advocate of the position as well. The difference between the two leaders had more to do with programmatics, that is, the means of achieving the goal, than the intricacies of philosophical differences.

Washington viewed the industrially useful man and what he termed the "representative black man" as inseparable, the latter being of beneficial value to both races. Washington preached that industrial education would bring forth his vision of the industrial man. In his book *The New Negro for a New Century*, Washington stated that the country was bringing forth a new Negro who would replace the "old type Negro," that is, the one who came out of slavery. One was shaped and motivated by the value system of industrial education; the other's character and motivation were formed by ignorance and agitation. In a sense Washington saw himself as an educational midwife aiding the birth of what he called the "new useful Negro type for a new century."[9]

Utility and Character

Character was the critical variable in the language of all those who advocated the philosophy of the industrially useful man. Such fundamental character traits as self-industriousness, self-dignity, and love have been used in black literature to characterize the industrially useful type.[10] An authentic attribute of the useful man type must be seen in his ability to submit hands, head, and heart to the disciplining process of industrial education. The subsequent step in the process was to be able to apply skillfully the principle of the three *h*s (hands, head, and heart) to the project of racial uplift.

Washington advocated that blacks subscribe to a version of suffering-servant love that would empower them to redeem white people. For him, this amounted to the politics of compromise.

Character and Compromise

Washington called for moral character that would be nonthreatening to the political order. The philosophy of political compromise in the matter of race dominated Washington's thought, and he used industrial education to teach his philosophy. The Tuskegee educator developed this position to counter what he viewed as the "lazy Negro," who was the creation of slavery and its aftereffects. He observed that the forced labor system of slavery left blacks morally underdeveloped and therefore deficient in character. It robbed black people of the spirit of self-initiative that was necessary for them to become a free people. Washington believed that functional illiteracy, mandated by slavery, made black people vulnerable to the systemic racist powers of the society. In other words, poverty and ignorance were the actual fruits of functional illiteracy. These factors placed blacks at the margins of human civilization. The lack of literacy skills prevented recently freed slaves from becoming significant players in the progressive stream of human civilization. Washington touted industrial education as the panacea for the nation's racism, poverty, and ignorance.[11]

Washington viewed character transformation as one of the main objectives of industrial education and thought of himself as a counselor for his race's individual and collective development through character and industriousness. As a counselor, he reflected, "I have advised my race to give attention to acquiring property, intelligence and character, as the necessary base of good citizenship."[12] He reasoned that Christian intelligence fostered healthy individuals and races and was the foundation of brotherhood. Responding to a government leader of South Carolina, Washington observed that "only ignorance could allow whites to live side by side with the 'brother in black' and yet have no acquaintance with him beyond the slight knowledge gained of those serving in menial capacities."[13]

A Theological Perspective

Advocates of the utility theory recognized the God of white civilization as their Creator and Lord, and Christ as their elder brother and Savior. Also portraying God as the captain of industry, they believed that God had made all human beings to contribute constructively to the common good. Illiteracy led to one's failing of both God and humanity, and laziness had no place in God's world. Indeed, laziness was viewed as the consequence of sin against God. In other words, there was no place in God's social order for the healthy man or woman who chose being lazy over work. For leaders like Washington, the functional value of the Christian religion was to improve the moral fiber of the individual and society.

An Ethical Perspective

The dominant ethical principle for advocates of the utility theory was that God endows all people with the educable capacity to choose the useful life over the unuseful. Whites thought that making blacks useful to society, rather than socially and politically equal, was the virtue necessary for subjugating blacks. In other words, becoming useful to society was viewed as the proper way for blacks to work out their own civil salvation, which whites had predefined for them, with trembling and fear. Being useful meant being saved in the kingdom of white America through the merits of good works. Ironically, whites inevitably always rewarded blacks' sacrificial efforts by raising the civic hurdles to impossible heights. Whites defined both the moral goal of brotherly behavior and its means of attainment.

The utility perspective valued whites' understanding of agency. They doubted that blacks had anything constructive to offer to the decision-making process. At best, whites thought that blacks could merely be good imitators of their own behavior. In response, black leaders advocated a copycat morality predicated first on the notion that whites had given humanity all the high things of civilization and second on the belief that blacks were merely emotional beings incapable of cognitive decision making. Characterizing blacks as lacking in cognitive skills in comparison to whites, black leaders concluded that at best blacks had contributed to white civilization the capacity to love. A prominent black clergy leader at the turn of the twentieth century said:

> Humility, fidelity, patience, large-heartedness, love—this is Africa's contribution to Christianity. If the contribution of the Saxon is Pauline, that of the African is Johannine. Paul

with his consuming energy, carrying the gospel to the utter-most parts, stands for the white man; John, the man of love, leaning on his master's bosom, is typical of the black. The white man and the black are contrasts, not contraries; complimentary opposites, not irreconcilable opponents.

The Jew has given us ethics; the Greek philosophy; the Roman, law; the Teuton, liberty. These the Saxon combines. But the African—"latest called of nations, called to the crown of thorns, the scourage, the bloody sweat, the cross of agony"—the African, I say, has the deep gushing wealth of love which is yet to move the great heart of humanity.[14]

Advocates of the utility theory instigated an either/or ideological dilemma in black consciousness. As apologists of the race, these leaders always ran the risk of having their ideas misconstrued by the media. The public struggle for ideological brotherhood was never simple.

The Dialectic Self-Conscious Man: W. E. B. DuBois

Critical self-awareness is the place to start in DuBois's work for discussing the notions of manhood and brotherhood. Most scholars refer directly to DuBois's famous double consciousness principle when addressing the issue of race and critical self-consciousness:

It is a peculiar sensation, this double consciousness, this sense of always looking at one's self through the eyes of others, of measuring one's soul through the tape of a world that looks on in amused contempt and pity. One ever feels his twoness,—an American, a Negro; two souls, two thoughts, two unreconciled strivings; two warring ideals in one dark body, whose dogged strength alone keeps it from being torn asunder.[15]

DuBois believed that critical self-consciousness was foundational for developing black manhood and brotherhood. His critically crafted phrase "two unsuccessful strivings in one dark body" is the antithesis of the submissive type of self that slavery produced and sustained.[16]

DuBois's theory of black critical self-awareness grew out of the race's collective and individual historical struggle for being and belonging in a racist society. His is a dialectical struggle for self-critical identity in the most ironic historical situation:

> The history of the American Negro is the history of this strife—this longing to attain self-conscious manhood, to merge his double self into a better and truer self. In this merging he wishes neither of the older selves to be lost. He would not Africanize America, for America has much to teach the world and Africa. He would not bleach his Negro soul in a flood of white Americanism, for he knows that Negro blood has a message for the world. He simply wishes to make it possible for a man to be both a Negro and an American, without being cursed and spit upon by his fellows, without having the door of opportunity closed roughly in his face.
>
> This, then, is the end of his striving; to be a co-worker in the kingdom of culture, to escape both death and isolation, to husband and use his best powers and his latent genius. These powers of his body and mind have in the past been strangely wasted, dispersed or forgotten.[17]

DuBois's three fundamental longings or strivings characterize his complex understanding of the critical black self-conscious type: (1) longing to attain self-conscious manhood, (2) longing to merge his double self into a better and truer self, and (3) longing to be a coworker in the kingdom of culture. These three typological objectives of black strivings provide the hermeneutical key for engaging DuBois's religious and ethical understandings of the black self.

Longing to Attain Self-conscious Manhood

For DuBois, a liberal arts education, as opposed to Booker T. Washington's model of industrial education, was foundational for the development of critical self-conscious manhood. DuBois's convictions of the merits of this kind of education are illustrated in his essay

"The Coming of John" in his book *Souls of Black Folk*. John, the main protagonist of the story, typifies one who makes the radical transition from a precritical understanding of self to a critical one. After slavery, John was born to a sharecropper on a south Georgia sea island plantation. John, whose father is a former slave, is one of two Johns on the island. His contemporary is a white John, whose father is the owner of the plantation. The white John's father sent him off to Princeton University to be educated. The black community sent their John off to a small black southern college. Their doing so defied the white community's belief that education would spoil the black John by introducing him to new horizons of truth, which would make him a misfit to the oppressive ways of white folks.

DuBois gives us two different portraits of John: one is the precritical John who enters college; the other is the self-critical John who graduates from the college. The precritical John is for DuBois rather "crude and ignorant"; he lacks the light of self-critical reasoning to which college would expose him. DuBois's portrayal of the self-critical John at the school's graduation ceremony mirrors his own philosophy of character-building education:

> He looked now for the first time sharply about him, and wondered why he had seen so little before. He grew slowly to feel for the first time the veil that lay between him and the white world; he first noticed the oppression that had not seemed oppressive before, differences that erstwhile seemed natural, restraints and slights that in his boyhood days had gone unnoticed or been greeted with a laugh. He felt angry now when men did not call him "Mister," he clenched his hands at the Jim Crow cars, and chafed at the color-line that hemmed in him and his. A tinge of sarcasm crept into his speech and a vague bitterness into his life; and he spent long hours wondering and planning for his way around these crooked things.[18]

DuBois' self-critical John is caught in the both/and dilemma. On the one hand, the self-critical John is better off in the sense that he now sees the truth of racism that the veil of ignorance once hid from his eyes. On the other hand, the self-critical John is worse off since he will never be able to make peace with a world that denies his human-ity. DuBois' self-critical John must find a constructive way to use his troublesome emotions of anger, sarcasm, and bitterness.

Longing to Merge His Double Self into a Better and Truer Self

How to merge an ideal American self with an opposing Negro self was for DuBois the foremost critical question of black existence. It struck deep at the heart of blacks' quest for the remaking of them-selves for the New World. This dilemma, too, is dramatized in DuBois's story "The Coming of John." DuBois's John, after college graduation, faces the dialectical challenge of being/becoming, that is, of actuality/potentiality, in a racist society. Cast in deontological terms, the challenge for John is how to lead and educate his people to become better and truer selves in the closed society. The racist nature of American society would not let John escape the dilemma of race even in the entertainment district of New York City. An evening at the theater brings him rather surprisingly in contact with the white John, who was his childhood playmate on the south Geor-gia plantation where both were reared. The white John's racist remarks, in their encounter at the theater, evoked in the black John critical feelings of the "double self." White John had remarked to his lady friend within hearing of black John while standing in line at the theater: "Be careful, you must not lynch the colored gentleman sim-ply because he is in the way." The white John had compared the tol-erance for blacks in the North, in terms of public accommodations, with what was not allowed in his native South. Then the white John told his girlfriend:

> "Why, I remember my closest playfellow in boyhood was a little Negro named after me, and surely no two,-well!" The man stopped short and flushed to the root of his hair, for there directly beside his reserved orchestra chairs sat the Negro he had stumbled over in the hallway. He hesitated and grew pale with anger, called the usher and gave him his card, with a few peremptory words, slowly sat down. The lady deftly changed the subject.[19]

The black John mirrors DuBois's notion of "a better and truer self" in his private struggles for truth and justice when he returns to the little south Georgia plantation of his nativity. John invariably had to struggle between his race's "actuality" and "potentiality." That struggle is heard in the dialogue between John and his sister near the end of the story. After John denounced his community's denominational differences over the interpretation of their respective baptismal rituals, which proved divisive, John admonished the gathered blacks at his reception: "Let's leave all that littleness and look higher."[20] DuBois concluded that the community's assessment of John's reentry speech was that he "had spoke an unknown tongue, save the last word about baptism; that they knew."[21] The story takes a turn when the old black preacher, with "the intense rapt look of a religious fanatic, . . . mount[s] the pulpit of the church and manipulate[s] the people into an emotional frenzy."[22] DuBois's characterization of John's response to that ritualistic moment of emotionality is revealing: "John never knew clearly what the old man said; he only felt himself held up to scorn and scathing denunciation for trampling on the true Religion, and he realized with amazement that all unknowingly he had put rough, rude hands on something this little world held sacred."[23] Following this experience of painful rejection, John left the little church, where the community had waited for his arrival, and went out into the night to the sea. He was pursued by his little sister. DuBois's crafted dialogue between the two shows the private rational struggle of John:

> "John," she said, "does it make every one unhappy when they study and learn lots of things?"
> He paused and smiled. "I am afraid it does," he said.
> "And, John, are you glad you studied?"
> "Yes," came the answer, slowly but positively.
> She watched the flickering lights upon the sea, and said thoughtfully, "I wish I was unhappy,-and-and," putting both arms about his neck, "I think I am, a little, John."[24]

DuBois gives the reader a black John who was caught between the black and white communities' different expectations of him.

John's dilemma is that of trying to live within the parameters of the black community's traditional religious definitions of truth and the white community's prescription of segregated social reality. Both communities, black and white, perceived him as a misfit. A college education had birthed and nurtured in black John a critical consciousness that was antithetical to the worldview of his native community. In short, he had become what that society perceived to be a "dangerous nigger." John had caught a vision of the kingdom of culture that was too big for the south Georgia sea island.

Longing to Be a Coworker in the Kingdom of Culture

DuBois considered being a coworker in the kingdom of culture a great moral challenge for both whites and blacks, for it called for an ethic of mutual cooperation between the races. Such an ethic had to be predicated on a philosophy of critical self-reflection. This belief has its roots in what might be called the integrationist side of DuBois's philosophy. He reasoned that slavery had rendered blacks to an involuntary status in the kingdom of culture; freedom would now give them voluntary membership in it. DuBois believed that the time had come in America when blacks could chose to merge into the kingdom of culture. In the earlier years of his life, he expressed greater hope for his race in America than did his ideological rival Marcus Garvey. The latter challenged blacks to develop a critical posture of self-confidence reflective of their having been created in the image of God.

The Self-confident Man: Marcus Garvey

Marcus Garvey thought of himself as a messenger of human redemption rather than a messenger of divine redemption, a philosophic statesman of his race.[25] He assumed that it was his task to guide his race through the wilderness of racist culture. Garvey envisioned bringing forth a type of black man who was self-confident that God had naturally endowed him with the same developmental capacities as whites. He boldly declared to his race: "You have the same opportunities to rise to the same level of any other man whom God ever made because he was just enough to endow you with the same facilities, the same sense, and more than all the same soul he gave to every other man is yours."[26] Garvey predicated his gospel of self-reliance on the doctrine that God created and equally distributed God's gifts to all human beings. For Garvey, blacks were to see God as the Creator and the equal distributor of justice both to the oppressed and oppressor. Blacks were challenged to make this doctrine the ground upon which they would build the self-reliant man. For Garvey, competition and cooperation were the two key attributes that characterized the self-reliant black man.

The Competitive Self

God endowed blacks with the gift of the soul, a unique capacity that even the harsh realities of slavery could not destroy. Garvey asserted that this gift allowed blacks to do more than survive slavery; it uniquely empowered them to compete with their former enslavers because God had also endowed blacks with a competitive spirit. Competition became the dominant concept in Garvey's philosophy of black self-reliance. The need of the black race to compete with the oppressor took precedence over its need to cooperate.

Garvey could not imagine a God of love and justice, a God who is no respecter of persons, who would create blacks with souls inferior to those of whites. He observed that "God could not be the God of love, the God of justice, the No-Respecter-of-Persons if he were to create among men superior intelligence and inferior intelligence, and expect them to battle equally for the right."[27] Countering the white racists of his day, Garvey argued that black people knew a God who favored them: "The God we know, the God of our race, the God we believe in, is too fair and just to discount the Negro in the competitive battles of life."[28] For this reason, Garvey cautioned blacks against blaming God for their predicament of victimization: "because God gave us our physical self and made us lords of creation on an equality with all other men; nor must we blame the white man who is similarly using the ability given him by God."[29] Attacking what he thought to be the superstitious beliefs of his race, Garvey said, "The fault is not in the stars, but in ourselves, that we are underlings."[30]

For Garvey, nothing short of being competitive with whites would prepare blacks to climb the mountain of economic, political, social and cultural prosperity as any other people. He went on to say: "It is nonsense to think that any real help will come from without. In fact it must come from within."[31] Garvey was concerned to move blacks from the status of being psychologically dependent upon whites to that of being psychologically independent. He said, "Let the Negro think independently, let him realize that he must not only build upon his own manhood, but he must build upon his own racial or national prestige."[32] Zealous for blacks to attain national respect as a people, Garvey concluded that only when the black man accomplishes this would "other peoples of the world . . . truly respect him and give him the honor due to every man of courage and character."[33]

Garvey believed that responsibility was one of the most critical elements necessary for blacks to attain competitive skills equal to those of whites. In that light, he said, "You stand and fall by your own acts, so do not blame anybody for your racial condition."[34] Garvey had no patience for blacks who felt it necessary to go in a begging posture to whites for everything. Rebukingly, Garvey said: "Negroes stop crying and be men and save yourselves. Crying is not going to help except in Hell."[35] For Garvey, the ethic of ethnic cooperation was the key to that salvation.

The Cooperative Self

Garvey did an interesting twist on a popular myth of his day, the one that said the black man was cursed by God. Adamantly denouncing whites' version of the myth, Garvey countered with a rather different interpretation of the curse: "It was the curse you brought upon yourselves by your hate of each other, which was not the spirit of love, which was not the spirit of God, and since man is of God by link of the spirit between himself and his God, you voluntarily separated yourselves from the blessing of God by doing that which was the opposite to the will of God."[36] Voluntary separation from God is the locus of sin for Garvey. This is the explanation why blacks express so much "hate, jealousy, malice and envy and dislike for themselves." Garvey reasoned conclusively, "You have tried in all forms and manners, and always, to add insult to injury, by even expressing your displeasure with God for his wisdom of even making you as you look, and so you have become the corrupted people of the world."[37]

Despite this charge, Garvey declared that black people were once the greatest people in creation.[38] He thought of blacks as being the chosen people of God, who had built up a wonderful civilization. His cyclical view of history assumed that God allows races to rise and fall on the great wheel of human destiny. Garvey concluded that blacks started at the top of the wheel but lost their place because of their voluntary separation from God. God permitted them to go into the wilderness of corruption and incivility. Garvey believed that God had promised in the Bible to bring the once premier people back to their rightful place among the other people of the world: "He promises that Princes shall come out of your land. It is the human cycle of sin and misunderstanding, and your time has come in this great cycle, as other people's time will come following others in the same cycle."[39]

Redemptive restoration of the race, Garvey proclaimed, would only take place when blacks become partners with God. This would happen when blacks, individually and collectively, learned to work for their own salvation. For Garvey, this could be accomplished through organized brotherhood.

The Ideal of Brotherhood

Garvey preached that the cooperative self could best be expressed organizationally. For its actualization, Garvey founded what he called the Universal Negro Improvement Association (UNIA). He envisioned this organization for the purpose of improving the condition of his race, with the condition of establishing a nation within Africa where Negroes will be given the opportunity to develop by themselves, without creating the hatred and animosity that now exist in countries of the white race through Negroes rivaling them for the highest and best positions in government, politics, and society.[40]

The UNIA advocated a rather egalitarian belief in the rights of all people, yellow, white, and black. Garvey, its president, argued that the black man had just as much a natural right to the pursuit of his own manhood as his white counterpart. Garvey envisioned, as did black leaders such as Alexander Crummell, the nationalization of black manhood in the same way that white manhood had been nationalized.[41] Understandably his model was that of the nationalization of white manhood in all parts of Europe. Garvey stated his philosophy of organizational brotherhood in the preamble to the UNIA's constitution:

> The Universal Negro Improvement Association and the African Communities League is a social, friendly, humanitarian, charitable, educational, institutional, constructive, and expansive society, and is founded by persons, desiring for the utmost to work for the general uplift of the Negro peoples of the world, and the members pledged themselves to do all within their power to conserve the rights of their noble race and to respect the rights of all mankind, believing always in the Brotherhood of man and Fatherhood of God.[42]

Garvey could not picture a brotherhood that was not predicated on the perfect unity of God. This motivated him to establish the UNIA and to choose for its motto the words "One God! One Aim! One Destiny!" Acknowledging this divine harmony, Garvey called upon all to let "justice be done to all mankind, realizing that if the strong oppresses the weak, confusion and discontent will ever mark the path of man, but with love, faith and charity toward all the reign of peace and plenty will be heralded into the world and the generation of man shall be called Blessed."[43] Garvey's description of the UNIA's objectives reveal the emphasis he placed on ethnic brotherhood. Belief in the brotherhood of man and the fatherhood of God became the cornerstone of Garvey's philosophy of the black man. Garvey thought of the UNIA as the means, rather than the preclusion, to a just society. His fundamental concern was that the basic rights of black people in every part of the world be protected. Garvey best states this belief in his assertion that the organization was to do the following among black people:

> To establish a Universal Confraternity among the race; to promote the spirit of pride and love; to reclaim the fallen; to

administer to and assist the needy; to assist in civilizing the
backwards tribes of Africa; to assist in the development of
Independent Negro Nations and Communities; to establish
a central nation for the race; to establish Commissaries or
Agencies in the principal countries and cities of the world
for the representation of all Negroes; to promote a consci-
entious Spiritual worship among the native tribes of Africa;
to establish Universities, Colleges, Academies, and Schools
for the racial education and culture of the people; to work
for better conditions among Negroes everywhere.[44]

Garvey was convinced that black people would have to build up their
own racial and national prestige. Only such cooperation would
assure his race the respect and honor due them from the other races
in the world.

Summary

Although they all believed in character-building education and character-building religion, apologists and ideologues of the race have
not been able to agree upon what constitutes the race's normative
self-hood. At least four typological understandings of the self have
been at the heart of the debate: (1) the generic type, (2) the utility
type, (3) the dialectic self-conscious type, and (4) the self-confident
type. These typical notions of the self have dictated the way that
blacks have appropriated theological and ethical beliefs about Jesus,
God, and the Holy Spirit. They have also influenced blacks' notions
of God's being for and with them spiritually and politically. This
issue is better illuminated in the ideas and actions of Malcolm X and
Martin L. King Jr., both of whom are considered moral and religious
icons of the black community. They are paradigms for salutatory
black manhood and brotherhood.

Chapter 8

Salutatory Brothers of New Paradigms
Martin and Malcolm

Martin L. King Jr. and Malcolm X each greeted black America in the names of justice, love, and peace. Each understood that these religious and ethical principles are foundational to the coexistence of the human community before God. Scholars have observed that Martin and Malcolm were more brothers in the spirit of human struggle for brotherhood than ideological enemies of any philosophy of civil rights protest. Their ideological warfare, often initiated and perpetuated by the white press, over the strategy of liberation must not be allowed to eclipse that fact. Although differing radically in social-protest strategies for liberation, Malcolm and Martin uncompromisingly called for the realization of justice, love, truth, and peace in the American society. Both committed their lives to these ideals. Malcolm's and Martin's sacrificial commitment to the realization of these principles won the hearts of black Americans.

Is God a respecter of persons? Or is God no respecter of persons? Or, more specifically, is God for and with black people both politically and spiritually? Is God for black people spiritually only? These questions must be heard afresh in the light of Martin's and Malcolm's commitment to the ideal principles of brotherly community. Both thinkers prophetically challenged white and black America's theological beliefs and practices about justice, love, and truth.

Martin Luther King Jr. and His God of Salutatory Reassurance

James Cone, a premier black theologian, has reminded us that King's faith was informed and shaped by the belief system of the black church tradition, although he was trained in Eurocentric liberal theology. The black church tradition taught him the place of the cross in God's salvation drama. King's experience of suffering, brought about by the Montgomery bus boycott, convinced him that God was for and with the oppressed both politically and spiritually. His conviction grew out of the faith of oppressed black people. King's own story of his encounter with Sister Pollard, following a Montgomery mass meeting, is instructive. He tells how Sister Pollard's query of his state of being, following one mass meeting, led to her personal expression of faith in God. On this particular occasion, Sister Pollard observed that King did not speak with his customary strength and power. In summary, the dialogue between Sister Pollard and King went like this:

> "Son, what's wrong with ya?" she asked following the meeting. "You didn't talk strong tonight." Although Martin responded, "Nothing is wrong Sister Pollard, I'm allright," she knew he was not allright. "You can't fool me," she said. "Somethin' wrong with ya. Is the white folks doin' somethin' to ya that ya don't like?" "Everything is going to be all right," Martin said, as he tried to cover up his depression. Finally Sister Pollard said, "Come close to me and let me tell you something one more time, and I want ya to hear it this time. Now I told ya we's with ya. Now even if we ain't with ya, the Lord is with ya. The Lord's gonna take care of ya."[1]

King's conviction of God's being for and with him spiritually and politically came in what has been referred to as his "kitchen experience" during the Montgomery bus boycott. Martin confessed that in the face of paralyzing fear, precipitated by whites' violent threats, it seemed as though he could hear the quiet assurance of an inner voice saying, "Stand up for righteousness, stand up for truth; and God will be at your side forever."[2]

King came from a people who believed that the God of Moses and of Jesus was more powerful than the forces of captivity. Black people resonated with King's celebration of God's being for and with them in their great political and spiritual crisis. They readily believed that if God could deliver those of the biblical world, God could deliver them from the Ku Klux Klan and other white hate groups. Cone insightfully concludes what this meant for blacks' faithful determination in the civil rights struggle of that period: "Faith in the God of the Bible, as revealed in the black religious experience, cast out black Christians' fear of whites and enabled them to take that long, courageous walk toward freedom, singing enthusiastically, 'Walk together children, do not you get weary, there is a great camp meetin' in the Promised Land.'"[3]

One of Martin's endearing salutatory expressions to whites was "our white brothers." This salutation grew out of his theological conviction of the parenthood of God and the brotherhood and sisterhood of humanity. He believed that God created blacks and whites for each other and not for separation from each other. Cone rightly observes that the religious claim of brotherly love was rooted in King's early experience.[4] King knew very well, from his black Christian experience, that we are all sisters and brothers because "God made of one blood all nations of people to dwell on the face of the earth."[5] For Martin, whites were worthy of these salutatory expressions because they were equally, with blacks, children of God.

Martin as Prophetic Brother

Martin prophetically challenged the practical beliefs of the American community's theological conceptions of justice, love, and truth in the classic biblical sense. The God of his Christian experience called upon King, in a private revelatory moment, to "stand up for truth." Cone says that "for Martin truth first and foremost meant love—the love of God and human love."[6] Martin prophetically challenged those he called "our white brothers" to practice their biblically based faith claims of human love. King was theologically convinced that "the church has a moral responsibility of being the moral guardian of society."[7] He reasoned that "the broad universalism standing at the center of the Gospel makes brotherhood morally inescapable. Racial segregation is a blatant denial of the unity we have in Christ. Segregation is a tragic evil which is utterly un-Christian."[8]

King denounced the eleven-o'clock worship hour of the white church as the most segregated hour in the week, which, for him, was empirical evidence of whites' inconsistency between their theological creed and practice. Martin reminded his fellow white brothers of the clergy that "all too often many have been more cautious than courageous and have remained silent behind the anesthetizing security of stained-glassed windows."[9] To those white ministers who failed to admonish their white members to comply with the desegregation decision because it was the law, King responded: "I have longed to hear white ministers declare: 'Follow that decree because integration is morally right and because the Negro is your brother.'"[8] He noted that the "church was content to stand on the sideline and mouth pious irrelevancies and sanctimonious trivialities"[10] during blacks' struggle. Cone has reminded us that King did not believe that the white churches' failure to follow the gospel had invalidated it. Cone observes, on the contrary, that King "believed that it obligated him and other Christians to bear witness more than ever to the universal message of the gospel so that the world might know that true Christianity is not only concerned with heaven over yonder but also with the quality of life here on earth."[11]

The Vietnam War

Against the background of the quality of life emerges the question of King's belief regarding God's being or not being for and with black people politically and spiritually. Cone's work on King is the only one of its kind that has critically addressed the multifaceted variables of King's religious thought. Cone reminds us that King's greatest prophetic contribution was to speak the truth to America in relation to the Vietnam War. King recognized a direct correlation between the impoverishment of black Americans and the American government's exploitative involvement in Southeast Asia. His public moral stand against that war clearly demonstrated his qualities as a prophet of truth in the biblical sense. Justice, love, and hope were the dominant principles that King drew upon as he critically responded to the war.[12] Cone proceeds with an interesting analytical observation of King's action and thought:

> King's qualified sympathy with the Black Power movement
> and his disappointment with whites were reinforced by his

growing distress over the war in Vietnam, which became an important theme in his public utterances during the last of his life. He was gripped by the suffering of the Vietnamese, especially the children; he was angered that Americans would deprive their own poor to pay for an unjust war; and he was saddened that his antiwar position alienated many of his allies, black and white, in the freedom movement. His discouragement over these developments led to an important change in his theology.[13]

Cone observes that at the same time when King began to consider the war, he began to "speak like a prophet, standing before the judgment, proclaiming God's wrath and indignation upon a rich and powerful nation that was blind to injustice at home and indifferent to world peace."[14] Prior to his prophetic stance against the Vietnam War, King had been enchanted by the American dream rhetoric, but the reality of the Watts uprising and the Vietnam War turned his dream into a nightmare. In King's great speech at Riverside Church in New York, "Beyond Vietnam," his prophetic voice in opposition to the Vietnam War became loud and clear. Cone has rightly observed that "in terms of moral courage it was his greatest hour, as he proclaimed America to be the 'greatest purveyor of violence in the world today.'"[15] King agonized over the fact that the media was supportive of his nonviolence stance against racism in America but not against the Vietnam War:

> They applauded us in the sit-in movement when we nonviolently decided to sit at lunch counters. They applauded us on the freedom rides when we accepted blows without retaliation. They praised us in . . . Birmingham and Selma, Alabama. Oh the press was so noble in its applause and . . . praise when I would say "Be nonviolent toward Bull Connor." "Be nonviolent toward Jim Clark." There is something strangely inconsistent about a nation and a press that would praise you when you say, "Be nonviolent toward Jim Clark," but will curse and damn you when you say, "Be nonviolent toward little brown Vietnamese children!"[16]

For Martin, the truth of God took preeminence over being popular as a leader. He told those blacks who criticized his stance on the Vietnam War: "I am not a consensus leader. I don't determine what is right and wrong by looking at the budget of the Southern Christian Leadership Conference, or by taking a Gallup Poll of the majority opinion."[17] King proceeded to say that "ultimately a genuine leader is not a searcher for consensus but a molder of consensus."[18] Cone rightly comments that King's sermons against the Vietnam War "reveal the decisive influence of the black and biblical tradition upon them."[19]

Responding to his critics about the wisdom of mixing peace and civil rights, King observed, "Before I was a civil rights leader, I answered a call, and when God speaks, who can but prophesy?"[20] King was very clear in his conviction that the courage to tell the truth was what it meant to be called by God: "I answered a call which left the Spirit of the Lord upon me and anointed me to preach the gospel. . . . I decided than that I was going to tell the truth as God revealed it to me. No matter how many people disagreed with me, I decided I was going to tell the truth."[21] In the black church tradition, speaking the truth constitutes the cornerstone of authentic faith in God and Christ. It is what the community expects of the preacher; it is what the preacher expresses to the community. Moreover, the truth must be told even in the face of the community's rejection of the truth when it is told. King expresses such truth in one of his sermons at Ebenezer Baptist Church:

> God anointed me! No member of Ebenezer Baptist Church called me to the ministry. You called me to Ebenezer, and you may turn me out of here. But you can't turn me out of the ministry, because I got my appointment from God almighty, and anything I want to say I'm going to say to you from the pulpit. It may hurt somebody. I do not know about that. Somebody may not agree with it, but . . . the word of God is upon me like fire shut up in my bones and when God gets upon me, I have got to say it. I have got to tell it all over everywhere. And God has called me to deliver those in captivity. Some people are suffering, . . . hungry, . . . [and] still living in segregation and discrimination this morning. I am

going to preach about it. I am going to fight for them. I'll die for them if necessary, because . . . the God that called me to preach told me that every now and then . . . I'll have to agonize and suffer for the freedom of his children, I may even have to die for it. But if that's necessary I'd rather follow the guidelines of God than to follow the guidelines of men.[22]

Martin as Priestly Brother

Basic to understanding King as a priestly brother is to see that he was an avid advocate of character-building education and a character-building religion. That is to say, King did not make an artificial distinction between faith and reason. The civil rights movement itself became a school for educating a generation of young blacks in the philosophy and practice of character building in relationship to the Christian gospel.

Martin's priestly challenge must be seen in his expressed sense of being both for and with the black and white community. In this sense, he was the priestly/prophetic one who stood in the moral gap for both races. (For a biblical perspective of standing in the gap for God, see Ezekiel 22:30.) The way that King conducted mass meetings demonstrates his priestly role. The mass meetings held during the Montgomery bus boycott reveal three critical elements that were always necessary for success: (1) self-discipline, self-dignity, and covenant making, (2) forgiveness and reconciliation; and (3) racial inclusion and ecumenism.

Self-dignity, Self-discipline, and Covenant Making

The mass meeting affirmed that a democratic space existed in the black community that permitted everyone the right of self-expression and questioning. Telling of how blacks in Montgomery reached the decision to launch its boycott, King observes the democratic way in which it was resolved: "As we listened to lively discussion, we were heartened to notice that, despite the lack of coherence in the meeting, not once did anyone question the validity or desirability of the boycott itself. It seems to be the unanimous sense of the group that the boycott should take place."[23]

The boycott itself became an experiment that challenged the black community's capacity for self-discipline, self-dignity, and covenant making. King became the high priest over this special moment in the lives of an oppressed people. One of his major priestly contributions was to make sure that the boycott method was used for ethical and Christian ends. It was King's intent to use "the method of boycott to give birth to justice and freedom, and also to urge men to comply with the law of the land."[24] Martin reasoned that "we were concerned not to put the bus company out of business, but to put justice in business."[25]

King led the people of Montgomery to see that they had a religious duty to "withdraw their cooperation from an evil system."[26] The mass-meeting forum became one of the most celebrative moments in the black revolutionary struggle. Martin's response to the people's self-disciplined commitment on the first day of the boycott is worthy of note:

> During the rush hours the sidewalks were crowded with laborers and domestic workers, many of them well past middle age, trudging patiently to their jobs and home again, sometimes as much as twelve miles. They knew why they walked, and the knowledge was evident in the way they carried themselves. And as I watched them I knew that there is nothing more majestic than the determined courage of individuals willing to suffer and sacrifice for their freedom and dignity.[27]

Using the mass-meeting forum, King's objective was to rally a people into becoming the symbol of moral courage. He told his audience: "If you will protest courageously, and yet with dignity and Christian love, when the history books are written in future generations, the historian will have to say there lived a great people—who injected new meaning and dignity into the veins of civilization."[28]

Forgiveness and Reconciliation

King used the mass-meeting forum as an occasion for the struggling community to experience forgiveness and reconciliation. Officially serving as president of the mass meetings, Martin said, "Our aim must never be to defeat or humiliate the white man, but to win his friendship and understanding."[29] A favorite scriptural passage of the mass meetings comes from 1 Corinthians: "And now abide faith, hope, love, these three; but the greatest of these is love" (1 Cor.13:13 NRSV). Another was the famous dialogue on forgiveness between Jesus and Peter (Matt. 18:21, NRSV). King observed, "For the mass meeting audiences, these Scriptural admonitions were not abstractions that came from a distance across the centuries; they had a personal and immediate meaning for them today."[30]

Martin himself became the exemplar of forgiveness and reconciliation. He stood, as it were, in the moral gap between white and black America. Nowhere was this more graphically demonstrated in his leadership than following the bombing of his home in Montgomery. Facing an angry black group who formed around his home in response to the bombing by white cowards, King taught the spirit of forgiveness and reconciliation. Here we see him fulfilling the role of the Christian priest in the finest sense of the word. In recalling his own response, King said, "In this atmosphere I walked to the porch and asked the crowd to come to order."[31] King's admonishment reflects his priestly role:

> Quietly I told them that I was all right and my wife and baby were all right. "Now let's not become panicky. If you have weapons, take them home; if you do not have them, please do not seek to get them. We cannot solve this problem through retaliatory violence. We must not meet violence with violence. . . . We must love our white brothers, no matter what they do to us. We must make them know we love them. Jesus still cries out in words that echo across the centuries: 'Love your enemies; bless them that curse you; pray for them that despitefully use you.' This is what we must live by. We must meet hate with love. Go home with this glowing faith and radiant reassurance."[32]

Racial Inclusion and Ecumenism

King came to see that the Montgomery bus boycott was accomplishing daily what the Christian Church had failed to accomplish on Sunday mornings. Rotating mass meetings from church to church fostered an ecumenical spirit among Christian blacks of the city. The speakers represented the various denominations, thus removing any grounds for sectarian jealousy. Baptist, Methodists, Lutherans, Presbyterians, Episcopalians, and others all came together with a willingness to transcend denominational lines. Martin said: "Catholic priests were actively involved in the protest, many of their parishioners took part. All joined hands in the bond of Christian love."[33]

Mass meetings during the civil rights movement in Montgomery, defying the status quo of a segregated society, were predicated upon the Christian ideals of the black church community. Martin summarized those ideals in this way:

> The mass meetings also cut across class lines. The vast majority present were working people; yet there was always an appreciable number of professionals in the audience. Physicians, teachers and lawyers sat or stood beside domestic workers and unskilled laborers. The Ph.D's and the no D's were bound together in a common venture. The so-called "big Negroes" who own cars and had never ridden a bus came to know the maids and the laborers who rode the buses every day. Men and women who had been separated from each other by false standards of class were now singing and praying together in a common struggle for freedom and human dignity.[34]

King as Christly Brother

King was unabashedly clear that his commitment was to help realize the beloved community in general. Interestingly, King was criticized by many of his critics for having what they termed a "messianic complex." Despite the criticisms, King interpreted fighting for the rights of black Americans to be a Christly act. King's Christ required that he offer himself to humanity as the brother of everybody in general, even of his oppressors. His faith was in a God who was faithfully for and with oppressed people. King believed that God required the oppressed to be trustfully for and with each other. Such belief led King to the ultimate sacrifice on behalf of oppressor and oppressed.

Convinced of God's love, King steered away from using negative salutatory metaphors when referring to whites. He instead used such amicable salutatory titles as "white friends" and "white brothers," even in the face of whites' hostility.[35]

Ultimately, King became committed to following the sacrificial example of Jesus Christ's life and teachings about the cross. For the believers of Christianity, Jesus is the elder brother of humanity, the only Son of God. King was charmed by the Christian idea that the cross, which symbolized redemptive suffering, is at the heart of the Christian faith. Christian brotherhood for King was predicated on the biblical notion of redemptive suffering. For this reason, King called upon those who claimed brotherhood with Christ to stand up for justice, love, and peace.

Given his belief in Jesus' unconditional love for humanity, King believed that as a believer in Christ, he was just as much responsible for the souls of his white brothers as for the souls of blacks. Being Christly for King was more than a creedal confession; it constituted the heart of his daily deeds. King preached a Christ whom he believed was universally receptive to all of humankind. Christ's universal receptivity to everybody anywhere meant that Christ was for and with every person in general and in particular. King best demonstrated his convictions about this principle in the ultimate sacrifice of his life for the striking Memphis garbage workers. By doing so, King radically shifted the theological and moral paradigm in America regarding what constitutes liberated manhood and brotherhood in God.

Black America's Response

Black America holds no other human leader, black or white, in the kind of adoration comparable to what it does Martin L. King Jr. As with Malcolm X, King is held up before black youth of America as the moral icon of true manhood and brotherhood. Black leaders reverently invoke King's name in their battles against black-on-black crime as well as drugs. He is often spoken of with ancestral reverence. Followers often invoke his name to condemn or bless the behavior of the nation. Civil rights leaders often tell us of that with which King would either be pleased or displeased.

Black Americans, regardless of their disposition toward nonviolence, still hold up King as the exemplary model of religious and moral leadership. They reverence King as the true practitioner of Jesus' love-forgiveness ethic. King was able to forgive both blacks and whites who sought his destruction. His ability to do so was for him, not a sign of weakness, but a sign of strength, a sign that the strength of God's love was embedded in his life. King's critical perception of Christian love enabled him to see the distinctions between the different kinds of love as identified in the Greek language. He was particularly interested in the distinction between the love of God and the love of self. Black artists have shown their appreciation of King's sacred place in history by placing him at the Last Supper with Jesus.

Black Americans see King as an exemplary brother of courage and faith. They marvel at King's having lived daily under threats of death upon his family and himself. Despite these threats, King did not surrender to the forces of evil. And black Americans unequivocally recognize King as anointed by God for the role of prophetic leadership. King was a hero who was bigger than life. Black America has thought of him as the modern Moses.

Malcolm X and His God of Retributive Justice

Malcolm's God of black manhood authored the law of revenge: "An eye for an eye, a tooth for a tooth, an arm for an arm, and a head for a head and a life for a life."[36] Drawing even upon Old Testament narratives, Malcolm envisioned a God who permits blacks to defend themselves against their oppressors. For Malcolm, God was working in collaboration with black people to defeat white people. Malcolm was unequivocally convinced that God is a respecter of black people because they are oppressed. He was convinced that God was for and with black people politically and spiritually. Malcolm concluded that "the 'solution' to the problem of racial justice 'will never be brought about by politicians,' but 'it will be brought about by God.'"[37]

In contrast to Martin, Malcolm focused on God's justice rather than God's love. His conclusion that blacks, because they had been victims of whites' injustice, needed a God who would repay the oppressor. Malcolm's God was to render judgment upon those whites who had victimized black people. God would, as it were, resurrect blacks from their American valley of dry bones. Malcolm characterized blacks as a valley of dry bones who no longer knew their "names, language, homeland, God, or religion."[38] In short, he saw them as a people of death.

Malcolm was unequivocally convinced that the God that white people worshiped was an enemy of black people spiritually and politically. This God had proven historically to be an absolute enemy of blacks.

Malcolm's Salutatory Dilemma

Malcolm despised the word "Negro" as a term of self-designation. He often made light of it by frequently using the phrase "so-called Negro." He told a Los Angeles audience, "You were re-named Negro by the same man, who had kidnapped and robbed you of your own culture."[39] Malcolm preferred the designations "African," "black," and "Afro-American," reminding blacks in his salutatory responses to them: "You ain't nothing but an African. You were denied the oldest culture man knows."[40]

Malcolm believed that "Almighty God Allah has declared that HE HIMSELF shall remove . . . this murderous, beast-like, wicked white race . . . from the planet earth."[41] Malcolm called for blacks uniting unto themselves: "We should get unto our own kind and seek to get on God's side and to integrate with God and imitate God instead of running around here foolishly trying to integrate with the white man."[42]

Malcolm sought to turn the game of using negative stereotypical salutatory metaphors back upon whites. In doing so, he publicly designated whites as "devils," "beasts," and "snakes," which "was his technique in trying to get blacks to love each other."[43] Unfortunately, Malcolm's earlier negative salutatory technique would not allow him to see distinctions among whites. Cone has carefully observed that Malcolm could not see the difference between those whites who sacrificed themselves in the civil rights movement and whites of the Ku Klux Klan.

Malcolm as Prophetic Brother

Blacks idealized Malcolm, just as they did Martin, because they believed him to be a leader in word and deed. In short, they believed that he practiced what he preached and vice versa. Malcolm was not content merely telling black people that he loved them. He dared to die a martyr at the hands of his own ethnic brothers. If it seems that Martin took the idea of sacrificially loving white people to the extreme, Malcolm took to the extreme the idea of ultimate sacrificial love for his own ethnic brothers. Cone summarizes the paradox of these two leaders: "Revolutionary prophets, like Malcolm and Martin, often do not live to become old men. They are usually killed by the forces they are seeking to change. Malcolm X was killed by blacks he loved and seeking to set free from racism."[44] Unlike any other black leader except King, Malcolm was an embodied symbol of both the prophetic brother and the priestly brother for black America.

Malcolm was, and still is, viewed as a prophetic brother who was trustingly for and with the black masses spiritually and politically. He must be seen as the prophetic brother who, because of his commitment to truth, ultimately laid down his life for his ethnic brothers. Malcolm's overall prophetic contribution must be seen in (1) his constructive critiques of blacks' own self-hatred and (2) his critique of whites' refusal to include blacks in their application of the Christian and democratic ideals of the American society. As a prophetic brother, Malcolm went to the black masses in the name of Allah calling for the restoration of the authentic black man. He was of the conviction of his mentor, Elijah Muhammad, that whites' subjugation of blacks, during slavery, had robbed the latter of their ancient glory. Malcolm was convinced that whites had accomplished a whitenization of blacks in the name of Jesus, and he deemed the white Christ of Christianity as an enemy of black people. The white Christ was the spiritual tool that the slave master used to theologize the institutionalization of slavery and subserviency following its demise. Malcolm believed that the white man's version of Christianity had contributed to blacks' own self-hatred and social alienation among themselves as a people.

For Malcolm, the God of the white man's Christianity was radically antiblack. This God explicitly showed disfavor toward blacks and favor for whites. Malcolm's prophetic insight taught blacks that the God of whites could not be for and with black people either spiritually or politically. If so, God would have to become an enemy of white people. For Malcolm, blacks' serialized experiences of slavery, legalized segregation, and institutionalized racism were all indications that the white man and God were in coalition against blacks. Based upon his conviction that white Christianity was racist, Malcolm offered Islam, which Robert Franklin rightly calls the "liberating faith."[45] Malcolm expressed his faith in Islam as the cure-all religion for black Americans: "The religion that the Honorable Elijah Muhammad is teaching us here in America, today, is designed to undo in our minds what the white man has done to us. It's designed to undo the type of brainwashing that we have had to undergo for four hundred years."[46]

Following his hajj to Mecca, Malcolm came to a more inclusive understanding of human anthropology, a broader understanding of brotherhood/sisterhood. Subsequently, he sought to articulate his broader view to the American public. He observed, "True Islam removes racism, because people of all races who accept its religious principles and bow down to one God Allah, also automatically accept each other as brothers and sisters, regardless of differences in complexion."[47] Robert Franklin has rightly interpreted the impact of Islam upon Malcolm:

> Both during and after his years in the Nation of Islam, Malcolm believed profoundly that Islam was the only true religious system capable of providing firm, practical rules for moral living and high self-esteem for struggling blacks. He believed that Islam was able to generate the "moral reformation necessary to up the level of the so-called Negro community by eliminating the vices and other evils that destroy the moral fiber of the community."[48]

Malcolm as Priestly Brother

Malcolm's primary concern was that blacks be for and with each other spiritually and politically. Concerned that blacks learn to love and forgive each other, Malcolm believed that black people being trustingly for and with each other politically was fundamental to their survival. His black nationalist dream was to lead black people into a utopian unity. Malcolm's life and words as a priestly brother are clearly reflected in his rhetoric of black nationalism. It is the later Malcolm who demonstrates such a radical notion of priestly concern for black Americans. His litmus test, however, comes in the face of adversarial challenges from brothers in the black Muslim movement itself. This painful reality drove Malcolm to become a martyr for his ethnic brothers.

Theologically and ethically Malcolm was forced, by the confrontation between him and his Muslim brothers, to face the challenge of becoming a victim of fratricide. His unalloyed commitment to the freeing of black people took Malcolm to the point of the Rubicon in the stream of life. At the core of his being, Malcolm was the black brother of all black brothers. He dared love blacks with a, if not unconditional, self-sacrificing love. He dreamed of seeing blacks cleansed of their slavery ways. Malcolm lamented the fact that blacks were so poisoned by their own self-hatred.

One of Malcolm's great strengths was his aggressive advocation of character-building education and a character-building religion. For him, brotherhood and manhood had to be predicated on the proper kind of education and religion.

Black America's Response

Despite the fact that Malcolm X was killed more than thirty years ago, the black community still invokes his name as its paradigm for salutatory black manhood and brotherhood. This is particularly the case when leaders are appealing to black males of the ghetto to transcend the dead-end world of the ghetto. Such leaders invoke Malcolm's name as the exemplary model of real black manhood and cite him, whether fairly or not, as the classic example of a black male who rose from the underworld of crime and debauchery to that of public dignity and respect. Malcolm is, also, referred to as the black male who loved black people by precept and example. The community always runs the danger of romanticizing Malcolm as the self-made man, as a kind of savior figure. Malcolm did not himself, however, make any such preposterous claim.

Malcolm publicly credited his own rescue from the underworld to the honorable Elijah Muhammad, whom he recognized as his spiritual father. Little critical attention has been given to the fact that Malcolm's rescue was the result of the communal efforts of the black Muslim nation, that is, black Muslims who sought to transform black male prisoners. Black Muslims' salutatory greeting of the prisoner as brother is a message in itself that bestows dignity upon the inmate.

Malcolm's self-transformation took place through exposure to both a character-building religion and a character-building education. This happened when Elijah Muhammad mentored him for leadership. The goal of the black Muslim religion was not just to save Malcolm for the afterlife but also to save him from his own illiteracy. Malcolm subsequently adopted the Muslims rather puritanical moral beliefs and practices. By his own admission, he needed a religion that taught very strict moral codes, that would help him find Allah's moral moorings.

Malcolm personifies for black America the ideal fearless, manly brother. He is the black man who rose from the gutter of the streets to speak publicly with blacks about their hopes and fears in a racist society. Malcolm is the black male who never forgot the black masses, even when he spoke in the face of television cameras. He saw himself as a model of character-building education and character-building religion. Contemporary followers of Malcolm have preached his beliefs to prison inmates and street toughs as well as to youngsters of the black middle class.

Blacks continue to affirm Malcolm's ethical response to white violence. It was Malcolm's "By any means necessary" ethic that appealed to blacks' moral sensibilities. His was a consolatory response that grew out of blacks' moral fatigue with whites' barbarous reaction to their nonviolent strategies. Malcolm's "By any means necessary" ethic was the very antithesis of King's "love thy neighbor as thyself" ethic.

In Malcolm's ethic, many blacks heard a voice of strength; in King's "love thy neighbor as thyself" ethic, numerous blacks heard a voice of weakness. Malcolm's survival ethic appealed more to blacks' proclivity to natural law instincts of self-preservation. It demanded that white Christians reassess their racist presuppositions about manhood and brotherhood. Prior to Malcolm, the parameters for whites of what constituted authentic manhood and brotherhood were defined by race. Theological and ethical insights were informed by race, class, and gender. While his protest approach did not dismantle racism, classism, and sexism, Malcolm's rhetoric served as an agitator to bring some whites of good will to the table of dialogue. Understandably, blacks concluded that whites were taking their strength to love, displayed by nonviolence, as a sign of weakness.

Summary

The teachings and exemplary lives of Martin L. King Jr. and Malcolm X have presented black Americans with new theological and ethical challenges. Blacks could not have known either leader without struggling afresh with the critical questions that have guided this study: Is God faithfully for and with black people? Can black people be trustingly for and with each other? For the first time in history, black Americans (even members of predominantly white denominations) withdrew from whites and sought to discuss these questions among themselves. From this time on emerged what has became known as the phenomenon of the black caucuses in major church denominations. In such settings, blacks rediscovered among themselves the power of saluting each other with such affectionate titles as "brotherman" and "soul brother." They rediscovered the reward of being creators and re-creators of their own salutatory metaphors. Hence, this made them partners with God in their own liberation efforts.

Chapter 9

Creative Liberation Metaphors
Creators and Re-creators

The necessity, then, of those "lesser breeds without the law"—those wogs, barbarians, niggers—is this: one must not become more free, nor become more base than they: must not be used as they are used, not yet use them as their abandonment allows one to use them: therefore they must be civilized. But when they are civilized, they may simply "spuriously imitate [the civilizer] back again," leaving the civilizer with no satisfaction on which to rest.—James Baldwin, "The Devil Finds Work"[1]

Paul Ricoeur's theoretical insights on the metaphorical nature of language has proved most helpful in constructing this chapter. His notion of metaphorical reality sharpened my perception of how black males, in particular, have created and re-created themselves through their own salutatory metaphors. Black males' metaphorical acts of creation and re-creation reflect their creative ability to play the oppressors' language, rather than merely to be played by it, for their own liberation. Such salutatory metaphors as "soul brother" and "brotherman," which are uniquely black American creations, have allowed blacks to rename themselves as well as their relationships to each other. These acts of salutatory renaming and relating reflect blacks' challenge of being and doing in a racist society. They point to ontological and deontological concerns that have both theological and ethical implications.

Blacks' uniquely creative salutatory metaphors for referring to themselves and the nature of their social relationships must be seen as more than subcultural acts of verbal defiance against mainstream language use. These metaphors must really be seen as blacks' linguistic attempts to create and re-create themselves in the face of social death. For instance, a salutatory metaphorical expression such as "soul brother" seeks to restore to the other, in the moment of social encounter, the divine capacity for trustful human relations that systemic racism robbed from black males. "Soul brother" serves prophetic notice on white Christians' refusal to include blacks in their circle of brotherly embrace.

Black males' audacity to rename themselves and their relationship to each other must be seen against the oppressive ethos of the old racist salutatory paradigm. The dominant feature of the latter paradigm authorized whites to name blacks and the relationship between whites and blacks.

The Old Racist Salutatory Paradigm

Richard Wright brilliantly captures a feel for the infectious racist ethos out of which the old racist salutatory paradigms arose. Wright shows us what it was like for black males to be and do in that type of society. Writing in the decades of the 1930s and 1940s, Wright once said, "The Negro is the metaphor of America."[2] Michael Fabre, the leading biographer on Wright, has observed that Wright meant by this claim that

> the experience of the black American crystallizes a more universal problem of western culture created by the tradition from a family-oriented, and still somewhat feudal, rural existence, to the anonymous mass civilization of the industrial centers. The history of the black people of the United States reflects the material progress and cultural evolution of the country at the same time that it anticipates (by years, decades or even centuries) a similar evolution in other nations of the world.[3]

If Wright is correct, blacks not only have their being in America, but a part of the nation's being is rooted in them. Wright's fictional writings invaluably mirror black males' struggle for manhood under the old racist salutatory paradigm of systemic racism both in the South and North. A cursory examination of Wright's perception of the black male self, as reflected in several of his writings, illuminates our argument about the old racist salutatory paradigm.

Wright's *Black Boy*

Margaret Walker has called Wright's book *Black Boy* a blending of fact and fiction about his own life.[4] The book begins with Wright's southern youth and ends when he leaves the South for Chicago. For Wright, the black male struggled to forge his manhood out of a racially prohibitive southern ethos that ever sought to keep him a boy. The hostile nature of the southern white male "demanded that a black male conceal from all whites what he actually felt."[5] A prisoner of a racist South, Wright used the tools of literacy to fight his battle to become a manly self. Possessing a library card borrowed from an Irish Catholic who worked at the optical company with him in Memphis, Wright forged a note to the white librarian that read: "Dear Madam: Will you please let this nigger boy have some books by H. L. Mencken?"[6] This is how Wright obtained *A Book of Prefaces* and one volume of *Prejudices*. Wright asserts that reading these books brought about the transforming moment in his life. He discovered the power of words, not as just an escape or a compensation, but as a tool for rebuilding the world. Wright wrote:

> I was jarred and shocked by the style, clear, clean sweeping sentences. Why did he write like that? And how did one write like that? I pictured the man as a raging demon, slashing with his pen, consumed with his hate, denouncing everything American and extolling everything European, or German, laughing at the weaknesses of people mocking God, authority. . . . Could words be weapons? Well, yes, for here they were. Then maybe, perhaps, I could use them as a weapon. No. It frightened me. I read on and what amazed me is not what he said, but how on earth anybody had the courage to say.[7]

Wright immersed himself in the reading of American novels, which gave him "the means to analyze the society he lived in, to bridge the gap between himself and the white world created by igno-rance alone."[8] In addition, "it also enabled him to start separating white people, who had hitherto appeared collectively as a unified threat, into social and psychological categories."[9] The undeniable fact was that literature was often Wright's means of escape from the real world: "The plots and stories in the novels did not interest me so much as the point of view revealed. I gave myself over to each novel without reserve, without trying to criticize it; it was enough for me to see and feel something different. And for me, everything was something different. Reading was like a drug, a dope. The novels cre-ated moods in which I lived for days."[10]

Reading also reminded Wright of the unbearable limitations that racism had placed upon blacks:

> It buoying me up, reading also cast me down, made me see what was possible, what I had missed. My tension returned, new, terrible, bitter, surging, almost too great to be con-tained. I no longer felt that the world about me was hostile, killing; I knew it. A million times I asked myself what could I do to save myself, and there were no answers. I seemed for-ever condemned, ringed by walls.[11]

The Old South that Wright knew created an environment that was "too small to nourish human beings, especially Negro human beings."[12]

Wright recognized that the ethic of Jim Crow was foundational to the old racist salutatory paradigm. In every encounter of black males with white males, custom itself demanded that black males respond in a nonoffensive way. It often demanded neutrality. Recall-ing an experience in Jackson, Mississippi, Wright tells of being cor-nered by two fellow workers. One of them said, "Richard, Mr. Mor-rie here tells me you called me Pease."

> I stiffened. A void seemed to open up in me. I knew this was the show-down.
>
> If I had said: No, sir, Mr. Pease, I never called you Pease, I would have been automatically calling Morrie a liar. And if I had said: Yes, sir, Mr. Pease, I called you Pease, I would

have been pleading guilty to having uttered the worst insult
that a Negro could utter to a southern white man. I stood
hesitating, trying to frame a neutral reply.[13]

Framing neutral replies so as not to offend was what whites wanted
blacks to do. Better than any other writer, Wright wrote about what
might be termed "old racist salutatory metaphors." His narrative
accounts provide insight into the ways that the black masses heard
and internalized them.

Wright and God

Nature was God for Richard Wright. For this reason, Wright was not
concerned with the questions of God's being for and with black people. He would not have troubled himself with the question of whether
God was with and for black people spiritually and politically. He
would have been more inclined to entertain the question of black people's inability to be trustfully with and for each other politically. Black
spiritual unity was less a concern since Wright was highly influenced
by communist belief. For this reason, Wright rejected all association
with the formal expressions of religion. He expressed faith only in a
radical humanistic ethic in defiance of all expressions of racism.

Wright saw traditional black religion as the enemy of black people. This is evident in Bigger Thomas's voice in the novel *Native Son*.
The communist attorney, Max, asked Bigger why he could not feel
at home in the black church. Bigger's answer reflects Wright's own
disposition toward the black church's eschatological view of happiness: "I wanted to be happy in the world, not out of it. I didn't want
that kind of happiness. The white folks like for us to be religious,
then they can do what they want with us."[14] Although reared in a
very conservative religious family in the South, Wright sought to
deny his religious heritage. Despite this denial, one of his biogra-
phers and literary friends, Margaret Walker, paradoxically characterizes Wright as a rebel and a puritan:

Wright felt that religious belief or faith and superstition
blinds man's insight into the human problems because of

dependency on God rather than on himself (and the god within himself), and that false religion keeps man divided against himself by race, creed, and class. But if man really wants to be healed and cured of hatred, racism, fascism, and cruel imperialism, he can find a common ground of humanity through the use of his reason and will.[15]

Wright embraced a naturalistic belief that was based on individualism. He dreamed of the emergence of a rationally self-determined black man who would fearlessly organize against racist America.

Wright's *Native Son*

Wright's protagonist, Bigger Thomas, lacks the trained capacity for rational actions. The white society, because of Bigger's race and ignorance, saw him as a black predator who preys upon white women. Wright portrayed Bigger as the type of black male who rebels against the closed society that whites created for blacks. Bigger would not submit himself totally to the old racist salutatory paradigm. He is as much a reaction to the white world as he is its creation. Analyzing him as a creation of the white world, Margaret Walker wrote of Wright's *Native Son* and Bigger Thomas: "*Native Son* was a powerful testament to American racism, for it openly declared that the young black criminal—illiterate and poverty-stricken—was a direct result of the society. The environment of a slum and the fear of crossing the white man's sexual and civil laws bred young black criminals. This was the thesis of *Native Son*."[16]

Wright's Bigger Thomas struggled within the ontological structures of fear, flight, and fate. Walker sees psychological parallels between Wright's protagonist and his own struggle as a black male within the vortex of American racism:

In his creative writing process and effort, Wright and Bigger become momentarily the same; emotionally they are the same. Wright not only becomes deeply involved with Bigger as a character, he expresses his own subliminal desires, and in the creative process of transforming reality into fiction he translates these desires into those of his character, Bigger Thomas. Who else but a Mississippi boy, who had lived in rural and urban Mississippi and been wounded by the painful sting of white racism, circumscribed and constrained to a poverty-stricken black world of ignorance and superstition, who had observed the weekly Saturday night razor cutting scrapes and the drunkenness of tortured and powerless black men killing their own and craving to kill the white man whom they blamed for their depth of degradation and racial impotence, who else but a Mississippi black boy could write with such authenticity of the tormented depths in the soul of a black youth? Wright knew how Bigger felt because he knew how he as a black male felt, and he knew how to express feelings of shame, fear, rage, and rebellion.[17]

Wright knew that the white world saluted Bigger as "a boy," "a primitive Negro," "a black clown," and "nigger." He expressed that knowledge in his novel through a portrayal of Bigger by the *Chicago Tribune:*

"He looks exactly like an ape!" Exclaimed a terrified young white girl who watched the black slayer being loaded onto a stretcher after he fainted.

Though the Negro killer's body does not seem compactly built, he gives the impression of possessing abnormal physical strength. He is about five feet nine inches tall and his skin exceedingly black. His lower jaw protrudes obnoxiously, reminding one of a jungle beast. . . .

All in all, he seems a beast utterly untouched by the softening influences of modern civilization. In speech and manner he lacks the charm of the average, harmless, genial, grinning southern darkey so beloved by the American people.

But the brutish Negro seemed indifferent to his fate, as though inquests, trials, and even the looming certainty of the electric chair held no terror for him. He acted like an earlier missing link in the human species. He seemed out of place in the white man's civilization.[18]

Wright presents Bigger's defense attorney's arguments as futile in the face of a white racist judicial system. Max, who is a liberal white communist lawyer, argues to no avail that Bigger is really a victim of white American racism. The lawyer, instead, is merely a lone white liberal voice crying in the racist wilderness of America. The prosecuting attorney symbolizes the racist will of white Americans. He speaks out of the old racist salutatory paradigm. His salutatory metaphors for referring to Bigger Thomas, the criminally accused, as a "maddened ape," an "infernal monster," and a "treacherous beast" all illustrate this.[19]

The New Poeticized Salutatory Paradigm Shift

The civil rights struggle symbolized the birth of a new creative linguistic moral energy that inevitably erupted out of the souls of black Americans. Earlier we showed that the King-led civil rights movement, which was predicated on the biblical notion of brotherhood, was the litmus test of white Christian's profession of brotherhood. King evoked such utopian hospitable images as "all of God's children sitting at the welcome table" and "the beloved community" in which men and women would not be judged by skin color or religious affiliation. He challenged his followers, by precept and example, to work for the realization of Christian brotherhood. His words and life were so authentic that, following his death, many black Americans became cynical of pious white Christians' brotherly salutations. In a word, King's assassination marked the end of blacks' long sacrificial struggles of presenting themselves, brotherly and sisterly, as living sacrifices for the soul of the nation. Many concluded that this was proving too costly. Pessimism provoked the question of what it would take to convince whites that blacks were endowed by the Creator for fully inclusive brotherhood and sisterhood.

After King's death, Malcolm X's rhetoric of militant black manhood dominated the language and behavior of young black males. If Martin symbolized the brother who presented himself as a living sacrifice for the soul of the white nation, Malcolm symbolized the brother who gave himself as a living sacrifice for the soul of the black nation. Malcolm's militant verbal cliches, such as "black power" and "by any means necessary," became more popular to young black males than King's benevolent call for "nonviolence" and the "beloved community." Malcolm was clear that he was in no position to sacrifice himself for the redemption of white people, which for him amounted to black people hating themselves and loving their oppressor. King's death caused blacks to wonder if they loved their oppressors too much and demanded a revisitation of the old theological and ethical questions of black people's faith in God and their trust of each other. Was God for and with the oppressed, rather than the oppressor, spiritually and politically? Could blacks be trustfully for and with each other? Revisiting these questions drove James Cone to write and publish his first book, *Black Theology and Black Power*.[20] This marked the genesis of a new intellectual black religious consciousness in the academy. It produced a genre of intellectual scholarship that still struggles to balance the tension between the poetic creativity of the folk and the academic reflectivity of the scholars. When black scholars of religion sacrifice one for the other, they hermeneutically miss the deeper theological and ethical insights into the phenomenon of blacks' social expressions.

The Birth of Poeticized Brotherly Metaphors

Social encounters between blacks, males in particular, took on new ritualistic significance following King's death. Brotherly poeticized salutatory expressions emerged out of these encounters that exhibited the black community's new religious creativity and reflectiveness. Unique fraternal expressions such as "soul brother," "blackman," and "brotherman" all reflect this poeticized creativity of black male consciousness for coping in a systematically racist society. These salutatory metaphors would constitute a different response to the questions of God's being for and with black people as well as blacks being for and with each other.

We observed initially in this study that salutatory metaphors such as "brotherman," "soul brother," and "blackman" reflect a spirit of ethnic kinship. They mirror blacks social struggle to be and belong for each other. A phenomenological study of "soul brother," "blackman," and "brotherman" will show that these concepts mirror black males' deeper religious and ethical concerns of being and relating and that these concepts evolve from black males' collective and individual deontological, ontological, and teleological needs. In other words, it will show that black males have been unable to separate their being for and with God politically and spiritually from that of being trustfully for and with each other. Standard mainstream language has always failed blacks in this struggle in the face of whites' historical efforts to devalue blacks' humanity, as evident in the negative names that they have called blacks since slavery.

No scholarly studies exist on such pedestrian terms as "soul brother," "brotherman," and "blackman." Amazingly these terms seldom show up in the scholarly literary sources produced by black males; neither do they appear in standard dictionaries, although books that specialize in naming and defining black idioms generally include these terms. The lack of written materials on these concepts has inevitably made the task of defining them rather difficult.

The Soul Brother Salutation Type

What have blacks meant by the salutatory expression "soul brother"? Pedestrian black users of the metaphor "soul brother" have often been more creative than reflective in their use of it. The term has its genesis in their creative poeticization of the language. For instance, the black jazz culture has been where much of the creative appropriation of the language has taken place. Ironically, lexicographers of black linguistic phrases have been insensitive in the definitions of certain terms that have emerged in black speech. A classic example is the term "soul brother." The term, which was very much in vogue among jazz musicians as early as the 1930s, is defined in total disregard of any possible influence of the black religious imagination:

> Soul brother (1930s–1960s) is a form of address for one black man to another; an expression of cultural solidarity. Also, often used by white males on the hip scene in addressing black males, in fact, white speakers had by the mid-sixties taken over the phrase entirely. Rare among black speakers after the mid-sixties.[21]

One might just say it is "a generic reference to an African American man."[22] There is no indication from the definition that the term has any roots in black spirituality.

I would contend here that "soul brother" is a salutatory social expression that has primarily signified a ritualistic verbal exchange between two black males. Although physical gestures are important in the social encounter, the ritual of verbal exchange is most critical. The latter exchange of verbal salutations (e.g., soul brother) elicits and affirms a potential or actual spiritual kinship bond between two black males.

Vincent Harding, in his insightful book *There Is a River,* traces the genesis of the spirit of this brotherly kinship bond back to slaves crossing what came to be known as the Middle Passage of the Atlantic Ocean. Harding thinks that it was this bond, forged out of the crucibles of common suffering, that enabled blacks to transcend the divisive barriers of tribal tongues, religions, and cultural differences. It was blacks' shared empathy for the common experience of each other's suffering on those slave ships that welded them together emotionally into a community of brothers and sisters.[23]

"Soul brother" is a modern term of greeting, just as "blackman" and "brotherman" are. In the mouths of black males, the term "soul brother" is pronounced as one word "soulbrother." This style of speaking often reflects the poetic creativity of pedestrian black male speakers. Creating and reconfiguring words tend to be natural in the pedestrian population of the black community. This seems to be particularly true as it relates to terms that are used in salutatory moments of social encounter. Acts of creating and reconfiguring words tend to make possible a needed psychological distance between oppressed people and their oppressors. It allows the oppressed to maintain some degree of definitive control over their social beings. In the call-and-response act of the salutatory moment, the oppressed take the liberty to create or reconfigure, from the dominant society's language, a salutatory metaphor that embraces their humanity, as well as elicits its brotherhood/sisterhood challenges. In other words, the oppressed are in search of salutatory liberation metaphors that mutually affirm each other's potential for being manly brothers and brotherly men.

In the call-and-response act of creating and reconfiguring the salutatory language, the implicit, if not always explicit, objective of black males' salutatory ritual becomes that of manly and brotherly restoration. During the salutatory ritual, oppressed brothers in the moment of social encounter seek to restore unto each other their real dialogical selves. It is the real dialogical self, among the oppressed, that is lost under the experience of oppression; that is to say, oppressed people lose an authentic voice for speaking and being heard by each other. Internalized oppression dictates that the oppressed must only speak through the master's voice and hear through the master's ears. The restoration of the dialogical self can only take place when the oppressed creates an alternative salutatory structure for speaking and hearing in the initial social encounter.

This study has shown that the oppressor's use of such an ethical term as "brother" was intended to appeal to the dialogical selves of black Americans. Whites used it, at best, to imply the voice of the elder speaking to the younger, the greater speaking to the lesser, the superior speaking to the inferior. In this sense, the notion of the monological self is exalted.

I observed above that King's death symbolized for black males the need to revisit what it means to be both for and with each other. In short, it harkened back to the old problem of whether black people were inherently more loving and trusting of white people than of each other. Following King's death, "soul brother" became a salutatory expression of endearment that black males made a primary part of their greeting repertoire. White males, following King's death, often felt excluded from this verbal ritual of social exchange. They often failed to understand that black males needed a language for bonding with and for each other.

The salutatory metaphor "soul brother" implied black male's individual and collective need to struggle with such ontological questions as, "Who am I?" "Where did I come from?" These questions took on a new kind of intensity following the death of black America's icons of brotherhood and manhood, Martin and Malcolm. "Soul brother" as a salutatory expression begged the correlating question of the black man's ethnic image and ontological existence. Resolving this issue has been problematic since the days of slavery. The haunting questions have been, Did the black man have a soul that reflected the image of God? Did God endow black men with brotherly potential?

The salutatory expression "soul brother" was black males' creative response to white males' denial that they actually had souls and were made in the image of God. It has been their way of affirming that God is faithfully for and with them in their daily social encounters. For black males, this has been more than superfluous rhetoric; rather, it has been a ritualistic act of socially re-creating themselves to be trustfully for and with each other. Blacks males' creation of the greeting "soul brother" was their way of restoring, by renaming each other in the social encounter, what whites had sought to destroy by naming it incorrectly (e.g., "boy" and "nigger").

Questions about the term "soul brother" still remain. If the word "brother" presupposes that one has a soul, why call another "soul brother"? Are we not to assume that every soul made by God is a potential brother or sister? Poeticized creative genius played a role in black Americans' critical attempt to restore each other from the oppressive language of alienation. Black men knew that there was a radical difference between whites' use of the term "brother" and their kinship expression "soul brother." They saw "brother" as a salutatory social ascription, when used among white church groups when relating to blacks, that was often no more than a verbal expression of politeness. The term "brother," for white Christians, meant whatever they wanted it to be. Consequently when whites called blacks "brother," blacks knew that whites did not mean that they were accepting them as social equals.

Blacks often experienced more genuine brotherly acceptance among white patrons of jazz than among white church members who piously called each other "brother." For blacks, the notion of "brother" has been rooted in their profound experience of God and humanity. Being a brother is inseparable from the relationship with God and Jesus. White jazz players, even in the 1930s and 1940s, used the term "soul brother" to salute their fellow black jazz players and vice versa. Ironically, there has often been more brotherly fellowship among white and black musicians than Christians of the two races. In the jazz community the term "brother" became an individual and corporate creative response to suffering that gave black and whites the sense of being "soul brothers." It gave them a sense of affirming and being affirmed by each other's dialogical selves. These creative responses generated the religious and moral energy that grows out of being the community of the stigmatized, that constitutes the life force that ensouled blacks, the extra gift (e. g., feeling, hearing, and seeing) for being faithfully for and with each other. It is not an accident that, perhaps, the jazz community gave the larger black society the salutatory expression "soul brother" since jazz is a creative inclusive communal language of the soul.

The "soul brother" salutation symbolized black men's willingness to recognize each other's potential for mutual love and trust. It was an attempt to reclaim in each other the gift of agency. "Soul brother" as a fraternal salutation was black males' radical way of calling each other to a higher level of mutual love and trust. One criticism that whites had of black males was that, since they were devoid of a soul or possessed an inferior one, they were untrustworthy. The "soul brother" salutation constitutes black males' challenging call to trust and love each other mutually. King and Malcolm had become for them classic examples of the personifiers of love and trust.

King was the exemplary embodiment of love and trust on behalf of white America. Following his death, blacks lifted King to messianic status. They constantly reminded whites that King's sacrificial death was more or as much on their behalf as it was those of his race. Many believed that King's movement did more for whites than for the black masses. Without question, King symbolized the messianic figure who stood in the moral gap on behalf of a recalcitrant white nation. Many hoped that his death would nudge the nation's heart unto repentance for its moral, economic, and political sins toward black Americans. Undeniably King personified to white America, following the emergence of Malcolm X, the black man's capacity for love and trust. He has become an American icon of sacrificial love. Blacks have taken pride in the fact that King taught all people both how to love and trust in the face of persecution. Ironically, King loved and trusted a nation that officially conspired for his ruination.

Malcolm was no less a teacher of love and trust to the black community in particular. He worked against that deadly stereotype in the black community that said that blacks do not trust or love each other. Malcolm's constant fear was that blacks had a history of trusting white people better than they did each other. His speeches and addresses were replete with the dominant theme of ethnic love and trust. In short, Malcolm saw himself as Allah's messenger to the lost house of black America. His soul was on fire for the salvation of his people.

The Blackman Salutation Type

The Muslim Perspective

"Blackman" is another salutatory expression that has dominated speech patterns among black males since the rise to prominence of the Black Muslims in the 1960s. I have not been able to find the term in any dictionary. The lack of any formal literary recognition of this expression has not prevented the black urban community's embrace of it. In fact, exclusion by white America often increases the currency value of minority groups' marginal verbal expressions. In the 1960s, the salutatory expression "blackman" was popularized by young black male Muslims who sold their religious newspapers on street corners in the black sections of large urban areas. The word "blackman" was used generically to salute any black man in general and every black man in particular. In the compounded term "blackman," "black" is not an adjectival modifier of the word "man." Instead, the word "black" is inseparable from "man," for "black" is what constitutes his manly being.

To black Muslims, "blackman" meant the original man. Elijah Muhammad taught that those of African descent were the real "blackman": "The original man, Allah has declared, is none other than the black man. The black man is the first and the last, maker and owner of the universe. From him came all brown, yellow and red and white people. By using a special method of birth control law the black man was able to produce the white race."[24] Muhammad dared counter the white man's myth of superiority. He called black America to its mythic beginning.

Naming the Beginning

In the light of Black Muslim mythology, we might argue that the salutatory word "blackman" signifies a conscious struggle to restore ontologically the hiatus between primal blackness and manhood. It was certainly a creative response to the artificial separation that whites had made between blackness and manhood. This creative linguistic response has been seen as an ideological overreaction to whites' racist denial that real men can be black. Nothing has been more disturbing to blacks than this denial. Conversely, Elijah Muhammad, leader of the Black Muslims, taught his followers that the "blackman" is the only normative man. He chided black males for wanting to be white. Muhammad attributed this desire to what he characterized as the black man's amnesia of his rich African history.

Call to Self-love

Minister Elijah Muhammad of the Nation of Islam taught that one of the greatest enemies of black Americans was the lack of self-love. In fact, the lack of self-love was the cause of a disharmony among blacks that neared crisis proportions:

> One of the greatest handicaps among the so-called Negroes is that there is no love for self, nor love for his or her own kind. This not having love for self is the root cause of hate (dislike), disunity, disagreement, quarreling, betraying, stool pigeons and fighting and killing one another. How can you be loved, if you have not loved self? And your own nation and dislike being a member of your own, then what nation will trust your love and membership.[25]

Muhammad took to task the biblical teachings on self-love and the love of neighbor, charging that the Bible's directives on this subject had misled black people. He denounced the black man's "I love everybody" claim as untrue. Muhammad's counterclaim was, "Love for self comes first." In the face of this, the minister gives his own interpretation of what the Bible says about love:

> The Bible, the book that you claim to believe says, "Love the brotherhood" (1 Peter 2:17). "Love one another" (John 15:17). Love of self comes first. The one who loves every-

body is the one who does not love anyone. This is the false teaching of the Christians for the Christians war against Christians. They have the Bible so twisted by adding in and taking out of the truth that it takes only God or one whom God has given the knowledge of the book to understand.

The Bible puts more stress upon "love for thy neighbor" than "love for thy brother." When asked "Who is my neighbor?" the answer was contrary and incorrect. Jesus' answer was that of two men who were on a journey. They were not from the same place. One was from Jerusalem, the other was a Samaritan. The Samaritan came to where the man from Jerusalem lay wounded by the robbers who had stripped him of his possessions. The Samaritan showed sympathy for the fellow traveler. (He was not a neighbor in the sense of the word. A neighbor can be an enemy.) Many enemies live in the same neighborhood of a good neighbor. But, the answer that Jesus gave was a futile one which could be classified as a parable of the so-called Negro and their slave-masters.[26]

As an expression of greeting, "blackman" was the call of the so-called Negro people back to primal love. This is why Minister Muhammad could say to his followers: "Let us refrain from doing evil to each other, and let us love each other as brothers, as we are the same flesh and blood."[27]

Antecedents of the Type

Confidently, Black Muslims addressed the question of naming and renaming the race and its individual members as though blacks were the first. The Black Muslims created such salutatory metaphors for referencing themselves as blackman, brotherman, and X. Self-designation and relating have been a critical problem for blacks since the nineteenth century. Black history professor Sterling Stuckey calls it the problem of "Identity and Ideology: The Names Controversy."[28] Black people in the nineteenth century called themselves such names as "African, Ethiopian, Free African, Colored, Negro, Children of Africa, Sons of Africa, Colored American, people of color, free people of color, blacks, Anglo-African, African, African-American, Afro-American, American, Aframerican, Africo-American, and Afro-Saxon."[29]

The Brotherman Salutation Type

Earlier in chapter six it was stated that a white leader had used the term "brother man." Black males later compounded the words for the purpose of renaming and recreating themselves. The contention of this study is that the term "brotherman," when used by black Americans, has had both religious and moral implications.

Like the expression "blackman," "brotherman" is both spoken and written as one word. In this case as well, "brother" does not modify "man." Instead, "man" and "brother" constitute a compound noun that names the being of the person. Logicians of the English language might rightly question the superfluousness of the compound noun. Has not every "man" the potential to be a "brother"? Is not every "brother" assumed to be a "man"? The term "brotherman" here is used in defiance of whites' religious and moral claims of brotherhood in relationship to blacks. Whites have been insensitive to the need to recognize blacks as men and brothers.

Who qualifies to be called a brotherman? Definitions in the black community are not always clear. The one thing that is certain, however, is that "brotherman" is a salutatory expression used in the black community for addressing another black male, for calling him to a sense of a new relationship.

The Call to New Being

"Brotherman" as a salutatory expression is an attempted corrective response to a racist society's disregard for the being of blacks. It has been black males' linguistic attempt to restore themselves to normative humanity, their creative attempt to redeem the concepts of both "man" and "brother" from their oppressors' desecrated mouths, from whites' insensitive misuse of them. "Brotherman" has been the black community's attempt to offset whites' degradation of black men as "boy."

White men, particularly in the South, felt that they had the license to call any black man "boy." If he were a very elderly man, they would call him "uncle." In a rescue attempt, black men sought to make "brother" and "man" one. They sought a primordial restoration of "brother" and "man." They knew that every "brother" is not necessarily manly, and every "man" is not always brotherly. Blacks, by using the term, sought to bring forth a new black man. Critical scholars such as Vincent Harding sought to describe this new "black man" during the era of the birth of the black power awareness movement.

The Call to Trust

"Brotherman" as a salutatory expression was a call of the black man to both manly and brotherly duty. It demanded that blacks recognize that they can be trustingly for and with each other in the struggle for the social re-creation of themselves in their own image. The Million-Man March was a classical social expression that publicly demonstrated black males' willingness to trust each other in the ritualistic call to accountability.

Summary

This chapter has shown the rich contribution that blacks have made to the salutatory phenomenon. Black males have unabashedly re-created salutatory formulas of the culture for the preservation of their human dignity. Black males' contribution to this social phenomenon of creativity must be seen in comparison to black females' creation of their own salutatory metaphors.

Chapter 10

Salutatory Metaphors of Womanhood, Sisterhood, and Friendship

Black males, through creative salutatory language, have re-created themselves socially, religiously, and morally. This is clearly evident in the perennial "I am a man" cry that has dominated black American males' public protest rhetoric for centuries. Such subjective declarations of manhood will continue in the struggle for freedom until it has been realized in the society as a whole. Historically blacks have begged whites to recognize them as having constitutional rights to assert publicly their manly and womanly capacities. I make the case here that black males' social creation and re-creation of themselves have been intentional. In other words, black males' salutatory declarations of being faithfully for and with each other reflect their creative understanding of language, as evident in primary black literary sources.

Black women's verbal expressions for referring to each other have been no less radical in many ways. Just as black men have had to fight to have their manhood recognized, black women have had to fight to have their womanhood affirmed. Collectively and individually, black women have kept Sojourner Truth's "Ain't I a Woman?" question before the American public. Marcia Riggs has rightly observed of Sojourner Truth that "she challenged the definition of womanhood that excluded the black woman as she modeled the strength and resilience of black femininity."[1] Black women have shown their own flair for creativity in creating their own verbal greeting language. The primary premise of this chapter is that black women have created rich poetic salutatory metaphors reflective of their own race and gender struggles. Collectively and individually, black women have found it necessary to reach out and bond with white women, each other, as well as the men of their race, in their fight against systemic racism. Black feminist scholars such as bell hooks have voiced radical criticism against white and black women's philosophy and practice.

Black Womanist Salutations

Black women's ethnocentric salutations, like those of black males, reflect a linguistic creativity that subtly critiques such conventional salutatory metaphors as "sister" and "girl." Playful salutatory metaphors such as "girlfriend" and "sistergirl" are creative greeting titles that are unique to black women. Such verbal greeting rituals must be seen as more than exercises of expressive frivolity. Cultural critics must be aware of the fact that this creative language provides the linguistic infrastructure for black women bonding with each other in the time of crisis. It is the creative language that black women summon each other to be for and with each other in the face of the oppressor. It is the creative language that black women draw upon to challenge each other to speak critically against each others' unacceptable behavior.

Black women's primary literary sources portray their affirmative embrace of sisterhood, womanhood, and friendship. Their public voices, whether militant or conciliatory, have challenged the Christian Church and nation to affirm the noblest ideals represented by these concepts. Desire for salutatory recognition and respect has been at the heart of black women's struggle. An exciting body of scholarly literature, documenting and interpreting the struggles of black women, continues to be produced. Examples include Joan M. Martin's most valuable work *More than Chains and Toil: A Christian Work Ethic of Enslaved Women*, as well as Traci West's poignant study of black women, *Wounds of the Spirit: Black Women, Violence, and Resistance Ethics*.

First, this chapter will deal with some of the negative salutatory metaphors that white America has used to greet black women. Second, it will name and analyze some of the poetic salutatory metaphors that black women have used to refer to each other. Third, it will deal with the primary theological and ethical questions of black people's faith in God and their trust in each other. All three aspects of the chapter will be dealt with in light of the theological and ethical questions that frame this study, which have been worded here to relate specifically to black women: Have black women understood God to be both faithfully for and with them spiritually and politically? Have black women understood God to be faithfully with them spiritually but not faithfully for them politically? Have black women understood God to be neither faithfully for nor with them spiritually or politically? Have black women understood sisterhood to mean that they are trustfully for and with each other spiritually and politically? Have black women understood sisterhood and friendship to mean that they are trustfully for and with each other spiritually but not trustfully for and with each other politically?

Black women's creative salutatory metaphors, when used in their social relationships with each other, have primarily reflected their humanistic, moral, and religious sensibilities. Religious and moral sensibilities are not necessarily absent even in black women's social moments of saluting each other as "girlfriend" and "sistergirl." These expressions, perhaps, say more than males are aware of regarding the bonding that takes place among black women in the salutatory moment of social encounter. They are code expressions that permit black women creatively to talk womanist talk trustfully for and with each other. I will say more about this later.

The primary sources, produced by black women, under investigation will show that they have been very much critically engaged in public discourses about suffering and race, individually and collectively. Black women's experiences of slavery and systemic racism, as with their black male counterparts, have contributed to their militant spirit of social protest. These racist experiences have tested black women's faith in God and their trust in each other.

Racist Salutatory Metaphors

A growing genre of literature addresses the abuses and stereotypes of black women in America since the crossing of the Atlantic's Middle Passage during the slave trade era until the present. White society's large numbers of stereotypes for referring to black women says much about its inability to accept them as equals socially, politically, and religiously. Denigrative salutations such as "mammy," "matriarch,"

"Jezebel," and "welfare mother" have all contributed to the blem-
ished perception of black women. The common consensus among
black scholars is that use of such denigrations aimed to deny the
black woman acceptable status alongside the white woman. Patricia
Hill Collins notes that "these controlling images are designed to
make racism, sexism, and poverty appear to be natural, normal, and
a part of the everyday life."² Such images suggest that it was abnormal to think that black women could attain those virtues delineated
by the cult of true womanhood: "piety, purity, submissiveness, and
domesticity."³ Elite white women and those of the emerging middle
class were encouraged to aspire to these virtues. The reality was that
"ladylike" behavior was totally irreconcilable with most white people's concept of black womanhood. No story demonstrates this fact
any better than that told by Adele Logan Alexander's relatives.
Alexander recalls the story, as it was told to her, in the following way:

> In the early 1940s, . . . a well-known educator and official in
> the Roosevelt administration, was traveling one day by train
> through the segregated South. She was a very dark-skinned
> woman, and there was no mistaking her African American
> (or at that time, Negro) heritage. She dressed and groomed
> herself meticulously, was corseted, and in public wore her
> ever present hat and gloves, and carried both pocketbook and
> umbrella, like all "respectable ladies" of the period—and
> much like the ladies when I grew up. Her posture was ram-
> rod straight, and she appeared, in short, both utterly refined
> and indomitable.
>
> At the time, of course most schools and parks and play-
> grounds, theaters, hotels, drinking fountains, means of
> transportation, and other public facilities, throughout the
> southern United States were strictly segregated by law and
> practice. But on this particular day in this particular depot
> in this particular unidentified city, the white station master
> was stunned when Mrs. Bethune, an apparition of imperi-
> ous rectitude, started to walk unswervingly across his expan-
> sive "White only" waiting room. Feeling obligated to assert
> his power in order to maintain the rigidly established racial

hierarchy, he called out to the elegant yet determined inter-
loper, "Hey there! You can't do that." Mrs. Bethune lifted
her chin higher, but never once hesitated. "Yes, you know
who I talkin' to, old colored woman. You just can't come
marchin' through here," he shouted waving his arms and
shaking his fists. "This room reserved for white folks." Still
no response at all from Mrs. Bethune who kept moving
toward her destination. By now other travelers were staring
in amazement at the drama unfolding between the increasingly frantic white male agent of authority and the well-
dressed black woman blatantly flouting established racial
practices. Finally, in disbelief that his vigorous admonition
had gone unheeded, and realizing that he was unable to pre-
serve the segregated sanctity of his waiting room, the station
master turned in puzzled frustration to the slack-jawed clerk
standing beside him and asked, "She is a nigger, ain't she?"[4]

The Double Handicap

Black women have had to overcome the double handicap of gender
and race. This factor has undoubtedly determined black women's
self-perception as well as their perception of friendship and sisterhood.[5] Scholars of the humanities have, in the past thirty years, contributed immensely to literature that addresses the stereotypes and
abuses of black women in America. An intellectual and emotional
awareness of the black woman's double handicap of gender and race
is evident in these publications.

Denigrative titles such as "mammy," "matriarch," "Jezebel," and
"welfare mother" have had a way of controlling black women's behavior and self-perception.[6] While "mammy" has represented the good
black mother, "matriarch" symbolizes the bad black mother.[7] The latter, Collins notes, is seen "as aggressive, unfeminine, black matriarchs
who allegedly emasculate their lovers and husbands."[8] Another controlling image, according to Collins, is that of the welfare mother.
Comparing the matriarch image with the welfare mother image,
Collins writes: "Like the matriarch, the welfare mother is labeled a bad
mother. But unlike the matriarch, she is not too aggressive. . . . In short

the welfare mother represents another failed mammy, one who is unwilling to become 'de mule uh de world.'"[9] "Jezebel" is equally as controlling in a negative way. Black women have been called "Jezebel" to suggest that they are by nature whores who are sexually aggressive. The image derives from slavery when black women were portrayed as being sexually aggressive wet-nurses.[10] In order for us to fully understand the destructive power of these images, it is necessary to take a closer look at slavery and paternalism.

Genovese's Mammy Theory

"Mammy" was an affectionate name that plantation masters reserved for a certain type of black woman on the slave plantation. Although a mammy was the master's property, the master understood the need to share some of his authority with her. Eugene Genovese's theoretical analysis of slavery reveals that the plantation mammy remained "the most illusive and important person in the Big House. . . . To understand her is to move toward understanding the tragedy of plantation paternalism."[11] Primary literary sources by whites who were reared during the time of slavery clearly illustrate the pivotal role that they perceived their black mammies to play in their socialization experience. As one white male said of his black mammy:

> She was the first to receive us from the doctor's hands, and was the first to proclaim, with heart bursting with pride, the arrival of a fine baby. . . . The mammy first taught us to lisp and walk, played with us and told us wonderful stories, taught us who made us and who redeemed us, dried our tears and soothed our bursting hearts, and saved us many well deserved whippings.[12]

Mammy played the role of punisher, consoler, and forgiver. In the system of plantation paternalism, mammy was a rather complex figure to be reckoned with both by slaves and master:

> She gave the whites the perfect slave, loyal, faithful, contented, efficient, conscientious member of the family who

always knew her place, and she gave the slaves a white-approved standard of black behavior. She also had to be a tough, worldly-wise, enormously resourceful woman; that is, she had to develop all the strength of character not usually attributed to Aunt Jane.[13]

Was mammy just "a white man's nigger, some pathetic appendage to the powerful whites of the Big House?"[14] Genovese warns of the danger of oversimplifying her, observing that the real tragedy of the black mammy of the plantation was "not in her abandonment of her own people, but in her inability to offer her individual power and beauty to black people on terms they could accept without themselves sliding further into a system of paternalistic dependency."[15]

DuBois's Mammy Theory

The prominent black intellectual W. E. B. DuBois arrived at conclusions about the mammy image different from those of Genovese. DuBois began to study the family around the turn of the twentieth century. His conclusive assessment was that the black mammy figure had no admirable attributes because of the chasm that her role created between the black woman and her children. DuBois described the mammy as "one of the most pitiful of the world's Christs. . . . She was an embodied Sorrow, an anomaly crucified on the cross of her own neglected children for the sake of the children of the masters who bought and sold her as they bought and sold cattle."[16] In short, "mammy" was the antithesis of the Hagar-type black woman. The Hagar-type symbolized black women of the slavocracy who were kept at servant status for its population. For a scholarly treatment of this subject, see Delores Williams's book *Sisters in the Wilderness*.

From an ethical standpoint, the harshness of DuBois's assessment of the mammy type perhaps has some foundation. For her, God was not perceived as being both for and with black people spiritually and politically. Blacks of the mammy type also did not see the need to be trustfully for and with each other spiritually and politically. The black mammy, driven by an unconditional love-forgiveness ethic, saw and experienced God's justice through the eyes of her master.

Commercialized Racism

Negative female images of black women are highly visible in the technological society of rap culture that exploits the erotic sensibilities of youth culture. Capitalist sponsors and benefactors of this cultural phenomenon of misogynist assaults on black women's dignity have tended to be oblivious to any public criticism. In the name of artistic creativity, some contemporary black musical groups have commercialized the old racist salutatory metaphors that were once used on plantations for addressing black women. This has been particularly true for what has come to be called in the music industry gangsta rap.

Many of the song lyrics of hard-core gangsta rappers refer to women as "whores" and "bitches." Though these terms have long had strong currency in the black ghetto cultures of urban areas, it has only been with the emergence of gangsta rap that misogynous lyrics are being openly marketed. Driven by large economic profit, many young artists tend to ignore the protest voices of conventional wisdom.

Some blacks have been very critical of this misogynous language; others have tried to explain it away as harmless. Still other blacks have maintained a posture of indifference toward the whole thing. Defenders of the producers of this language have been hard-pressed to convince the rest of the population that such verbal violence against black females is justified. Robin D. G. Kelley, a social scientist, tries to soften the bite of hustler poetry:

> Given the central place that misogyny occupies in the gangsta/baadman aesthetic, it would be hard to trust a straight sociological answer to the question of open distrust and aggressive hatred of women. Furthermore, I do not believe that rap music can or ever intended to represent the true and complex character of male/female relations among black urban youth. Too many critics have taken the easy way out by reading rap lyrics literally rather than developing a nuanced understanding of actual social relations among young people, in all of their diversity and complexity. And there is no reason in the world to believe that any music

constitutes a mirror of social relations that can be general-
ized for entire groups of people.[17]

Kelley's sociological explanation weakens in the face of the mounting
moral and social challenges facing the population that is so enamored with this music. Temptations to produce more sociological
explanations for the problem abound in the society.

Interpretations such as Kelley's provoke the question, have black
intellectuals given so much energy to explaining the racist reasons for
blacks' deviant behavior that they have none left for the work of social
transformation? This often seems to be the case. If so, this is the radical
difference between earlier black educators, such as DuBois, Benjamin
Mays, and Mary McLeod Bethune, and contemporary ones. The complexity of the moral challenge of the black community is undeniably
persuasive. There is no human way to solve it all in one sweep! Long-
term and short-term constructive approaches are necessary. A critical
assessment of salutatory metaphors in the language of the black religious community is a step in the right direction. This is definitely the
case as it relates to the biblical name Hagar, which was once used to per-
sonify the faith, courage, and love of the black woman. Other positive
biblical names include Esther, Mary, and Deborah. For a study of the
way women are transvaluated see Renita Weems's *Just a Sister Away.*

Hagar: Sacred Metaphor for the Phenomenal Black Woman

The Hagar-type female represents a black woman who perceives God
as being both faithfully for and with black people spiritually and
politically. She subscribes to a God of unconditional love and forgiveness, upon which she bases her ethic. Hagar's faith that God
would take care of her even in the house of her oppressor is a dominant factor in the biblical narrative. Black womanist theologian
Delores Williams, through her study and clear theological insight,
has helped us to understand better the symbolic implications of
Hagar's name and her experiences for black American women.
Williams draws her inspiration from her own personal sufferings in
relationship to her faith in God, as well as from the sufferings of her

mother's grandmother and of the mostly female worshipers who influenced the faith development of her childhood. About the faith experience of her maternal ancestors, Williams writes: "They expressed their belief that God was involved in their history, that God helped them make a way out of no way. And they shared their trials, tribulations and blessings, they asked the other communicants to pray for them. Their testimonies suggested they believed their lives were about more than white people's oppression of black people."[18]

Williams's account of the believers of her childhood sharing their faith communally is a clear example of the value that blacks placed on the need for spiritual community. More than merely a ritualistic moment of testifying, worship for the women of Williams's early life required bonding and sharing one's faith with each other. Williams speaks to the intergenerational aspect of this community when she links her own testimony to the personal faith construction of her womanist ancestors. As a professional theologian, Williams speaks of the ethical and cathartic value of the community of sisterhood even in adulthood. She says that community has strengthened her during her own personal struggles of life:

> Many times the painful moments would not have been healed were it not for the road I traveled to faith—learning to trust the righteousness of God in spite of trouble and injustice; learning to trust women of many colors regardless of sexism, racism, classism and homophobia in our society; learning to believe in the sanctuary-power of family defined in many ways in addition to nuclear; discovering love in a variety of forms that heal, but also believing serious political action is absolutely necessary for justice to prevail in the world of my four black children and other motherless children.[19]

The theological and ethical questions that have guided my study of salutatory metaphors have also been the concern of women: Is God a respecter of persons? Is God faithfully for and with black people spiritually and politically? Must black people be trustfully for and with each other? Can they be trustfully for and with whites without being against themselves? Prophetic/priestly religious voices of black women of both the nineteenth and twentieth centuries have clearly demonstrated black women's commitment to their race, to God, and even to those who oppressed them. Williams has given us a radically new appreciation for this reality in her theological interpretation of the Hagar-type woman in black consciousness. In her book *Sisters in the Wilderness,* Williams identifies Hagar as one of the more useful ethnocentric metaphors for an apical understanding of black womanhood. For Williams, Hagar typifies the faith, courage, and love of the black woman.

Faith, Courage, and Love

In traditional black consciousness, the name Hagar has unequivocally symbolized a devout woman of religious faith, courage, and love. Black scholars have tended to address the Hagar-type black woman, the one who had the courage to be in the wilderness with her child, poetically rather than analytically. The poets Maya Angelou and Langston Hughes have given rare poetic portraits of the Hagar-type black woman's faith, courage, and love.

Angelou's poetic portrait of the prototype black woman, whom she calls "Our Grandmothers," indicates that every elderly black woman who is faithful and courageous in her struggle for freedom exemplifies the virtues of faith and courage of our ancestral "grandmother" type. Angelou celebrates the black woman who, in her being and doing, has risen above the vitriolic tongues of her oppressor. The true grandmother type understood herself to be bigger than the negative names that she was called. She defied being stereotyped in the salutatory encounter:

> She heard the names
> swirling ribbons in the wind of history:
> nigger, nigger bitch, heifer,
> mammy, property, creature, ape, baboon,
> whore, hot tail, thing, it.
> She said, But my description cannot
> fit your tongue, for
> I have a certain way of being in this world.[20]

Comparing and contrasting our grandmother type to the biblical character Hagar, without naming her, Angelou observes:

> *No angel stretched protecting wings*
> *above the heads of her children,*
> *fluttering and urging the winds of reason*
> *into the confusion of their lives.*[21]

Our grandmothers often became clandestine conductors of their children's escape to freedom through diverse ways: "underground, overland, in coaches, and / shoeless."[22] They commissioned their children to be getters and givers of the resources of life:

> *When you learn, teach.*
> *When you get, give.*[23]

For Angelou, a grandmother's strength originates in the fact that she is "clothed in the finery of faith."[24] The grandmother's faith was undaunted by the inhospitality of white Christians

> *when she appeared at the temple,*
> *no sign welcome*
> *Black Grandmother. Enter here.*[25]

Whites' lack of Christian hospitality was unable to stymie the grandmother's faith in God's providential care. In the face of rejection, the grandmother resolved:

> *No one, no, nor no one million*
> *ones dare deny me God. I go forth*
> *Alone, and stand as ten thousand.*
> *The divine upon my right hand*
> *Impels me to pull forever*
> *at the latch on Freedom's gate.*
> *The Holy Spirit upon my left leads my*
> *Feet without ceasing into the camp of the*
> *Righteous and into the tents of the free.*[26]

Our grandmother's resolve throughout history in America has been, "I shall not be removed." This has been her resolution even in the face of death. She has taught her children no less. Grandmother has looked her oppressor in the face and said:

> *You have tried to destroy me*
> *and though I perish daily,*
> *I shall not be moved.*[27]

This grandmother type signifies a combination of strong faithfully courageous black women of both the past and present:

> *She is Sheba and Sojourner, Harriet and Zora,*
> *Mary Bethune and Angela*
> *Annie and Zenobia.*[28]

Margaret Walker caught the spirit of this type of black woman in her poem "Lineage." Lamentingly she speaks of the primal strength, stamina, productivity, nurturing gift, and creativity of black women:

> *My grandmothers were strong.*
> *They followed plows and bent to toil.*
> *They moved through fields sowing seed.*
> *They touched earth and grain grew.*
> *They were full of sturdiness and singing.*
> *My grandmothers were strong.*
> *Why I am not as they?*[29]

Langston Hughes's poem "Mother to Son" captures the faith, courage, and work ethic of the Hagar-type black female. The black mother of Hughes's poem is a model of perseverance and hope that is evident in a personal testimony to her son:

> *Well, son, I'll tell you:*
> *Life for me ain't been no crystal stair.*[30]

She confesses that her life has been punctuated by unnatural impediments of "tacks, splinters, torn up boards and carpetless floors."[31] Rather than dwell on these realities of her life, Hughes's mother type accents the black matriarch's gift of coping strength in the face of life-negating circumstances:

> *But all the time*
> *I'se been a-climbin' on,*
> *and reachin' landin's,*
> *And turnin' corners,*
> *and sometimes goin' in the dark*
> *Where there ain't been no light.*[32]

The persevering mother admonishes her son to have hope in the face of despair, for faith has taught her that hope can triumph over the dark and uneven emotional terrain of life. This hope is echoed in her admonishing words to her son to persevere in spite of life's impediments:

> *So boy don't you turn back.*
> *Don't you set down on the steps*
> *'Cause you find it kind of hard.*
> *Don't you fall now—*
> *For I's still goin', honey,*
> *I's still Climbin',*
> *And life for me ain't been no crystal stair.*[33]

Hagar in Black Art and Literary Sources

There is no feminine salutatory metaphoric expression in the language of the black experience comparable to that of Hagar. Blacks of previous generations well understood the complimentary value of this title when referring to the religious faith, moral courage, and sacrificial spirit of black women in the face of adversity. That black women and men thought proudly of themselves as Hagar's children has been deemed as an honorable salutation. It has enabled blacks religiously and morally to make sense of the nonsense of their struggle.

The name "Hagar" rang poetic in the ears of earlier generations of black Americans, as seen in their artistic and literary imaginations as well as in the naming of their children. Examples of the use of the name abound. The following are but a few of the examples: (1) Edmonia Lewis, a nineteenth-century African American sculptress, who worked in Italy, carved a famous statue named "Hagar in the Wilderness." (2) Paul Laurence Dunbar wrote about the members of the Afro-American Sons of Hagar social club. (3) Novelist Richard Wright referred to the African American family as Hagar's children. (4) E. Franklin Frazier titled one chapter in *The Negro Family in America* "Hagar and Her Children." (5) African American anthropologist John Langston Gwaltney dedicated his collection of urban narratives *Drylongso* to "Lucy and all other flowers in Aunt Hagar's garden." In the glossary of this book, Gwaltney describes Aunt Hagar as a "mythical apical figure of the core black American nation." (6) Maya Angelou's poem "The Mothering Blackness" alludes to the woman as "black yet as Hagar's daughter."[34] (7) Delores Williams shows that black people, in reading the Hagar story of the Bible, clearly identified with her. As a rereader of the biblical story herself, Williams concludes that "Hagar in the wilderness as an image of womanhood—poor, hardworking, strong, self-reliant, autonomous, committed to her family, communicating with God—continues to live and thrive in the African-American world."[35] Therefore when blacks have affectionately called the black woman "Hagar," they have dared name her attributes as industry, strength, self-reliance, autonomy, commitment to her family, and openness to God. She is a moral paragon of sisterhood even across racial lines.

From Hagar to A Moral Phenomenon of Sisterhood

Black women of the North, as early as the beginning of the nineteenth century, sought to become sisters of white women. Some of them had been educated at such predominantly white schools of that day as Oberlin College. Most of them joined organizations for white women. Black women's salutatory expression "We are your sisters" became their motto for reaching out to white women. Sarah L. Forten's poem, which she contributed to the Convention of American

Women held in New York in 1837, expresses black women's desire to
be the sisters of white women:

> *We are thy sisters. God has truly said,*
> *That of one blood the nation he has made.*
> *O, Christian woman! In a Christian land,*
> *Canst thou unblushing read this great command?*
> *Suffer the wrongs which wring our inmost heart,*
> *To draw one throb of pity on thy part!*
> *Our skin may differ, but from thee we claim*
> *a sister's privilege and a sister's name.*[36]

Black women of the North who were members of white female
groups, albeit few in number, were very committed to the principle
"a sister's privilege and a sister's name." Many black women, however, experienced bitterness from being treated as second-class citizens
by white women and from the effects of slavery on them and their
race. Such bitterness is evident in this quotation from an unknown
domestic day worker speaking to audiences of domestic workers and
day laborers:

> O, ye fairer sisters, whose hands are never soiled, whose nerves
> and muscles are never strained, go learn by experience! Had
> we had the opportunity that you have had to improve our
> moral and mental faculties, what would have hindered our
> intellects from being as bright, and our manners from being
> as dignified as yours? Had it been our lot to have been nursed
> in the lap of affluence and ease, and to have basked beneath
> the smiles and sunshine of fortune, should we not have natu-
> rally supposed that we were never made to toil? And why are
> not our forms as delicate and our constitutions as slender as
> yours? Is not the workmanship as curious and complete?[37]

Prophetic/Priestly Voices

It was not uncommon for black women of the post-slavery period to
organize themselves formally as "Africa's Daughters" or "Daughters

of Africa," though, as Sterling Stuckey reminds us, these groups were African in name rather than substance.[38] Nevertheless, organized groups of black women became what I would characterize as prophetic/priestly voices starting in the early part of the nineteenth century, prophetic/priestly voices that daringly advocated the idea of sisterhood both within and outside of their race.

I have designated the voices of black women as being prophetic *and* priestly. I hold this view contrary to the informative studies of Marcia Riggs and Gayraud Wilmore, who recognize prophetic voices alone. Riggs has studied the prophetic voices of black women from the nineteenth century to the present. Her scholarship, in an area where very few religious scholars have probed, has proven to be of immense value. Riggs understands herself to be chronicling black women's lives as faithful witnesses to the prophetic dimensions of the gospel: "I chronicle black women's lives as faithful witnesses to the prophetic dimensions of the Gospel using significant sociohistorical moments (slavery, emancipation, urbanization) and movements (e.g., the Great Awakenings, abolition, temperance, suffrage, women's clubs, women's missionary efforts) as implicit principles of selection for this volume."[39] I would argue that black women have had to struggle with the prophetic/priestly dialectic, just as their male counterparts have. It is not enough to speak of the prophetic voices of black men or women as though they were devoid of a priestly dimension.

During the black power era, black scholars tended to read the primary black nineteenth-century sources as though all militant leaders, such as Bishop Henry McNeal Turner and Frederick Douglass, were purely prophetic voices. I read Gayraud Wilmore's seminal study of black religious radicals somewhat in this way. Acknowledging her indebtedness to Wilmore's study, Riggs asserts the following about black female prophetic voices: "The prophetic voices of the African American women . . . are voices which are confessional, sermonic, political, and poetic—all witnesses to their God as the one who created, redeemed, and sustained them and who creates, redeems and sustains us for the work of liberation."[40] I would sharpen Riggs's claim by calling for a recognition of the priestly side of these voices, which is heard in the rhetoric of spiritual purification.

Spiritual Purification

Black women have not merely demanded that white people free black people from political bondage. These sisters have called upon black people to cleanse themselves from the stain of slavery and ignorance. This is the priestly side of the story. Acts of cleansing and purifying the race were looked upon by black female, as well as male, leaders of the nineteenth century as prerequisites for being favored by God. The common expression that those in the nineteenth century used to characterize the consequences of the stain caused by ignorance and slavery was "the lack of character." Character acquisition, produced by character-building education and religion, was understood as the means to the social and spiritual purification of the race.

Nineteenth-century black leaders were forced to try and make a rational connection between the suffering caused by their own enslavement and the Christian doctrine of original sin. Invariably they wondered how it was that God would allow the enslavement of a people of African descent. The answers of nineteenth-century black leaders have been less than satisfactory to those in the late twentieth century. Early leaders, believing that God used whites to enslave blacks for the purpose of Christianizing their souls for heaven, concluded that slavery itself was an indication that God was faithfully for and with black people spiritually. This belief, however, did not answer all the questions. Did whites enslave Africans because of their disobedience to God? Or did whites enslave Africans because God had made them lesser human beings?

The Priestly Response

Although some black women did engage publicly the theological debate of the enslavement of black people, many more freely entered the public arena to assist in the cleansing of their race from the sins of ignorance caused by slavery. Those committed to the task represented the moderate conservative conviction of black female leadership. The ultraconservative believed that the stain of sin and ignorance originated primarily in the degenerative nature of the African, who was a savage. Advocates of this view asserted that slavery actually was the social experiment that started to improve blacks' nature.

Black female missionaries to blacks generally internalized and taught these same kinds of stereotypes about the theological cause of their people's social and spiritual condition. A black female missionary's expressed sense of undying loyalty to her outcast race illustrates the claim: "No thought of suffering, and privation, nor even death, should deter me from making every effort possible, for the moral and intellectual elevation of those ignorant and degraded people."[41] Some white missionaries such as Sara G. Stanley expressed a deep priestly compassion reflective of many whites' attitude to bring "the poor outcast from the pale of humanity, into the family of man."[42] Others thought of the missionary effort as "the regeneration of a down-trodden and long suffering people."[43]

Blacks sought to accomplish this transformation of the sin-stained self through a character-building philosophy of education based on the teachings of the Scriptures. Male and female leaders of this period tended to take the message of the Scriptures at face value, as did their white counterparts. Those who lacked seminary training commonly depended upon the Holy Spirit for their interpretations of the Bible.

I would argue that the female strand of the priestly tradition struggled with the challenge of making their race spiritually and socially fit for acceptance by a white society. Following the Civil War, white religious leaders of the North led in that crusade, teaching blacks the necessary prerequisites for acceptable social and spiritual purification. White men, such as Clinton B. Fisk, were in charge of making and regulating the policies of educating women. Fisk, the popular head of the Freedman's Bureau in Tennessee, admonished black female members of his audience regarding the rules for making its members socially fit:

> Do not think of getting married until you know how to knit
> and sew, to mend clothes and bake good bread, to keep a nice
> clean house and cultivate a garden, and to read and write.
>   A wife should take good care of her person, be clean,
> neat, tidy, and look as pretty as possible. I do not see how a

man can love a slovenly woman, who goes about with her heels out of her stockings, her dress unpinned, her hair uncombed with dirt under her finger nails and snuff or tobacco in her mouth. A wife must do her best to help her husband make a living. Much of the beauty and happiness of home depends on the good sense, economy, and industry of the wife.[44]

Proponents of the social and spiritual purification theory always ran the danger of blaming the victim. In the nineteenth century, black leaders were always caught in the dilemma of trying to give the priestly formula for realizing freedom as an ethnic group while prophetically condemning white America for its racial injustices.

Finally, black female voices of the priestly type, particularly in the nineteenth century, constantly reminded their people that they were suffering economically for having violated their relationship with God. A primary danger of this message is leading people to believe that a personal relationship with God is all that God requires. The corporate notion of salvation, which is also a part of the biblical tradition, is ignored.

The Prophetic Voice

The phrase "prophetic voice" is seldom used to refer to the spoken word of females. The term "prophetic voice" is often made synonymous, sometimes unconsciously so, with the speech of men. Despite this fact, the prophetic voice of women is a very authentic reality in the primary sources of the black experience. Naturally, it has had to overcome more adversity than the prophetic voice of their black male counterparts. Black female voices have often dared to prophesy deliverance in the face of white and black male opposition. Black males have too often imitated their white male counterparts as oppressors. This fact is vividly demonstrated in the black women's accounts of black males' opposition to them preaching the gospel of Jesus Christ. The painful truth is that even black male leaders of the Christian church have been oppressors of their women, refusing to share power with them. According to black women of the nineteenth century, an experience with God that convicted them to "fear no man" was the litmus test that would prove that God had prepared them to prophesy deliverance. This experience would bring them to the unconditional conviction that God was for and with them as bearers of the prophetic word. Marcia Riggs's characterization of black women's prophetic voices is instructive:

> First, like biblical prophets, the women relate faith and history; they were individuals who brought "faith out of the temple or sanctuary into the market place of human affairs where history was in process; history—the present and immediate future viewed in the light of the past. . . ."
>
> Second, the women's voices are consistent with a black prophetic tradition rooted in a relationship between religion and radicalism found in the "prophetic wing of the black church." This tradition is in evidence from the slave era through contemporary civil rights era and is earmarked by (1) re-appropriation of the revolutionary language of the Declaration of Independence and the Constitution; (2) espousal of providential agency; (3) a theology of national redemption emphasizing social transformation through moral reform; (4) a critique of the practice of democracy in the United States while yet asserting a "mutual dependency between church and state"—the former, being the agent of Christian love and the latter, the agent of social justice.
>
> Third, the voices of these women express a prophetic hermeneutic which seems inextricably bound up with their conversion into Christianity and appropriation of biblical traditions to judge their reality.[45]

The reality of sexism has demanded that black women since slavery struggle with the *God being for, with and against* dilemma and vice versa. Inevitably, it meant that black women struggled with this relationship dilemma in terms of *gender* as well as *race* and *class*. When it came to being prophets of the word of God, black women had to face such troubling questions as: (a) Is God for and with black women preaching the gospel of liberation? (b) Ought black women who are desirous of speaking for and with God to do so in a society that denies women of that right? (c) Ought black women speak for but against black men who prohibit them from preaching the prophetic word? Given the nature of this study, we can only briefly comment on each question. Black women of both the nineteenth and twentieth centuries are very clear about what it means to struggle with the theological and ethical questions just mentioned.

God Being For and With

The conversion language of black Americans in the nineteenth century makes it very clear that God was for black women. Numerous women's conversion stories in the primary literature of the nineteenth century narrate accounts of God's converting and commissioning of them for prophetic work. These stories take the same shape as those of men. Formally literate black women used autobiography, as another narrative form, to tell of their experiences of having been converted and commissioned by God to preach the gospel of Jesus Christ. Speaking of her own consciousness of God's being with and for her, Jarena Lee observed:

> The Lord gave his handmaiden power to speak for his great name, for he arrested the hearts of the people, and caused a shaking amongst the multitude, for God was in the midst.[46]

Sojourner Truth argued that if God could use a woman to bring Jesus Christ into the world for its salvation then a woman ought not be excluded from any right given to a man.[47] Harriet Tubman gave one of the most intriguing accounts of God being for and with the black female dilemma. Reared by very religious parents, Tubman recalled that she talked to God as a man talks with his friend. The following account was recorded by Tubman's biographer:

> "As I lay so sick on my bed, from Christmas till March, I was always praying for poor ole master. Pears like I din't do nothing but pray for ole master. 'Oh, Lord, convert ole master;' 'Oh dear Lord, change dat man's heart, and make

him a Christian.' And all the time he was bring men to look at me, and dey stood ther saying what dey would give, and what dey would take, and all I could say was, 'Oh, Lord, convert old master.' Den I heard dat as soon as I was able to move I was to be sent with my brudders, in the chain-gang to de far South. Then I changed my prayer, and I said, 'Lord, if you ain't never goint to change dat man's heart, kill him, Lord, and take him out of de way, so he won't do no more mischief.' Next thing I heard ole master was dead; and he died just as he had lived, as wicked bad man. Oh, den it 'peared like I would give de world full of silver and gold, if I had it, to bring date pore soul back, I would give myself; I would give eberting! But he was gone, I couldn't pray for him no more."[48]

Speaking for God

Against great odds, black women dared to proclaim that God had called them to preach the gospel of Jesus Christ. Rather than try and prove this with Scripture, black women generally appealed to some personal experience that they had had with God in a dream. They often experienced being healed by God from some peculiar sickness. In a word, black women used the same genre that men used to explain their experience of having been called by God to preach the gospel (see *God Struck Me Dead*). Julia A. J. Foote's story of how God converted her to preach the gospel is a case in point. Foote tells of having been taken in a dream to the spiritual world where she saw God the father, the Son, and the Holy Spirit sitting under a tree. Then the Father said to her, "Before these people make your choice, whether you will obey me or go from this place to eternal misery and pain."[49] In the dream, Foote is baptized by Christ, fed fruit from the tree by the Holy Spirit, and commissioned by God. What takes place between the newly commissioned Foote and God reassures her that she must speak for God:

Then God the father said to me: "You are now prepared, and must go where I have commissioned you." I replied, "If

I go, they will not believe me." Christ then appeared to
write something with a golden pen and golden ink, upon
golden paper. Then he rolled it up, and said to me: "Put this
in your bosom, and wherever your go, show it, and they will
know that I have sent you to proclaim salvation to all." He
then put it into my bosom, and they all went with me to a
bright, shining gate, singing and shouting. Here they
embraced me, and I found myself once more on earth.[50]

Foote was just as certain about the realness of her conversion and com-
mission to bear God's prophetic word as any man of that day no doubt
would have been.

For but Against

Converted and commissioned black women of the prophetic word
were uncompromising in their convictions even with their black men.
Such black women chose to be for and with God even if it meant having to stand for but against men who denied them the right to their
preaching space. Virginia W. Broughton, an ardent advocate for the
rights of women, was from Tennessee. She was bitterly opposed by
black ministers for her efforts of trying to raise the consciousness of the
black women of her day to see themselves in the Scriptures. Broughton
was a Baptist missionary and teacher who may be characterized as the
forerunner for womanist biblical interpretation.[51] Broughton organized groups of women into what she called Bible Band work. She and
her women condemned those things of her day that worked against
strong family life. Broughton understood that black ministers and laymen often opposed her because she was a woman:

Ministers and laymen, who looked with disdain upon criticism that came from a woman, all those who were jealous of
the growing popularity of the woman's work, as if there was
some cause of alarm for the safety of their own positions of
power and honor, all rose up in their churches, with all the
influence and power and speech they could summon to
oppose the woman's work and break it up if possible.[52]

Despite the opposition, women such as Virginia Broughton were able to convert some men who opposed their work. Broughton cites a number of cases when such happened to the men who publicly opposed their work.[53] The beauty of such stories is that these black women were quick to form alliances with those black men who accepted them as bearers of God's prophetic word. Some men even became partners with them in this work. In the truest sense, black women worked for and with God for the elevation of their race. They were just as dedicated on working for and with their black male counterparts for the elevation of the race. The exception occurred when black males opposed them.

Sisterhood and Friendship

"Soul sister," "sistergirl," "sisterfriend," and "girlfriend" are affectionate salutations that black women have used for greeting each other. They are somewhat analogous to the creative terms "homeboy" and "boy" that black males use. These ethnocentric salutatory metaphors have been used most often in informal situations. I use the term "ethnocentric" to refer to those concepts that are peculiar to blacks' linguistic expressions. Research for this project has left me wondering why black scholars have given practically no theological or ethical interpretation to ethnocentric salutatory metaphors that are named in this study. Black female salutatory expressions are just as critical to the social formation of the self as are those used by males. Neither can afford to overlook the value of salutatory expressions in the renaming ritual. Black female scholars are in a better position than I to explain the dynamics that take place between each other in the greeting ritual. This is because salutatory ethnocentric metaphors between black women are an encoded language. Evidenced in the encoded salutatory metaphors between black women is an intuitive understanding of each other's being that is unique to their experience.

Salutatory expressions such as "sistergirl" or "sisterfriend" must be seen as having a kind of therapeutic value. It might be an expression that a group of black women might use to encourage a troubled sister in a season of emotional stress. Unlike men's salutatory metaphors, such as "brotherman," black females seldom, if ever, use the term "woman" in the salutatory moment of encounter. This might have to do with the different emotional needs of the genders. Was it easier for white America to deny black males the right of manhood than black women the right of womanhood? Some would answer that the ever present threat of literally castrating black males was always a threat to their manhood. Given this, it is understandable that being recognized as a man has been a constant preoccupation of black men. However, the attempt to undermine womanhood was much more difficult since black women in slavery were used to birth children for whites and blacks; to nurse and nurture the children of the slave holder as well as their own; and to care for and develop both households and communities. For women, salutatory metaphors such as "girlfriend," "sistergirl," and "sisterfriend" have had to do more with spatial relationships of community between black women than their being as woman. It is a matter of black women being for each other.

The "for Us or "with Them" Dilemma

Birth of the white feminist movement presented black women with a "for us/with them" dilemma unlike they had experienced previously. The intellectual black woman has sought to live creatively with the tension generated by this dilemma. Gloria Wade Gayles has stated the black intellectual woman's challenge in clear poetic terms. Gayles recalls living with a deception about how white feminist groups perceived the papers and speeches that she gave at conferences. In her poem "A Black Woman's RSVP," she writes:

> *You must understand my reasons*
> *or can you?*
> *You see*
> *I thought they were proud*
> *Of the papers and the speeches*
> *I gave at conferences they didn't call.*[54]

Gayles confesses the personal enjoyment of being white women's

> *dark child integrating panels*
> *being "the expert" who knew it all*
> *and said it well in language*
> *they never spoke.*[55]

It is Gayles's unavoidable encounter with the sermonic truth of Miss Rosie from her old neighborhood that brings her to a new level of critical self-consciousness about her role with white feminists:

> *Until*
> *Miss Rosie from my old neighborhood*
> *stood down in her hips*
> *and preached to me*
> *Her words like rolling pins*
> *smoothing out the truth:*
> > *"How you gone get anything done for us*
> > *Sitting on the platform with them?"*[56]

Miss Rosie voices the ethical question that every black intellectual female and male must confront. Her question goes to the heart of the problem of black leadership and responsibility to the black community. The old woman is aware that it is the highly educated black women who have the intellectual resources to represent and uplift their race. Gayles is correct to place the question in the mouth of the old woman from her neighborhood, for blacks who have the credentials to sit on platforms with whites can easily forget the importance of race representation and uplift.

Gayles observes that Miss Rosie had heard about

> *Black women*
> *waiting our turn to talk about men*
> *(our fury came out in stereotypes)*
> *and when we finished*
> *(our speeches were the longest)*
> *we tossed our heads as if our afros*
> *could move in the winds.*[57]

Miss Rosie knew that these women had been assimilated. She observes that black women sit on those platforms

> *to talk about men*
> *Black men*
> *how they oppress us*
> *enslave us*
> *abuse us*
> *never having us*
> *in the first place.*[58]

Miss Rosie helps Gayles to see the critical ethical questions that black women of the next millennium must not ignore:

> *Black women,*
> *so busy talking on their platforms*
> *we have no time*
> *for Black conferences*
> *Black schools*
> *Black communities*
> *and Black women*
> *who need our bonding*
> *more than white women*
> *need our words*[59]

Interestingly enough, Miss Rosie is under no illusion about black women being able to transform white women. She compares white women's intransigent disposition toward the issue of race to be as unchangeable as the nature of the magnolia tree:

> *You know about this tree?*
> *Don't never change.*
> *Gonna always be magnolia.*[60]

The magnolia tree is known for its fragrant flowers and aromatic bark and is much cultivated for ornament. In the poem, Miss Rosie compares the magnolia tree to white women's false assumption that they have natural petal status over black women:

> *Got its own history*
> *its own flowers*
> *Don't never change.*
> *Born magnolia*
> *Gonna stay magnolia.*
> *They like that.*
> *Born a certain way.*
> *Got their history and roots*
> *branches and . . . .*
> *Don't never change.*[61]

It is no accident that Miss Rosie makes the transition in the conversation from speaking of magnolia trees and their flowers to "acorns . . . and oak trees and faith and Black women."[62] The oak tree has no flowers or anything else that would give it premier status in society. Gayles unequivocally concludes that she will attend no more white women's meetings until she has given back to the black community:

> *RSVP:*
> *I won't attend the conference*
> *this year*
> *or next year*
> *or ever until . . .*
> *I*
> *AM*
> *GOING*
> *HOME.*[63]

Gayles has expressed what the masses of black women have felt about the white feminist movement. Bettye Collier-Thomas has stated it in more academic terms when she says that "black women's racial ideologies have taken precedence over any feminist leanings":

Black women continue to view the most critical issue in their lives as being racial oppression. In a white patriarchical society that has economically, politically, and socially oppressed blacks, black women have largely been unwilling to side with white feminists, or even with black feminists who argue that women must fight for their freedom and equality. Many black women cannot see how their family's economic status would benefit materially from feminist protest.[64]

Summary

Black women have made a unique contribution to ethnocentric linguistic salutatory expressions. Religious and moral concern have been at the heart of them. The study has shown that black women have struggled in their own way with the question of God's being a respecter or nonrespecter of persons. Black women have wrestled with the question of whether God has been faithfully for and with them spiritually and politically. Ethically black women have had to reckon with what it means to be trustfully for and with each other spiritually and politically, as have their male counterparts.

Afterword

This study of ritual, God, and brotherhood/sisterhood challenges in the black experience is my own special contribution to the conversation of black religious experience and language. The idea grew out of my receptiveness to the pedestrian terms that blacks have used to greet each other in their informal social encounters. Blacks have inevitably made their most creative contributions to everyday salutatory language in the face of whites' racist assaults. Much of this has grown out of their struggle for ethnic cohesiveness. I have tried to show that out of blacks' struggles against the phenomenon of racist language major theological and ethical issues have emerged and warrant further scholarly investigation. A critical engagement of the relevant theological and ethical questions must continue. These questions include the following: Is God both faithfully for and with black people spiritually and politically? Is God only faithfully for and with black people spiritually? Can blacks be both trustfully for and with each other spiritually and politically? Or can blacks only be trustfully for and with each other spiritually?

This study initially introduced some of the metaphorical phrases that blacks have used in their attempts to relate to God since slavery. It also addressed some of the salutatory metaphorical phrases that blacks believed God used to refer to them in the moment of encounter. I have considered the creative expressions that blacks have used in greeting each other in the moment of social encounter and the creative linguistic imagination of blacks in their brotherhood/sisterhood challenges. This study presents us with some basic theological constructs that are critical for doing theological and ethical reflection.

God's Faithful Partiality

The guiding theological question of this study has been, Is God a respecter of oppressed persons? Or, stated another way, Has God been both faithfully for and with black people spiritually and politically? I have shown that blacks have had different opinions about this question.

All black Christians are not in agreement with the idea that God favors the oppressed and curries their loyal affections, because it is a very complex issue. The Black Muslims certainly have been extremely critical of blacks' assumption that the white man's God has favored the oppressed. Instead, they have argued that Allah, the God of Islam, has been the only true friend of the oppressed. Black Muslims base their claim on the premise that Allah is the only true God.

Future study must critically explore this question: If God favors the oppressed, how has this favoritism manifested itself? For instance, if God favors them for liberation, was God favorable toward black people in creation? This has been the most difficult question for blacks to answer. Black Muslims respond to the issue by concluding that the original man was black. Their argument is that the white man is a perverted version of the original black man.

The fundamental theological question must be, What has God uniquely invested in the black man that warrants God's favoritism? In other words, has God been faithful toward blacks both in creation and redemption? If not, how do we account for God's faithfulness in the creation of black people and the lack of it in their liberation? Does this constitute an antimony in God's nature?

God's Faithful Impartiality

Is God a nonrespecter of persons? That is to say, does God love all people in general and none in particular? If this is true, what is the explanation for God's seeming to favor some groups of people above others? Ironically, oppressed people tend to teach the oppressed that God is a nonrespecter of persons. Oppressors behave toward the oppressed, of course, as though God made the latter inferior to themselves.

Oppressors delight in the claim that God made them superior in creation itself. This inevitably gives them superior status in the created order. The oppressors' notion of created superiority assumed that they, even after the fall of humanity, were still superior in every way to what they call "inferior races." From the perspective of the oppressor, God's creation reflected no sign of a theological antimony in the divine nature. Instead, it was consistent with the belief that God was the author of racial superiority. This question of God's impartiality left those blacks who believed in God's faithful partiality with the question of God's trustworthiness, which has given rise to the ethical questions that guided this study: Can blacks be trustfully for and with each other spiritually and politically in the salutatory moment? Can blacks be trustfully for and with whites spiritually and politically in the salutatory moment of social encounter without being against themselves?

Ethnocentric Trust

Blacks' lack of trust for and with each other spiritually and politically has been for them the primary critical ethical challenge. Why this distrust? has been the haunting question. Some have said that it originates in the fact that God created blacks inferior. Others have asserted that this distrust has grown out of blacks' long history of oppression. They made the case that the pathological distrust is a consequence of oppressive socialization, which bred self-hatred in the victimized. Some blacks have sought to overcome this trust/distrust challenge by invoking Jesus Christ as the new paradigm of trust. Slaves never mentioned Jesus' color in their relationship with him. Instead, they were convinced that Jesus could be trusted because he had taken on their "little man" or "little one" status.

Black Muslims' response has been that Jesus cannot be trusted because he is a friend of the white oppressor and, thus, should be viewed as the enemy of black people. Malcolm X called upon blacks to discard the white Jesus as their Lord. Instead, Malcolm and Elijah Muhammad called upon the black man to love himself. Self-love is thought to be the means of blacks' building a bridge of trust between each other in the salutatory moment in the black community.

Ethnocentric trust would determine blacks' notion of love and forgiveness. Race would condition the way that blacks would love and forgive each other. Ethnocentric blacks advocated a conditional love-forgiveness ethic, of which Malcolm X certainly became the embodiment. Adherents of this ethic make it very clear that they only love those who love them in return. They do not come with a surplus of love. Surplus love for the other potential enemy has no place in their love portfolio.

Christocentric Trust

The conditional love-forgiveness ethic of the Black Muslims is antithetical to the unconditional love-forgiveness ethic that grows out of the Christocentric notion of trust. This challenging perspective of ethics, which is found in the New Testament, requires that we treat every person in the moment of salutatory encounter as a potential Christ figure.

The idea of Christocentric trust has its origin in the New Testament perspective of Jesus Christ as every person's brother. Christ-centered brotherhood/sisterhood overcomes ethnocentric loyalty. Even the enemies of Christ must be responded to as potential siblings in Christ.

Christocentric trust teaches an unconditional love-forgiveness ethic. If Malcolm X embodies the conditional love-forgiveness ethic, Martin L. King Jr. exemplifies the unconditional love-forgiveness ethic. Adherents of this ethic behave with the conviction that, through Christ, they have a surplus of love that enables them to love those who despitefully use them. They get their strength from the exemplary life and teachings of Jesus, who in the words of the black slave community was "called everything but a child of God."

Endnotes

Introduction

1. Sterling Stuckey, *The Slave Culture: Nationalist Theory and the Foundations of Black America* (New York: Oxford University Press, 1988), 201.

2. Ralph Ellison, *Shadow and Act* (New York: Vintage Books, 1972), 147–148.

3. Riggins R. Earl Jr., *Dark Symbols, Obscure Signs: God, Self, and Community in the Slave Mind* (Maryknoll, N.Y.: Orbis, 1993).

4. Paul Ricoeur, *Figuring the Sacred* (Minneapolis: Fortress, 1995), 79.

5. Raymond Firth, "Verbal and Bodily Rituals of Greeting and Parting," in *The Interpretation of Ritual: Essays in Honor of A. I. Richards* (ed. J. S. La Fontaine; London: Tavistock, 1972).

6. Ricoeur, *Figuring the Sacred*, 53.

Chapter I: Jesus' Salutatory Peace and Muslims' Salutatory *Assaluma Alaykum*

1. David Rensberger, *Johannine Faith and Liberating Community* (Philadelphia: Westminster, 1988).

2. Jacquelyn Grant, "Servanthood Revisted: Womanist Exploration of Servanthood Theology," in *The Papers of the Henry Luce III Fellows in Theology ATS* (ed. Jonathan Strom; Atlanta: Scholars Press, 1997), 2:25–40.

3. Wes Howard-Brook, *Becoming Children of God: John's Gospel of Radical Discipleship* (Maryknoll, N.Y.: Orbis, 1994), 336.

4. Ibid.

5. Colin Brown, ed., "Brother, Neighbor, and Friend," in *The New International Dictionary of New Testament Theology* (Grand Rapids: Zondervan, 1975), 1:257.

6. Carter G. Woodson, ed., "Stray Thoughts and Meditations," in *Works of Francis James Grimke* (Washington, D.C.: Associated Publishers, 1942), 3:355.

7. Ibid., 359.

8. Kiel Hans Windisch, "Jesus' Rules of Greeting," in *Theological Dictionary of the New Testament* (ed. Gerhard Kittel and G. Friedrich; trans. G. W. Bromiley; Grand Rapids: Eerdmans, 1964), 1:499.

9. Ibid.

10. Howard-Brook, *Becoming Children of God,* 457.

11. Ibid.

12. Ibid.

13. Iman Al-Ghazali, *The Duties of Brotherhood in Islam* (trans. Muhtar Holland; Leicester, U.K.: Islamic Foundation, 1997), 26–27.

14. Ibid., 27.

15. Ibid.

16. Ibid., 32.

17. Ibid.

18. Ibid., 33.

19. Mattias Gardell, *In the Name of Elijah Muhammad: Louis Farrakhan and the Nation of Islam* (Durham: Duke University Press, 1996), 156.

20. Mohammad M. Siddiqi, *Assalam Alaykum: Meaning and Commentary* (Baltimore: Muslim Community Services, 1996).

21. Muhammad 'Atiqul Haque, *Islam: The Religion of Peace* (Lahore, Pakistan: Sh. Muhammad Ashraf, 1990), 1.

22. Ibid., 1.

23. Ibid., 7.

24. Siddiqi, *Assalam Alaykum,* 4.

25. Ibid.

26. Ibid., 5.

27. Ibid., 4.

28. Ibid., 11.

29. Ibid., 10–11.

30. Al-Ghazali, *The Duties of Brotherhood in Islam,* 50.

31. Ibid., 21.

32. Ibid.

33. Ibid., 23.

34. Ibid., 54.

35. Ibid., 54–55.

36. Ibid., 46.

37. John L. Esposito, *Islam: The Straight Path* (expanded ed.; New York: Oxford University Press, 1991), 26–27.

38. Holland, *Duties of Brotherhood in Islam,* 66.

Chapter 2: Ritual, God, and Salutation

1. Garth Kasimu Baker-Fletcher, *Xodus: An African American Male Journey* (Minneapolis: Fortress, 1996).

2. Paul Ricoeur, "The Hermeneutic of Symbols and Philosophical Reflection," trans. Denis Savage, *International Philosophical Quarterly* 2, no. 2, trans. Denis Savage (May 1962): 192–193.

3. Paul Ricoeur, "Word, Polysemy, Metaphor: Creativity in Language," in *A Ricoeur Reader: Reflection and Imagination* (ed. Mario J. Valdes; Toronto: University of Toronto Press, 1991), 78.

4. C. Eric Lincoln, *The Black Muslims in America* (Grand Rapids: Eerdmans, 1994); see also Wilson Jeremiah Moses, *Black Messiahs and Uncle Toms: Social Literary Manipulations of a Religious Myth* (University Park: Pennsylvania State University Press, 1993).

5. Alex Haley, *The Autobiography of Malcolm X* (1965; repr., New York: Ballantine, 1987).

6. William R. Jones, *Is God a White Racist?* (New York: Anchor/Doubleday, 1973).

7. Anthony B. Pinn, *Why, Lord? Suffering and Evil in Black America* (New York: Continuum, 1995).

8. I know of no studies to date that have critically addressed the contribution of black church leadership to such prominent organizations among black people as the National Association for the Advancement of Colored People.

9. J. W. E. Bowen, *What Shall the Harvest Be?* (Washington, D.C.: Howard University Press, 1892), 23.

10. Ibid.

11. Ibid.

12. Ibid., 23–24.

13. Cain Hope Felder, ed., *Stony the Road We Trod: African American Biblical Interpretation* (Minneapolis: Fortress, 1991).

14. Stuckey, *Slave Culture.*

Chapter 3: Revelation, Race, Class, and Reason

1. Martin L. King Jr., "Remaining Awake through a Great Revolution," in *A Testament of Hope: Essential Writings of Martin L. King, Jr.* (ed. James Melvin Washington; San Francisco: Harper & Row, 1986), 273–275. King brilliantly uses the principles of this parable to critique America's insensitivity to the poor.

2. Victor Anderson, *Beyond Ontological Blackness: An Essay on African American Religious and Cultural Criticism* (New York: Continuum, 1995); see also Charles Long, *Significations: Signs, Symbols, and Images in the Interpretation of Religion* (Philadelphia: Fortress, 1986); and Delores S. Williams, *Sisters in the Wilderness: The Challenge of Womanist God-Talk* (Maryknoll, N.Y.: Orbis, 1993).

3. This might be why black literature has contributed some unique categorical insights for doing black theological reflection in general.

4. "He's Got the Whole World," in *Black Song: The Forge and the Flame* (ed. John Lovell Jr.; New York: Macmillan, 1972), 395.

5. Maurice Natanson, *Anonymity: A Study in the Philosophy of Alfred Schutz* (Bloomington: Indiana University Press, 1986), 24.

6. Ibid., 25.

7. Lovell, *Black Song*, 395.

8. "Knocks Like Jesus," *Black Song*, 292.

9. "Hush! Hush! There's Some One Callin' Mah Name," *Black Song*, 308.

10. "I'm So Glad I Got My Religion in Time," *Black Song*, 316.

11. Lovell, *Black Song*, 292.

12. Abbey B. Munro, ed., *The Laing School Visitor* 9, no. 9 (November 1900): 3.

13. William Pickens and William L. Andrews, *Bursting Bonds: The Heir of Slaves: The Autobiography of a "New Negro"* (Bloomington: Indiana University Press, 1991), 31–32.

14. *God Struck Me Dead* in *The American Slave: A Composite Autobiography*, vol. 19 (Westport, Conn.: Greenwood, 1972), 16.

15. "Go Tell It on the Mountain," black spiritual in the public domain.

16. "Lord, I Want to Be a Christian in My Heart," *Black Song*, 191.

17. See Peter Paris, *The Social Teachings of the Black Churches* (Philadelphia: Fortress, 1985).

18. For a sociological explanation of this point of view, see Joseph Washington, *The Politics of God* (Boston: Beacon, 1967).

19. Henry Hugh Proctor, "Up from the South," Along Our Stream of Freedom papers, Amistad Research Center, Tulane University Library, New Orleans, box 4, folders 4–6, 1–42.

20. For a more comprehensive and constructive analysis of hermeneutics of Scripture, see Felder, *Stony the Road We Trod*.

21. Marcus Garvey, "Garvey Closes Convention with Classic Speech: A New Philosophy Expounded," *The Black Man: A Monthly Magazine of Negro Thought and Opinion* 1, no. 6 (November 1934): 18.

22. Ibid.

23. Ibid.

24. Ibid., 16.

25. Marcus Garvey, *Philosophy and Opinions of Marcus Garvey*, vol. 2 (ed. Amy Jacques Garvey; New York: Atheneum, 1969), 37.

26. Ibid., 38.

27. Mattias Gardell, *In the Name of Elijah Muhammad and the Nation of Islam* (Durham, N.C.: Duke University Press, 1996), 59.

28. Ibid.

29. Ibid.

30. Ibid., 165.

Chapter 4: Dark Kinship Metaphors: Dishonorable and Honorable Salutations

1. Stanley Elkins, *Slavery: A Problem in American Institutional and Intellectual Life* (Chicago: University of Chicago Press, 1959).

2. Earl, *Dark Symbols*.

3. Austin Steward, *Twenty-two Years a Slave, and Forty Years a Freeman* (New York: New American Library, 1967), 97.

4. Abraham Maslow, *Religion, Values, and the Peak Experience* (Columbus: Ohio State University Press, 1964).

5. Raymond Firth, "Verbal and Bodily Rituals of Greeting and Parting," in *The Interpretation of Ritual: Essays in Honor of A. I. Richards* (ed. J. S. La Fontaine; London: Tavistock, 1972).

6. Leon F. Litwack, *Been in the Storm So Long: The Aftermath of Slavery* (New York: Knopf, 1979), 267.

7. John W. Blassingame, *The Slave Community* (New York: Oxford University Press, 1972), 133.

8. Ibid., 134.

9. Ibid.

10. Ibid., 151.

11. Ibid., 153.

12. Litwack, *Been in the Storm So Long,* 255.

13. George P. Rawick, ed., *God Struck Me Dead* (vol. 19 of *The American Slave: A Composite Autobiography;* Westport, Conn. Greenwood, 1972), 2.

14. Ibid.

15. Ibid., 3.

16. Ibid.

17. Ibid., 50.

18. Ibid.

19. Ibid., 63.

20. Ibid.

21. C. G. Jung, *Memories, Dreams, Reflection* (New York: Vintage Books, 1989), 185. I am grateful to my friend Dr. Walter Fluker for calling my attention to this reference.

22. Rawick, *God Struck Me Dead,* 24.

23. Ibid.

24. Ibid., 39.

25. Lovell, *Black Song,* 304.

26. For a brilliant analysis of this phenomenon in relationship to the black experience, see Thee Smith, *Conjuring Culture* (New York: Oxford University Press, 1994).

27. Ibid., 305.

28. Harold A. Carter, *The Prayer Tradition of Black People* (Valley Forge, Pa.: Judson, 1976), 61.

29. Ibid.

30. Ibid., 62.

31. Peter Randolph, *Sketches of Slave Life* (Boston: James H. Earle, 1855), 68. See also Walter E. Pitts, *Old Ship of Zion: The Afro-Baptist Ritual in the African Diaspora* (New York: Oxford University Press, 1993).

32. Erskine Peters, ed., *Lyrics of the Afro-American Spiritual: A Documentary Collection* (Westport, Conn.: Greenwood, 1993), 350.

33. Ibid., 323–324.

34. Ibid., 380.

35. Ibid., 65–66.

Chapter 5: Brothers in White: The Minority Conscience of Salutatory Paternalists

1. Atticus G. Haygood, *Our Brother in Black: His Freedom and His Future* (1881; repr., New York: Books for Libraries Press, 1970), 54; see also Edward R. Carter, *The Black Side: A Partial History of the Business, Religious, and Educational Side of the Negro* (1894; repr., Atlanta: Books for Libraries Press, 1971), 17.

2. James M. McPherson, *The Abolitionist Legacy: From Reconstruction to the NAACP* (Princeton: Princeton University Press, 1995), 173.

3. Ibid.

4. Ibid.

5. Ibid., 54.

6. Ibid., 56.

7. Ibid.

8. D. G. W. Ellis, "The Unity of the Human Race," *Quarterly Review of the Methodist Episcopal Church, South* (July 1890): 310.

9. Ibid., 311.

10. Ibid., 310.

11. Haygood, *Our Brother in Black*, 251.

12. George Rawlinson, "The Duties of Higher toward Lower Races in a Mixed Community," *Princeton Review* (November 1878).

13. Beverly Waugh Bond, "The Duties of High Races to Themselves," *Quarterly Review of the Methodist Episcopal Church, South* 1 (July 1879): 461–475.

14. Ibid., 473.

15. Ibid., 474.

16. Ibid.

17. Ibid.

18. Ibid.

19. Ibid.

20. Haygood, *Our Brother in Black*, 41.

21. Ibid.

22. McPherson, *Abolitionist Legacy,* 56.

23. Ibid., 59.

24. Ibid., 54.

25. S. R. Thornton, "Character," *Quarterly Review of the United Brethren in Christ* 8, no. 4 (October 1897): 356.

26. Ibid., 357.

27. Ibid.

28. Ibid.

29. Ibid.

30. Eugene R. Hendrix, "Arnold of Rugby: A Character Study," *Methodist Review: A Bimonthly Journal Devoted to Religion and Philosophy, Science and Literature for the Methodist Church* 40 (September/October 1894).

31. Ibid.

32. Thornton, "Character," 358.

33. Ibid., 359.

34. W. S. Reese, "The Will and Its Culture," *United Brethren Review* 14, no. 3 (May/June 1903): 163–166.

35. Ibid.

36. Ibid., 165.

37. Leon F. Litwack, *Trouble in Mind* (New York: Knopf, 1998), 297.

38. Ibid.

39. Ralph E. Luker, *The Social Gospel in Black and White* (Chapel Hill: University of North Carolina Press, 1991).

40. For one of the more intriguing narrative studies of white minority Christians' contributions, see Taylor Branch, *Parting the Waters: America in the King Years, 1954–1963* (New York: Simon & Schuster, 1989).

41. See also John Griffin, *Black like Me* (Boston: Houghton Mifflin, 1961; repr., New York: Mass Market Publishers, 1997).

Chapter 6: Brothers in Black: The Priestly/Prophetic Type Conscience

1. Wilson Jeremiah Moses, *Alexander Crummell: A Study of Civilization Discontent* (New York: Oxford University Press, 1989); see also Stephen Ward Angell, *Bishop Henry McNeal Turner and African-American Religion in the South* (Knoxville: University of Tennessee Press, 1992).

2. Bowen, "What Shall the Harvest Be?" 42.

3. Ibid.

4. Ibid., 76

5. Ibid.

6. Ibid.

7. Ibid., 39.

8. Ibid., 42.

9. Ibid., 39.

10. W. Bishop Johnson, *The Scourging of a Race and Other Sermons and Addresses* (Washington, D.C.: Beresford, 1904), 8.

11. Luker, *Social Gospel in Black and White.*

12. Dorothy Sterling, ed., *The Trouble They Seen: Black People Tell the Story of Reconstruction* (New York: Doubleday, 1976), 2.

13. Litwack, *Been in the Storm So Long,* 171–172.

14. Irwin Sibler, ed., *Soldier Songs and Home-Front Ballads of the Civil War* (New York: Oak Publications, 1964), 41; see also Charles L. Perdue Jr., Thomas E. Barden, and Robert K. Phillips, eds., *Weevils in the Wheat: Interviews with Virginia Ex-Slaves* (1976; repr., Bloomington: Indiana University Press, 1980), 117, 212.

15. Litwack, *Been in the Storm So Long,* 171.

16. Sterling, *Trouble They Seen,* 65–66.

17. Reverdy C. Ransom, "The Race Problem in a Christian State," in *The Negro: The Hope or the Despair of Christianity* (Boston: Ruth Hill, 1935), 61.

18. Ibid., 77.

19. Ibid.

20. Ibid.

21. Robert E. Jones, "The Negro's Case Briefly Stated," December 30, 1909, Robert E. Jones Papers, Amistad Collection, Tulane University Library, New Orleans, 8.

22. Bowen, "What Shall the Harvest Be?" 19.

23. Ibid.

24. Ibid.

25. Ibid., 42–43.

26. Ibid., 71–72.

27. Ibid., 72.

28. Ibid., 42–43.

29. Ibid., 76.

30. Ibid.

31. Ibid., 77.

32. Robert E. Jones, "Saved by Serving," March 10, 1910, Robert E. Jones Papers, 2.

33. Ibid.

34. Ibid., 1–2.

35. Ibid.

36. Ibid.

37. Ibid., 2.

38. Ibid.

39. Robert E. Jones, "A Society of Good Cheer," September 9, 1910, Robert E. Jones Papers, 2.

40. Robert E. Jones, "New Year's Message to Negro Americans," December 29, 1910, Robert E. Jones Papers, 8.

41. Robert E. Jones, "The Easter Message," *Southwestern Christian Advocate* 43, no. 13 (April 8, 1909): 1.

42. Ransom, *The Negro*, 4.

43. Benjamin E. Mays, *Disturbed about Man* (Richmond: John Knox, Press, 1969).

44. Bowen, "What Shall the Harvest Be?" 76.

45. Ibid., 77.

46. Ibid., 79.

47. Ibid.

48. Ibid., 79–80.

49. Langston Hughes, *The Ways of White Folks* (New York: Vintage, 1962).

50. Ibid., 83.

51. Booker T. Washington, "The Colored Ministry—Its Defects and Needs," in *The Booker T. Washington Papers*, vol. 3, 1889–1895 (ed. Louis R. Harlan, Stuart B. Kaufman, and Raymond W. Smock; Urbana, Ill.: University of Illinois Press, 1974), 72–72.

52. McPherson, *Abolitionist Legacy,* 187.

53. Ibid.

54. Ibid., 186–187.

55. Ibid.

Chapter 7: Apologists and Idealogues of Black Manhood and Brotherhood

1. Theodore Roosevelt, *The Writings of Theodore Roosevelt 1858–1919* (ed. William H. Harbaugh; Indianapolis: Bobbs-Merrill, 1967), 3.

2. The five named types are for illustrative purposes only and are not intended to capture totally the thought of any one particular leader.

3. Robert S. Levine, *Martin Delany, Frederick Douglass, and the Politics of Representative Identity* (Chapel Hill: University of North Carolina Press, 1997). Levine's is an excellent comparative and contrasting account of the ideologies between Delany and Douglass.

4. Frederick Douglass, "The Nation's Problem: An Address Delivered in Washington, D.C. , on 16 April 1889," in *The Frederick Douglass Papers: Series One, Speeches, Debates, and Interviews* (ed. John W. Blassingame and John R. McKivigan; New Haven: Yale University Press, 1992), 5:412.

5. Martin Luther King Jr., "I Have A Dream," in *A Testament of Hope: The Essential Writings of Martin Luther King Jr.* (ed. James M. Washington; San Francisco: Harper and Row, 1986), 217).

6. Douglass, "The Nation's Problem," 5:413.

7. Ibid.

8. S. Kerr, "The Negro as a Christian," in *Twentieth Century Negro Literature* (ed. D. W. Culp; Miami: Mnemosyne, 1969), 321.

9. Booker T. Washington, *A New Negro for a New Century* (1900; repr., Miami: Mnemosyne, 1969).

10. Booker T. Washington, "The Story of My Life and Work, 1900" in *The Booker T. Washington Papers* (ed. Louis R. Harlan and John W. Blassingame; Urbana: University of Illinois Press, 1972), 1:31.

11. Booker T. Washington, "An Address to the Theological Department of Vanderbilt University, Nashville, Tenn, 29 March 1907," in *The Booker T. Washington Papers* (ed. Louis R. Harlan and Raymond W. Smock; Urbana: University of Illinois Press, 1975), 9:247. "Washington often proudly cited the fact that no holder of a diploma from Tuskegee Institute could be found in a single penitentiary in the country."

12. Booker T. Washington, "An Open Letter to the Louisiana Constitutional Convention, Tuskegee, Alabama, February 19, 1898," in The Booker T. Washington Papers (ed. Louis R. Harlan, Stuart B. Kaufman,

Barbara S. Kraft, and Raymond W. Smock; Urbana: University of Illinois Press, 1975), 4:381.

13. Washington, "The Story of My Life and Work," 88.

14. Kerr, "The Negro as a Christian," 319.

15. W. E. B. DuBois, *The Souls of Black Folk* (New York: First Vintage Books, 1990), 5.

16. Herbert Aptheker, ed., *Against Racism: Unpublished Essays, Papers, Addresses, 1887–1961 by W. E. B. DuBois* (Amherst: University of Massachusetts Press, 1985), 16.

17. DuBois, *The Souls of Black Folk*, 5.

18. Ibid., 191.

19. Ibid., 170.

20. Ibid.

21. Ibid.

22. Ibid., 174.

23. Ibid.

24. Ibid., 174–175.

25. Marcus Garvey, "Garvey Closes Convention," 18.

26. Ibid.

27. Marcus Garvey, "Negro Psychology," *The Black Man: A Monthly Magazine of Negro Thought and Opinion,* 1, no. 5 (May/June 1934): 14.

28. Ibid.

29. Ibid.

30. Ibid.

31. Marcus Garvey, "Outlook," *The Black Man: A Monthly Magazine of Negro Thought and Opinion* 1, no. 7 (June 1935): 3.

32. Ibid.

33. Ibid.

34. Marcus Garvey, "Marcus Garvey Opens International Convention with Great Speech: Sound Advice to the Race," *The Black Man: A Monthly Magazine of Negro Thought and Opinion* 1, no. 6 (November 1934): 11.

35. Ibid.

36. Garvey, "Garvey Closes Convention," 16.

37. Ibid.

38. Ibid., 17.

39. Ibid.

40. Garvey, *Philosophy and Opinions of Marcus Garvey,* 2:37.

41. Wilson Jeremiah Moses, *Classical Black Nationalism* (New York: New York University Press, 1995).

42. Garvey, *Philosophy and Opinions of Marcus Garvey,* 2:38.

43. Ibid.

44. Ibid.

Chapter 8: Salutatory Brothers of New Paradigms: Martin and Malcolm

1. James H. Cone, *Martin and Malcolm and America: A Dream or a Nightmare* (Maryknoll, N.Y.: Orbis, 1992), 236.

2. Martin Luther King Jr., *Stride Toward Freedom: The Montgomery Story* (New York: Harper & Row, 1958), 134–135.

3. Cone, *Martin and Malcolm and America,* 250.

4. Ibid., 126.

5. Ibid.

6. Ibid., 127.

7. Ibid., 133.

8. Ibid., 140.

9. Ibid., 141.

10. Ibid.

11. Ibid., 142.

12. Ibid., 235.

13. Ibid.

14. Ibid., 237.

15. Ibid.

16. Martin Luther King Jr., "Beyond Vietnam" (address given April 4, 1967, Riverside Church, New York City, sponsored by Clergy and Laymen Concerned about Vietnam), cited in Cone, *Martin and Malcolm and America,* 237.

17. Ibid., 238.

18. Ibid.

19. Ibid.

20. Ibid., 240.

21. Ibid.

22. Martin Luther King Jr., "Guidelines for a Constructive Church" (sermon delivered June 5, 1966, Ebenezer Baptist Church, Atlanta), cited in Cone, *Martin and Malcolm and America,* 242.

23. King, *Stride toward Freedom*, 47.

24. Ibid., 51.

25. Ibid.

26. Ibid.

27. Ibid., 54.

28. Ibid.

29. Ibid., 87.

30. Ibid.

31. Ibid., 137.

32. Ibid., 137–138.

33. Ibid., 85–86.

34. Ibid., 86.

35. Martin Luther King Jr., *Letter from the Birmingham Jail* (San Francisco: HarperCollins, 1994).

36. Cone, *Martin and Malcolm and America*, 104.

37. Ibid.

38. Ibid., 105.

39. Ibid., 106.

40. Ibid.

41. Ibid., 108.

42. Ibid.

43. Ibid.

44. Ibid., 243.

45. Robert Michael Franklin, *Liberating Visions: Human Fulfillment and Social Justice in African American Thought* (Minneapolis: Fortress, 1990), 91.

46. Malcolm X, *The End of White Supremacy* (ed. Benjamin Goodman; New York: Merlin House, Inc., 1971), 43.

47. Eugene Victor Wolfenstein, *The Victims of Democracy* (Berkeley: University of California Press, 1981), 309; see also Franklin, *Liberating Visions*, 92.

48. Franklin, *Liberating Visions*, 92.

Chapter 9: Creative Liberation Metaphors: Creators and Re-Creators

1. James Baldwin, "The Devil Finds Work," in *The Price of the Ticket: Collected Nonfiction, 1948–1985* (New York: Dell, 1972), 607.

2. Michael Fabre, *The Unfinished Quest of Richard Wright* (Urbana: University of Illinois Press, 1993), xxix.

3. Ibid.

4. Margaret Walker, *Richard Wright, Daemonic Genius: A Portrait of the Man, a Critical Look at His Work* (New York: Warner, 1988), 37.

5. Richard Wright, *Black Boy* (New York: Harper Perennial, 1993), 190.

6. Ibid., 216.

7. Ibid., 218.

8. Fabre, *Unfinished Quest of Richard Wright,* 68.

9. Ibid.

10. Wright, *Black Boy,* 219.

11. Ibid., 220.

12. Fabre, *Unfinished Quest of Richard Wright,* 252.

13. Walker, *Richard Wright, Daemonic Genius,* 37.

14. Richard Wright, *Native Son* (New York: New American Library, 1961), 329.

15. Walker, *Richard Wright, Daemonic Genius,* 37.

16. Ibid., 150.

17. Ibid., 148.

18. Wright, *Native Son,* 260.

19. Ibid., 376.

20. James H. Cone, *Black Theology and Black Power* (New York: Seabury, 1972).

21. Clarence Major, ed., *Juba to Jive: A Dictionary of African-American Slang* (New York: Penguin, 1994), 434.

22. Geneva Smitherman, *Black Talk: Word and Phrases from the Hood to the Amen Corner* (Boston: Houghton Mifflin, 1994).

23. Vincent Harding, *There Is a River: The Black Struggle for Freedom in America* (New York: Harcourt Brace, 1992).

24. Elijah Muhammad, *Message to the Blackman in America* (Chicago: Muhammad's Temple No. 2, 1965), 53.

25. Ibid., 32.

26. Ibid., 33.

27. Ibid.

28. Stuckey, *Slave Culture,* 193.

29. Ibid., 200.

Chapter 10: Salutatory Metaphors of Womanood, Sisterhood, and Friendship

1. Marcia Y. Riggs, ed., *Can I Get A Witness? Prophetic Religious Voices of African American Women: An Anthology* (Maryknoll, N.Y.: Orbis, 1997).

2. Patricia Hill Collins, "Mammies, Matriarchs, and Other Images in African Philosophy," in *African Philosophy: An Anthology* (ed. Emmanuel Chukwudi Eze; Malden, Mass.: Blackwell, 1998), 346.

3. Ibid.

4. Adele Logan Alexander, "She's No Lady, She's a Nigger: Abuses, Stereotypes, and Realities from the Middle Passage to Capitol (and Anita) Hill," in *Race, Gender, and Power in America: The Legacy of the Hill-Thomas Hearings* (ed. Anita Faye Hill and Emma Coleman Jordan; New York: Oxford University Press, 1995), 3–4.

5. Ibid., 6.

6. Collins, "Mammies, Matriarchs, and Other Images," 348.

7. Ibid., 350.

8. Ibid.

9. Ibid., 351.

10. Ibid., 352.

11. Eugene Genovese, *Roll Jordan Roll: The World the Slaves Made* (New York: Vintage Books, 1976), 353.

12. Ibid., 354.

13. Ibid., 356.

14. Ibid., 360.

15. Ibid., 361.

16. W. E. B. DuBois, *The Gift of Black Folk: Negroes in the Making of America* (New York: Washington Square Press, 1970), 188–189.

17. Robin D. G. Kelley, *Race Rebels: Culture, Politics, and the Black Working Class* (New York: Free Press, 1994), 216.

18. Williams, *Sisters in the Wilderness*, ix.

19. Ibid., x.

20. Maya Angelou, "Our Grandmothers," in *The Complete Collected Poems of Maya Angelou* (New York: Random House, 1994), 254–255.

21. Ibid., 254–255.

22. Ibid., 255.

23. Ibid.

24. Ibid.

25. Ibid.

26. Ibid.

27. Ibid., 254.

28. Ibid., 256.

29. Margaret Walker, "Lineage," in *The Poetry of Black America: Anthology of the Twentieth Century* (ed. Arnold Adoff; New York: Harper Collins, 1973), 148.

30. Langston Hughes, "Mother to Son," in *American Negro Poetry* (ed. Arna Bontemps; New York: Hill & Wang, 1963), 67.

31. Ibid.

32. Ibid.

33. Ibid.

34. Ibid., 245.

35. Ibid., 129.

36. Dorothy Sterling, ed., *We Are Your Sisters: Black Women in the Nineteenth Century* (New York: Norton, Company, 1984), 115.

37. Ibid., 155.

38. Stuckey, *Slave Culture*, 199–200.

39. Riggs, *Can I Get A Witness?* xi.

40. Ibid., xii.

41. Sara G. Stanley, "Sara G. Stanley's Letter to Rev. George Whipple," in *We Are Your Sisters* (ed. Sterling), 265.

42. Ibid.

43. Charlotte L. Forten, "Charlotte L. Forten's Letter to Lucy Chase," in *We Are Your Sisters* (ed. Sterling), 283–284.

44. Ibid., 320.

45. Riggs, *Can I Get A Witness?* xiii.

46. Ibid., 10.

47. Ibid., 20–21.

48. Ibid., 25–26.

49. Ibid., 54.

50. Ibid.

51. Ibid., 31–32.

52. Ibid., 35–36.

53. Ibid., 37.

54. Gloria Wade Gayles, "A Black Woman's RSVP," in *Anointed to Fly* (New York: Harlem River Press, 1991), 135.

55. Ibid.

56. Ibid.

57. Ibid.

58. Ibid., 136.

59. Ibid.

60. Ibid.

61. Ibid., 137.

62. Ibid.

63. Ibid.

64. Bettye Collier-Thomas, *Daughters of Thunder: Black Women Preachers and Their Sermons, 1850–1979* (San Francisco: Jossey-Bass, 1998), 37.

Bibliography

Abbott, A. R. *The Negro in His Own Defense*. Okolona, Miss.: Preacher-Safeguard Print, 1902.

Abercrombie, John W. "Vocational Education." Speech of Hon. John W. Abercrombie of Alabama in the House of Representatives. Washington, D.C., October 2, 1913. Reproduced from the collections of the Manuscript Division, Library of Congress.

Adoff, Arnold, ed. *The Poetry of Black America: Anthology of the Twentieth Century*. New York: Harper Collins, 1973.

Alexander, Adele Logan. "She's No Lady, She's a Nigger: Abuses, Stereotypes, and Realities from the Middle Passage to Capitol (and Anita) Hill." Pages 3–25 in *Race, Gender, and Power in America: The Legacy of the Hill-Thomas Hearings*. Edited by Anita Faye Hill and Emma Coleman Jordan. New York: Oxford University Press, 1995.

Al-Ghazali, Imam. *The Duties of Brotherhood in Islam*. Translated by Muhar Holland. Leicester, U.K.: Islamic Foundation, 1997.

Allen, A. R. "Thomas Dixon, Jr., and Political Religion: From Social Reformer to Racist." *Foundations* 14 (April–June 1971): 136–152.

Anderson, Victor. *Beyond Ontological Blackness: An Essay on African American Religious and Cultural Criticism*. New York: Continuum, 1995.

Andrews, Charles Green. "Education of the Colored Race." *Quarterly Review of the Methodist Episcopal Church, South* 23, no. 2 (April 1886): 271–283.

Angell, Stephen Ward. *Bishop Henry McNeal Turner and African-American Religion in the South*. Knoxville: University of Tennessee Press, 1992.

Angelou, Maya. *The Complete Collected Poems of Maya Angelou*. New York: Random House, 1994.

Aptheker, Herbert, ed. *A Documentary History of the Negro People in the United States*. 7 vols. New York: Citadel Press (vols. 1–4); Secaucus, N.J.: Carol Publishing (vols. 5–7), 1971–1992.

_____, ed. *Against Racism: Unpublished Essays, Papers, Address-es, 1887–1961, by W. E. B. DuBois.* Amherst: University of Massachu-setts Press, 1985.

Armstrong, M. F., and Helen W. Ludlow. *Hampton and Its Students.* New York: Putnam, 1874.

Baker, Lawrence W. *African American History in the Press, 1851–1899.* 2 vols. Detroit: Gale Research, 1996.

Baker-Fletcher, Garth Kasimu. *Somebodyness.* Minneapolis: Fortress, 1993.

_____. *Xodus: An African American Male Journey.* Minneapo-lis: Fortress, 1996.

Baldwin, James. *No Name in the Street.* New York: Dell, 1972.

_____. "The Devil Finds Work." In *The Price of the Ticket: Col-lected Nonfiction, 1948–1985.* New York: Dell, 1972.

Barrows, John Henry, ed. *The World's Parliament of Religions.* 2 vols. Chica-go: Parliament Publishing, 1893.

Bates, Edward. "Opinion of Attorney General Bates on Citizenship." Washington: Government Printing Office, 1862. Moorland-Spingarn Research Center, Howard University.

Beckett, L. M. "True Worshippers." Sermon delivered at Campbell A.M.E. Church. Anacostia, D.C., 1911. Moorland-Spingarn Research Cen-ter, Howard University.

Bigham, Robert W. "After the Battle of the Swords." *Quarterly Review of the Methodist Episcopal Church, South* 34, no. 2 (January 1892): 324–339.

Blassingame, John W. *The Slave Community.* New York: Oxford Universi-ty Press, 1972.

Bloch-Hoell, Nils E. "African Identity: European Invention or Genuine African Character?" *Journal of the International Association for Mission Studies* 9, no. 1 (1992): 98–107.

Bond, Beverly Waugh. "The Duties of High Races to Themselves." *Quar-terly Review of the Methodist Episcopal Church, South* 1 (July 1879): 461–475.

Bontemps, Arna, ed. *American Negro Poetry.* New York: Hill & Wang, 1963.

Bowen, J. W. E. "What Shall the Harvest Be?" Sermon delivered at Ashbury Methodist Episcopal Church. Washington, D.C., 1892.

_____. *An Appeal for Negro Bishops, But No Separation.* New York: Eaton & Mains, 1912.

Branch, Taylor. *Parting the Waters: America in the King Years, 1954–1963.* New York: Simon & Schuster, 1989.

Bristor, Julia M., Lee Gravois, and Michelle R. Hunt. "Race and Ideology: African-American Images in Television Advertising." *Journal of Public Policy and Marketing* 14 (April 1, 1995): 48.

Brown, Colin, ed. *New International Dictionary of New Testament Theology.* 4 vols. Grand Rapids: Zondervan, 1975–1985.

Brown, Robert Turner. *The Doctrines of Christ and the Church.* Jackson, Tenn.: Publishing House C.M.E. Church, 1898.

Bumstead, Horace. "The Freedman's Children at School." *Andover Review* (December 1885): 550–560.

Burke, J. W. "Individuality of Character." *Quarterly Review of the Methodist Episcopal Church, South* 16, no. 3 (July 1879): 405–415.

Burlin, Natalie Curtis. *Hymn of Freedom.* New York: G. Schirmer, 1918.

Burtner, C. A. "Character Building." *Quarterly Review of the United Brethren in Christ* 9, no. 3 (July 1898): 237–242.

Caes, David, ed. *Caring for the Least of These: Serving Christ among the Poor.* Scottdale, Pa.: Herald Press, 1992.

Carter, Edward R. *The Black Side: A Partial History of the Business, Religious, and Educational Side of the Negro.* 1894. Repr., Atlanta: Books for Libraries Press, 1971.

Carter, Harold A. *The Prayer Tradition of Black People.* Valley Forge, Pa.: Judson, 1976.

"Character and Success." *Outlook* (March 31, 1900).

Cheever, George B. "Rights of the Coloured Race to Citizenship and Representation; and the Guilt Consequences of Legislation against Them." Discourse delivered in the Hall of Representatives of the United States. Washington, D.C., May 29, 1864. New York: Francis & Loutrel, 1864. Moorland-Spingarn Research Center, Howard University.

Childs, John Brown. *The Political Black Minister: A Study in Afro-American Politics and Religion.* Boston: G. K. Hall, 1980.

"Christian Citizenship." Address before the Young Men's Christian Association, Carnegie Hall. New York, December 30, 1900.

Clark, D. W., and J. M. Walden. "Reports of the Freedmen's Aid Society of the Methodist Episcopal Church, 1866–1875." Cincinnati: Western Methodist Book Concern, 1867.

Clinton, George W. *Christianity under the Searchlight.* Nashville: National Baptist Publishing Board, 1909.

Cobbs, Price M., and William H. Grier. *The Jesus Bag.* New York: McGraw-Hill, 1971.

Collier-Thomas, Bettye. *Daughters of Thunder: Black Women Preachers and Their Sermons, 1850–1979.* San Francisco: Jossey-Bass, 1998.

Collins, Patricia Hill. *Black Feminist Thought.* New York: Routledge, 1990.

_____. "Mammies, Matriarchs, and Other Images in African Philosophy." Pages 346–354 in *African Philosophy: An Anthology.* Edited by Emmanuel Chukwudi Eze. Malden, Mass.: Blackwell, 1998.

Collyer, Robert. "We Would See Jesus." *Messiah Pulpit* 5, no. 28 (April 19, 1901). Reproduced from the collections of the Manuscript Division, Library of Congress.

Cone, James H. *Black Theology and Black Power.* New York: Seabury, 1972.

_____. *My Soul Looks Back.* Maryknoll, N.Y.: Orbis, 1990.

_____. *Martin and Malcolm and America: A Dream or a Nightmare.* Maryknoll, N.Y.: Orbis, 1992.

Crane, C. B. "Sermon on the Occasion of the Death of President Lincoln." Sermon delivered at South Baptist Church. Hartford, Conn., April 16, 1865. Hartford: Press of Case, Lockwood, 1865.

Crummell, Alexander. "The Eulogy on Henry Highland Garnet, D.D." Eulogy delivered to the Union Bethel Literary and Historical Association, 19th Street Baptist Church. Washington, D.C., May 4, 1882. Schomburg Center for Research in Black Culture, New York Public Library.

_____. *The Black Woman of the South: Her Neglects and Her Needs.* Cincinnati: Women's Home Missionary Society of the Methodist Episcopal Church, 1883. Schomburg Center for Research in Black Culture, New York Public Library.

Davis, B. J. "Putting the Most into Life." Delivered to the 13th B.M.C. Richmond, Va., October 2, 1906; Tifton, Ga., January 1, 1907, Emancipation Day. Reproduced from the collections of the Manuscript Division, Library of Congress.

De Jong, Mary G. "I Want to Be like Jesus: The Self-Defining Power of Evangelical Hymnody." *Journal of the American Academy of Religion,* vol. 54 (Fall 1986): 3, 461–493.

Dewey, John. "Interpretation of Savage Mind." *Psychological Review* 9, no. 3 (May 1902): 217–230.

"The Door of Opportunity." *Tuskegee Student* 17, no. 33 (October 21, 1905): 33.

Douglass, Frederick. *The Frederick Douglass Papers: Series One, Speeches, Debates, and Interviews.* Edited by John W. Blassingame and John R. McKivigan. 5 vols. New Haven: Yale University Press, 1979–1992.

DuBois, W. E. B. *The Gift of Black Folk: Negroes in the Making of America.* New York: Washington Square Press, 1970.

—————. *The Souls of Black Folk.* New York: First Vintage Books, 1990.

Earl, Riggins R., Jr. *Dark Symbols, Obscure Signs: God, Self, and Community in the Slave Mind.* Maryknoll, N.Y.: Orbis, 1993.

Elliott, Robert B. "Civil Rights." Speech of Hon. Robert B. Elliott of South Carolina in the House of Representatives. Washington, D.C., January 6, 1874. Moorland-Spingarn Research Center, Howard University.

Ellis, D. G. W. "The Unity of the Human Race." *Quarterly Review of the Methodist Episcopal Church, South* (July 1890): 309–317,

Ellison, Ralph. *Shadow and Act.* New York: Vintage Books, 1972.

Ellwood, Charles A. "The Theory of Imitation in Social Psychology." *American Journal of Sociology* 6 (May 1901): 721–741.

Esposito, John L. *Islam: The Straight Path.* Expanded Ed. New York: Oxford University Press, 1991.

Fabre, Michael. *The Unfinished Quest of Richard Wright.* Urbana: University of Illinois Press, 1993.

Fawcett, Edgar. "Plutocracy and Snobbery in New York." *Arena* 4, no. 2 (July 1891): 142–151.

Felder, Cain Hope, ed. *Stony the Road We Trod: African American Biblical Interpretation.* Minneapolis: Fortress, 1991.

Firth, Raymond. "Verbal and Bodily Rituals of Greeting and Parting." In *The Interpretation of Ritual: Essays in Honor of A. I. Richards.* Edited by J. S. La Fontaine. London: Tavistock, 1972.

Fishel, Leslie H., Jr., and Benjamin Quarles. *The Negro American: A Documentary History.* Glenview, Ill.: Scott, Foresman, 1967.

Fisher, John E. *The John F. Slater Fund: A Nineteenth Century Affirmative Action for Negro Education.* Lanham, Md.: University Press of America, 1986.

Flipper, J. S. *Pioneer Echoes: Six Special Sermons.* Baltimore: Hoffman, 1889.

Floyd, Silas Xavier. "National Perils." Address delivered. Atlanta, January 2, 1898. Augusta: Georgia Baptist Print, 1899.

_____. "Prodigal Young Men." Sermon delivered at Tabernacle Baptist Church. Augusta, Ga., January 28, 1900. Augusta: Georgia Baptist Print, 1900.

_____. *Life of Charles T. Walker.* Nashville: National Baptist Publishing Board, 1902.

Foraker, Joseph B. "The Black Battalion." Speech of Hon. Joseph B. Foraker of Ohio in the U.S. Senate. Washington, D.C., January 12, 1909.

Fordham, Monroe. *Major Themes in Northern Black Religious Thought, 1800–1860.* New York: Exposition Press, 1975.

Franklin, Robert Michael. "Religious Belief and Political Activism in Black America: An Essay." *Journal of Religious Thought* 43, no. 2 (fall–winter 1986–1987).

_____. *Liberating Visions: Human Fulfillment and Social Justice in African American Thought.* Minneapolis: Fortress, 1990.

Freitag, Walter, ed. *Festschrift: A Tribute to Dr. William Hordern.* Canada: University of Saskatchewan.

Gaines, Kevin K. *Uplifting the Race.* Chapel Hill: University of North Carolina Press, 1996.

Gaines, W. J. *The Gospel Ministry.* Atlanta: J. B. Rodgers, 1899.

Gardell, Mattias. *In the Name of Elijah Muhammad: Louis Farrakhan and the Nation of Islam.* Durham: Duke University Press, 1996.

Garrison, William Lloyd, ed. *Selection of Anti-Slavery Hymns, for the Use of the Friends of Emancipation.* Boston: Garrison & Knapp, 1834.

Garvey, Marcus. "Negro Psychology." *The Black Man: A Monthly Magazine of Negro Thought and Opinion* 1, no. 5 (May/June 1934): 1–20.

_____. "Garvey Closes Convention with Classic Speech: A New Philosophy Expounded." *The Black Man: A Monthly Magazine of Negro Thought and Opinion* 1, no. 6(November 1934): 14–19.

_____. "Marcus Garvey Opens International Convention with Great Speech: Sound Advice to the Race." *The Black Man: A Monthly Magazine of Negro Thought and Opinion* 1, no. 6 (November 1934): 4–12.

_____. "Outlook." *The Black Man: A Monthly Magazine of Negro Thought and Opinion* 1, no. 7 (June 1935): 3.

_____. *Philosophy and Opinions of Marcus Garvey.* 2 vols. Edited by Amy Jacques Garvey. New York: Atheneum, 1969.

Gates, Henry Louis, Jr. *Figures in Black.* New York: Oxford University Press, 1987.

Gay, Geneva, and Willie L. Baber, eds. *Expressively Black: The Cultural Basis of Ethnic Identity.* New York: Praeger, 1987.

Gayles, Gloria Wade. *Anointed to Fly.* New York: Harlem River Press, 1991.

Genovese, Eugene. *Roll Jordan Roll: The World the Slaves Made.* New York: Vintage Books, 1976.

Grace, Francis Mitchell. "From Bondage to Freedom." *Methodist Quarterly Review* 53, no. 1 (January 1904): 70–80.

Grant, Jacquelyn. "Servanthood Revisited: Womanist Exploration of Servanthood Theology." Pages 25–40 in *The Papers of the Henry Luce III Fellows in Theology ATS.* Vol. 2. Edited by Jonathan Strom. Atlanta: Scholars Press, 1997.

Grantham, Dewey W. "Theodore Roosevelt in American Historical Writing, 1945–1960." *Mid-America: An Historical Review* 43, no. 3 (January 1961): 3–35.

Griffin, John. *Black Like Me.* Boston: Houghton Mifflin, 1961. Repr., New York: Mass Market Publishers, 1997.

Griffin, Paul R. *The Struggle for a Black Theology of Education.* Black Scholars Series 4. Atlanta: ITC Press, 1993.

Grube, G. M. A., ed. *Plato's Republic.* Indianapolis: Hackett, 1974.

Haley, Alex. *The Autobiography of Malcolm X.* 1965. Repr., New York: Ballantine, 1987.

Haley, James T., ed. *Afro-American Encyclopedia or the Thoughts, Sayings, and Doings of the Race: Book 1.* Nashville: Winston-Derek, 1992.

_____. ed. *Afro-American Encyclopedia or the Thoughts, Sayings, and Doings of the Race: Book 2.* Nashville: Winston-Derek, 1992.

Hammond, Lily Hardy. "Human Races and the Race of Man." *Methodist Quarterly Review* 73, no. 4 (October 1924): 623–633.

Hampshire, Stuart. *Innocence and Experience.* Cambridge: Harvard University Press, 1989.

Haque, Muhammad Atiqul. *Islam: The Religion of Peace.* Lahore, Pakistan: Sh. Muhammad Ashraf, 1990.

Harbaugh, William H., ed. *The Writings of Theodore Roosevelt, 1858–1919.* Indianapolis: Bobbs-Merrill, 1967.

Harding, Vincent. *There Is a River: The Black Struggle for Freedom in America.* New York: Harcourt Brace, 1992.

Harley, Sharon. "When Your Work Is Not Who You Are: The Development of a Working-Class Consciousness among Afro-American Women." Pages 25–37 in *We Specialize in the Wholly Impossible: A Reader in Black Women's History*. Edited by Darlene Clark Hine, Wilma King, and Linda Reed. New York: Carlson, 1995.

Harmon, J. A. "The Negro: Our Duty and Relation to Him." *Methodist Quarterly Review* 75, no. 1 (January 1926): 56–66.

Harris, Michael W. *The Rise of Gospel Blues*. New York: Oxford University Press, 1992.

Harrison, William Pope. "The Race Problem in the South." *Quarterly Review of the Methodist Episcopal Church, South* 26, no. 2 (November 1887): 247–255.

Hartzell, J. C., ed. *Christian Educators in Council: Sixty Addresses by American Educators with Historical Notes upon the National Education Assembly, Held at Ocean Grove, N.J., August 9–12, 1883*. New York: Phillips & Hunt, 1883.

——————, ed. *Reports of the Freedmen's Aid Society of the Methodist Episcopal Church 1866–1875*. Cincinnati: Western Methodist Book Concern, 1893.

Haygood, Atticus G. *Our Brother in Black: His Freedom and His Future*. 1881. Repr., New York: Books for Libraries Press, 1970.

——————. *Sermons and Speeches*. Nashville: Southern Methodist Publishing House, 1883.

——————. "The Negro Problem." *Methodist Review* 42, no. 1 (September/October 1895): 40–53.

Hendrix, Eugene R. "Arnold of Rugby: A Character Study." *Quarterly Review Methodist Episcopal Church, South* (September/October 1894): 69–89.

Herrera, R. A., ed. *Mystics of the Book: Themes, Topics, and Typologies*. New York: Peter Lang, 1993.

Hill, Robert A., ed. *The Marcus Garvey and Universal Negro Improvement Association Papers*. Vol. 1. Berkeley: University of California Press, 1983.

Hodge, J. Aspinwall. "America and Africa." Annual discourse delivered at the seventy-first anniversary of the American Colonization Society. Washington, D.C., 1888.

Hollis, John P. "The Darkening Shadow of the Negro Problem." *Methodist Review Quarterly* 58, no. 4 (October 1909): 682–690.

Holsey, L. H. *Autobiography, Sermons, Addresses, and Essays of Bishop L. H. Holsey.* Atlanta: Franklin Printing and Publishing, 1898.

Hood, J. W. *The Negro in the Christian Pulpit: Two Characters and Two Destinies: Twenty-One Practical Sermons.* Raleigh: Edwards, Broughton, 1884.

Howard-Brook, Wes. *Becoming Children of God: John's Gospel of Radical Discipleship.* Maryknoll, N.Y.: Orbis, 1994.

Hughes, Langston. *The Ways of White Folks.* New York: Vintage, 1962.

Jackson, Crawford. "Character as Related to Flesh and Spirit." *Methodist Review* 41, no. 3 (July/August 1895): 327–334.

Johnson, Susanne, and Patricia H. Davis. "Dialogue and Advocacy: A Case Study of a Course on Human Sexuality." *Theological Education* 33, no. 2 (1997): 19–28.

Johnson, W. Bishop. *The Scourging of a Race and Other Sermons and Addresses.* Washington, D.C.: Beresford, 1904.

——————. "Address: In Introducing Dr. Booker T. Washington." Presented to National Baptist Convention. Nashville, September 19, 1913.

Jones, Jacqueline. *Soldiers of Light and Love: Northern Teachers and Georgia Blacks, 1865–1873.* Chapel Hill: University of North Carolina Press, 1980.

Jones, Robert E. Papers. Amistad Collection. Tulane University Library, New Orleans.

——————. "The Easter Message." *Southwestern Christian Advocate* 43, no. 13 (April 8, 1909): 1.

Jones, William R. *Is God a White Racist?* New York: Anchor/Doubleday, 1973.

Jordan, Philip D. "Josiah Strong and a Scientific Social Gospel." In *Iliff Review* 42/1 (1985): 25–31.

Jung, C. G. *Memories, Dreams, Reflection.* New York: Vintage Books, 1989.

Kelly, Robin D. G. *Race Rebels: Culture, Politics, and the Black Working Class.* New York: Free Press, 1994.

Kennedy, Ethelbert Sheldron. *The Negro Race.* Altoona, Pa.: Art Printery of H. & W. H. Slep, 1896.

Kerr, S. "The Negro as a Christian." In *Twentieth Century Negro Literature.* Edited by D. W. Culp. Miami: Mnemosyne, 1969, 315–330.

King, Martin Luther, Jr. *Stride toward Freedom: The Montgomery Story.* New York: Harper & Row, 1958.

_____. *Letter from a Birmingham Jail.* San Francisco: Harper-Collins, 1994. First published New York: Harper & Row, 1964.

Kittel, Gerhard, and G. Friedrich, eds. *Theological Dictionary of the New Testament.* Translated by G. W. Bromiley. 10 vols. Grand Rapids: Eerdmans, 1964–1976.

Leftwich, William. "The Race Problem in the South." *Quarterly Review of the Methodist Episcopal Church, South* 29, no. 1 (April 1889): 86–96.

Lerner, Gerda, ed. *Black Women in White America.* New York: Vintage Books, 1972.

Levine, Robert S. *Martin Delany, Frederick Douglass, and the Politics of Representative Identity.* Chapel Hill: University of North Carolina Press, 1997.

Lewis, David Levering. *W. E. B. DuBois: Biography of a Race, 1868–1919.* New York: Henry Holt, 1993.

Lincoln, C. Eric. *The Black Muslims in America.* Grand Rapids: Eerdmans, 1994.

Litwack, Leon F. *Been in the Storm So Long: The Aftermath of Slavery.* New York: Knopf, 1979.

_____. *Trouble in Mind.* New York: Knopf, 1998.

Locke, Alain, ed. *The New Negro.* New York: Atheneum, 1968.

Long, Charles. *Significations: Signs, Symbols, and Images in the Interpretation of Religion.* Philadelphia: Fortress, 1986.

Lovell, John, Jr. *Black Song: The Forge and the Flame.* New York: Macmillan, 1972.

Luker, Ralph E. *The Social Gospel in Black and White.* Chapel Hill: University of North Carolina Press, 1991.

Macklin, G. P. "Civic Redemption: A Duty of the Modern Christian." *United Brethren Review* 13, no. 4 (July/August 1902): 221–223.

Major, Clarence, ed. *Juba to Jive: A Dictionary of African-American Slang.* New York: Penguin, 1994.

Manning, Joseph C. "Letting the South Alone: Class Government That Defrauds Whites and Blacks." Speech delivered to the Middlesex Club. Boston, April 27, 1903. Reproduced from the collections of the Manuscript Division, Library of Congress.

Marshall, C. K. *The Colored Race: Weighed in the Balance.* Nashville: Southern Methodist Publishing House, 1883.

Martin, Sandy Dwayne. *For God and Race.* Columbia: University of South Carolina Press, 1999.

Maslow, Abraham H. *Religious, Values, and the Peak Experience.* Columbus: Ohio State University Press, 1964.

May, Herbert G., and Bruce M. Metzger, eds. *The New Oxford Annotated Bible.* New York: Harper & Row, 1963.

Mays, Benjamin E. "Veterans: It Need Not Happen Again." *Phylon* 6, no. 3 (July–September 1945): 205–210.

_____. *Disturbed about Man.* Richmond: John Knox, 1969.

_____. "Obligations of Negro Christians in Relation to an Interracial Program." *Journal of Religious Thought.* Vol. 24. No. 2 (1967–1968): 4–12.

McKinney, William, ed. *The Responsibility People.* Grand Rapids: Eerdmans, 1994.

McLean, Roderick Michael. *The Theology of Marcus Garvey.* Washington, D.C.: University Press of America, 1982.

McPherson, James M. *The Abolitionist Legacy: From Reconstruction to the NAACP.* Princeton: Princeton University Press, 1995.

Mebane, George Allen. *"The Negro Problem" As Seen and Discussed by Southern White Men.* New York: Alliance, 1900.

Mellon, Matthew T. *Early American Views on Negro Slavery, from the Letters and Papers of the Founders of the Republic.* Boston: Meador, 1934.

Montgomery, William E. *Under Their Own Vine and Fig Tree: The African-American Church in the South, 1865–1900.* Baton Rouge: Louisiana State University Press, 1993.

Moore, James Tice. "Redeemers Reconsidered: Change and Continuity in the Democratic South, 1870–1900." *Journal of Southern History* 44, no. 3 (August 1978): 357–378.

Moore, Lewis B. *How the Colored Race Can Help in the Problems Issuing from the War.* New York: National Security League, 1919.

Moore, Marcus Huston. "Force of Character and What Constitutes It." *Quarterly Review of the Methodist Episcopal Church, South* 4, no. 2 (May 1888): 209–217.

Morris, Samuel. *A Spirit-Filled Life.* Albion, Mich.: Golden Rule Publishing, 1908.

Moses, Wilson Jeremiah. *The Golden Age of Black Nationalism, 1850–1925.* Oxford: Oxford University Press, 1988.

_____. *Alexander Crummell: A Study of Civilization Discontent.* New York: Oxford University Press, 1989.

_____. *Black Messiahs and Uncle Toms: Social Literary Manipulations of a Religious Myth.* University Park: Pennsylvania State University Press, 1993.

_____. *Classical Black Nationalism.* New York: New York University Press, 1995.

Mott, A., and M. S. Wood, eds. *Narratives of Colored Americans.* New York: William Wood, 1875.

Muhammad, Elijah. *Message to the Blackman in America.* Chicago: Muhammad's Temple No. 2, 1965.

Munro, Abbey B., ed. *Laing School Visitor* 9, no. 9 (November 1900).

Murphy, Edgar Gardner. *The Larger Life: Sermons and an Essay.* New York: Longmans, Green, 1897.

Natanson, Maurice. *Anonymity: A Study in the Philosophy of Alfred Schutz.* Bloomington: Indiana University Press, 1986.

Newcomb, Harvey. *The "Negro Pew": Being an Inquiry concerning the Propriety of Distinctions in the House of God, on account of Color.* Freeport, N.Y.: Books for Libraries Press, 1971.

Newton, John C. Calhoun. "Certain Aspects of Christ's Character and Teaching We Forget." *Methodist Review Quarterly* 71, no. 1. (January 1922): 72–85.

Paris, Peter. *The Social Teachings of the Black Churches.* Philadelphia: Fortress, 1985.

Perdue, Charles L., Jr., Thomas E. Barden, and Robert K. Phillips, eds. *Weevils in the Wheat: Interviews with Virginia Ex-Slaves.* 1976. Repr., Bloomington: Indiana University Press, 1980.

Perry, Josiah B. "The Negro Question in the American Church." Speech of Rev. Josiah R. Perry, Rector of Trinity Church, Natchez, Miss., delivered (in part) before the General Convention. Richmond, Va., October 1907.

Peters, Erskine, ed. *Lyrics of the Afro-American Spiritual: A Documentary Collection.* Westport, Conn.: Greenwood, 1993.

Pickens, William. *Bursting Bonds: The Heir of Slaves: The Autobiography of a "New Negro."* Edited by William L. Andrews. Bloomington: Indiana University Press, 1991.

Pinn, Anthony B. *Why, Lord? Suffering and Evil in Black Theology.* New York: Continuum, 1995.

Pitts, Walter E. *Old Ship of Zion: The Afro-Baptist Ritual in the African Diaspora.* New York: Oxford University Press, 1993.

Porter, Dorothy. *Early Negro Writing, 1760–1837.* Boston: Beacon, 1971.

Powell, Jacob W. "Convention Addresses." Malden, Mass.: Massachusetts Sunday School Association, 1924.

Proctor, Henry Hugh. "Up From the South." Along Our Stream of Freedom papers. Amistad Research Center. Tulane University Library, New Orleans. Box 4, folder 4–6, 1–42.

——————. "Collected Items: Unpublished Address to Theodore Roosevelt." 1929.

——————. "Miscellany: Proctor Memorial." 1929.

——————. "Setting the World Record." 1929.

Randolph, Peter. *Sketches of Slave Life.* Boston: James H. Earle, 1855.

Ransom, Reverdy C. "The Industrial and Social Conditions of the Negro: A Thanksgiving Sermon." Delivered at the Bethel A.M.E. Church. Chicago, November 26, 1896. Rembert E. Stokes Learning Resource Center Library. Wilberforce University, Wilberforce, Ohio.

——————. "A Thanksgiving Address Delivered by Reverdy C. Ransom, D.D." Delivered at the Union Thanksgiving Service, Bethel A.M.E. Church. New Bedford, Mass., November 24, 1904.

——————. "Wendell Phillips." Centennial oration delivered at Plymouth Church. Brooklyn, N.Y.: November 29, 1911. Rembert E. Stokes Learning Resource Center Library. Wilberforce University, Wilberforce, Ohio.

——————. "Cripus Attucks: A Negro, the First to Die for American Independence." Address delivered at the Metropolitan Opera House. Philadelphia, March 6, 1930. Rembert E. Stokes Learning Resource Center Library. Wilberforce University, Wilberforce, Ohio.

——————. "The Race Problem in a Christian State." In *The Negro: The Hope or the Despair of Christianity.* Boston: Ruth Hill, 1935.

——————. Preface to *History of A.M.E. Church.* Nashville: A.M.E. Sunday School Union, 1950.

——————. *The Pilgrimage of Harriet Ransom's Son.* Nashville: A.M.E. Sunday School Union. [1900] 1983.

Rawick, George P., ed. *God Struck Me Dead.* Vol. 19 of *The American Slave: A Composite Autobiography.* Westport, Conn.: Greenwood, 1972.

Rawlinson, George. "The Duties of Higher toward Lower Races in a Mixed Community." *Princeton Review* 2 (November 1878): 804.

Reese, W. S. "The Will and Its Culture." *United Brethren Review* 14, no. 3 (May/June 1903): 163–166.

"Religious Influence at Tuskegee." *Tuskegee Student* 17, no. 23 (July 15, 1905): 23.

Rensberger, David. *Johannine Faith and Liberating Community.* Philadelphia: Westminster, 1988.

Ricoeur, Paul. *A Ricoeur Reader: Reflection and Imagination.* Edited by Mario J. Valdes. Toronto: University of Toronto Press, 1991.

_____. *Figuring the Sacred.* Minneapolis: Fortress, 1995.

_____. "The Hermeneutic of Symbols and Philosophical Reflection." Translated by Denis Savage. *International Philosophical Quarterly* 2, no. 2 (May 1962): 192–193.

Riggs, Marcia Y. *Awake, Arise, and Act.* Cleveland: Pilgrim, 1994.

_____. ed. *Can I Get a Witness? Prophetic Religious Voices of African American Women: An Anthology.* Maryknoll, N.Y.: Orbis, 1997.

Robinson, J. P. *Sermons and Sermonettes.* Nashville: National Baptist Publishing Board, 1905.

Rogers, Henry W. "The Status of the Negro." *Methodist Quarterly Review* 67, no. 4 (October 1918): 657–669.

Roman, C. V. "Racial Self-Respect and Racial Antagonism." *Methodist Quarterly Review* 62, no. 4 (October 1913): 768–777.

Roosevelt, Theodore. *The Writings of Theodore Roosevelt 1858–1919.* Edited by William H. Harbaugh. Indianapolis: Bobbs-Merrill, 1967.

Rose, Willie Lee, ed. *A Documentary History of Slavery in North America.* New York: Oxford University Press, 1976.

Rossi, Peter. "Skid Row Moves Downtown." *London Times* 4758 (June 10, 1994): 12.

Scarborough, W. S. "Our Political Status." Address delivered at the Colored Men's Inter-State Conference. Pittsburgh, April 29, 1884.

_____. "What Should Be the Standard of the University, College, Normal School, Teacher Training, and Secondary Schools." Paper read at the Conference on Education National Training School. Durham, N.C., November 21–24, 1916.

SenGupta, Gunja. *For God and Mammon: Evangelicals and Entrepreneurs, Masters and Slaves in Territorial Kansas, 1854–1860.* Athens: University of Georgia Press, 1996.

Sennett, Richard. "Something in the City." *London Times* 4825 (September 22, 1995): 13–15.

Sernett, Milton C. *Bound for the Promised Land.* Durham: Duke University Press, 1997.

Shannon, Alexander Harvey. "The Racial Integrity of the Negro." *Methodist Quarterly Review* 55, no. 3 (July 1906): 525–538.

Sherwood, W. H. *Sherwood's Solid Shot: A Few of the Sermons.* Boston: McDonald, Gill, 1891. Moorland-Spingarn Research Center, Howard University.

Sibler, Irwin, ed. *Soldier Songs and Home-Front Ballads of the Civil War.* New York: Oak Publications, 1964.

Siddiqi, Mohammad M. *Assaluma Alaykum: Meaning and Commentary.* Baltimore: Muslim Community Services, 1996.

Small, John B. *Practical and Exegetical Pulpiteer: Synopses of Discourses.* York, Pa.: P. Anstadt, 1895.

Smith, David. *Biography of Rev. David Smith of the A.M.E. Church.* Xenia, Ohio: Xenia Gazette Office, 1881.

Smith, N. Clark, ed. *New Jubilee Songs: For Quartette Choir or Chorus, Concert Church, and Home.* Chicago: Smith Jubilee Music Co., n.d.

Smith, Rembert G. "Methodism's Duty to the Southern Negro." *Methodist Review Quarterly* 57, no. 3 (July 1908): 529–536, 592.

Smith, Thee. *Conjuring Culture.* New York: Oxford University Press, 1994.

Smitherman, Geneva. *Black Talk: Word and Phrases from the Hood to the Amen Corner.* Boston: Houghton Mifflin, 1994.

Sobel, Mechal. *The World They Made Together: Black and White Values in Eighteenth-Century Virginia.* Princeton: Princeton University Press, 1987.

Soffer, Reba. "Nation, Duty, Character, and Confidence: History at Oxford 1850–1914." *Historical Journal* 30, no. 1 (1987): 77–107.

Sterling, Dorothy, ed. *The Trouble They Seen: Black People Tell the Story of Reconstruction.* New York: Doubleday, 1976.

_____, ed. *We Are Your Sisters: Black Women in the Nineteenth Century.* New York: Norton, 1984.

Stevens, George E. *Negro Segregation: A Measure to Assassinate a Race.* St. Louis: Antioch Baptist Association, 1915.

Steward, Austin. *Twenty-two Years a Slave, and Forty Years a Freeman.* New York: New American Library, 1967.

Steward, T. G. *The Tawawa Series in Systematic Divinity.* Philadelphia: Christian Recorder Print, 1884.

Stout, Jeffrey. *Ethics after Babel: The Languages of Morals and Their Discontent.* Boston: Beacon, 1988.

"The Strenuous Life." Speech before the Hamilton Club. Chicago, April 10, 1899.

Stroyer, Jacob. *My Life in the South.* Salem, N.C.: Salem Observer, 1885.

Stuckey, Sterling. *The Slave Culture: Nationalist Theory and the Foundations of Black America.* New York: Oxford University Press, 1988.

Stumme, Wayne, ed. *The Experience of Hope: Mission and Ministry in Changing Urban Communities.* Minneapolis: Augsburg, 1991.

Tanner, Benjamin Tucker. *The Dispensations in the History of the Church and the Interregnums.* Atlanta: National Library Bindery, 1898.

Thirkkield, Wilbur P. *The Negro and Organic Union of Methodism.* New Orleans: Louisiana Printing, 1916.

Thornton, S. R. "Character." *Quarterly Review of the United Brethren in Christ* 8, no 4 (October 1897): 356–359.

Thurman, Howard. *Jesus and the Disinherited.* New York: Abingdon-Cokesbury, 1949.

Tigert, John J. "Ethics: The Science of Duty." *Methodist Review* 47 (September/October 1898): 582–590.

Tindley, Charles Albert. *A Book of Sermons.* Philadelphia: Edward T. Duncan Agent, 1932.

Trawick, A. M. "The Good and Bad of Race Prejudice." *Methodist Quarterly Review* 74, no. 2 (April 1925): 243–258.

Von Grabill, S. Becker. (*Letters from Tuskegee, Being the Confessions of a Yankee.* 2d ed. Tuskegee: S. Becker Von Grabill, 1905.

Walker, C. T. "Fifty Years of Freedom for the Negro." Speech delivered at the Jubilee Celebration of the National Baptist Convention. Nashville, September 19, 1913. Georgia: Press of the Georgia Baptist. Reproduced from the collections of the Manuscript Division, Library of Congress.

Walker, George. "An Imperative Duty." *Methodist Quarterly Review,* 44 (September/October 1896): 158–160.

Walker, Margaret. "Lineage." In *The Poetry of Black America: Anthology of the 20ᵗʰ Century.* Edited by Arnold Adolf. New York: HarperCollins, 1973.

_____. *Richard Wright, Daemonic Genius: A Portrait of the Man, a Critical Look at His Work.* New York: Warner, 1988.

Washington, Booker T. "Education Will Solve the Race Problem: A Reply." *North American Review* 171 (August 1900): 221–232.

——————. "Fifty Years of Freedom." *Methodist Quarterly Review* 63, no. 2 (April 1914): 294–301.

——————. *The Booker T. Washington Papers.* 14 vols. Edited by Louis R. Harlan and Raymond W. Smock. Urbana: University of Illinois Press, 1975.

Washington, James M., ed. *A Testament of Hope: The Essential Writings of Martin Luther King, Jr.* San Francisco: Harper & Row, 1986.

——————. *Conversations with God: Two Centuries of Prayers by African Americans.* New York: HarperPerennial, 1994.

Washington, Joseph. *The Politics Of God.* Boston: Beacon, 1967.

Wayman, Alexander Walker. *Cyclopaedia of African Methodism.* Baltimore: Methodist Episcopal Book Depository, 1882.

——————. *My Recollections of African M.E. Ministers.* Philadelphia: A.M.E. Book Rooms, 1882.

West, Cornel, and Henry Louis Gates. *The Future of the Race.* New York: Knopf, 1996.

Williams, Delores S. *Sisters in the Wilderness: The Challenge of Womanist God-Talk.* Maryknoll, N.Y.: Orbis, 1993.

Willis, James E. *A Collection of Sermons Delivered by the Rev. James E. Willis.* Washington, D.C.: Vermont Avenue Baptist Church.

Wilmore, Gayraud S. *Black Religion and Black Radicalism: An Examination of the Black Experience in Religion.* New York: Doubleday, 1972.

Wolfenstein, Eugene Victor. *The Victims of Democracy.* Berkeley: University of California Press, 1981.

Woodson, Carter G., ed. *Works of Francis James Grimke.* 3 vols. Washington, D.C.: Associated Publishers, 1942.

Work, John W., ed. *American Negro Songs: 230 Folk Songs and Spirituals, Religious and Secular.* New York: Dover Publications, 1998.

Wright, Ellen, and Michel Fabre, eds. *Richard Wright Reader.* New York: Harper & Row, 1978.

Wright, Richard. *Native Son.* New York: New American Library, 1961.

——————. *Black Boy.* New York: Harper & Row, 1977.

——————. *Eight Men.* New York: HarperPerennial, 1996.

Young, Robert. "The African Stranger." Sermon delivered at London Wall, London, U.K. January 17, 1808.

Index